to

MSGR. George Vida

+ Thomas J. Dolensey

1987

John Paul II

in America

John Paul II
in America

**Talks given on the Papal Tour
September 1987**

Compiled and indexed by the
Daughters of St. Paul

Text:
Press Office of the Holy See

St. Paul Books & Media

ISBN 0-8198-3917-5

Printed in the U.S.A., by the Daughters of St. Paul
50 St. Paul's Ave., Boston, MA 02130

The Daughters of St. Paul are an international congregation of
women religious serving the Church with the communications
media.

CONTENTS

I Come as Pilgrim, Pastor, Friend

Greetings to the President, Church leaders and the American people at Miami International Airport—September 10, 1987.

Mr. President, dear Friends,
Dear People of America,

It is a great joy for me once again to be in your country, and I thank you for your *warm welcome.* I am deeply grateful to you all.

I express my special thanks to *the President of the United States,* who honors me by his presence here today. I thank *the Bishops' Conference* and *all the individual Bishops* who have invited me to their dioceses, and who have done so much to prepare for my visit.

My cordial greetings and good wishes go to *all the people of this land.* I thank you for opening your hearts to me and for supporting me by your prayers. I assure you of my own prayers.

To everyone I repeat on this occasion what I said on that memorable day in 1979, when I arrived in Boston: "On my part I come to you—America—with sentiments of friendship, reverence and esteem. I come as one who already knows you and loves you, as one who wishes you to fulfill completely your noble destiny of service to the world" (October 1, 1979).

Today, as then, I come *to proclaim the Gospel of Jesus Christ* to all those who freely choose to listen to me; to tell again the story of God's love in the world; to spell out once more the message of human dignity, with its inalienable human rights and its inevitable human duties.

Like so many before me coming to America and to this very city of Miami, I come as *a pilgrim:* a pilgrim in the cause of justice and peace and human solidarity—striving to build up the one human family.

I come here as *a pastor*—the pastor of the Catholic Church, to speak and pray with the Catholic people. The theme of my visit, "Unity in the work of service," affords me the welcome opportunity to enter into ever deeper communion with them in our common service to the Lord. It also enables me to experience ever more keenly with them their hopes and joys, their anxieties and griefs.

I come as *a friend*—a friend of America and of all Americans: Catholics, Orthodox, Protestants and Jews, people of every religion, and all men and women of good will. I come as a friend of the poor and the sick and the dying; those who are struggling with the problems of each day; those who are rising and falling and stumbling on the journey of life; those who are seeking and discovering, and those not yet finding, the deep meaning of "life, liberty and the pursuit of happiness."

And finally I come *to join you as you celebrate the Bicentennial* of that great document, the Constitution of the United States of America. I willingly join you in your prayer of thanksgiving to God for the providential way in which the Constitution has served the people of this nation for two centuries: for the union it has formed, the justice it has established, the tranquillity and peace it has ensured, the general welfare it has promoted, and the blessings of liberty it has secured.

I join you also in asking God to inspire you—as Americans who have received so much in freedom and prosperity and human enrichment—to continue to share all this with so many brothers and sisters throughout the other countries of the world who are still waiting and hoping to live according to standards worthy of the children of God.

With great enthusiasm I look forward to being with you in the days ahead. Meanwhile, my prayer for all of you, dear people of America, is this:

"The Lord bless you and keep you!

The Lord let his face shine upon you, and be gracious to you!

The Lord look upon you kindly and give you peace" (Nm. 6:24-26).

God bless America!

The Importance of Prayer

Address to clergy, religious and laity at St. Mary's Cathedral, Miami—September 10, 1987.

Dear Archbishop McCarthy and my other brother Bishops,
Dear Brothers and Sisters,
Dear Friends,

1. It is a great joy for me to begin my pastoral visit here in Miami, in this Cathedral of St. Mary's. This Church represents *a long history of faith and dedicated Christian life and witness* on the part of countless clergy, Religious and laity in this city and in the state of Florida.

In coming among you, I wish to commend you for the Jubilee Year of Reconciliation that you have observed in preparation for my visit, and for the Archdiocesan Synod that you are holding. These events are meant to be of *lasting spiritual value* for all of you of the Archdiocese, so that your Christian witness in everyday life may be ever more fruitful in the society of which you are a part. I also commend you for meeting the challenges of a rapidly expanding local Church. Over the years, you have welcomed hundreds of thousands of refugees, of different languages and cultures, fleeing religious or political oppression. You have struggled along with them and for them to build *a united community in Christ.* I urge all of you—the clergy, religious and laity of Miami, in communion with your Archbishop and with me— to continue seeking ways to deepen our ecclesial unity in the one Body of Christ.

This unity is expressed in many ways. It is unity in preaching the Gospel, professing the Creed, celebrating the liturgy and participating in the Sacraments, especially the Holy Eucharist. It is unity in going forward as a missionary Church to evangelize the world. But our very presence in this house of God reminds us of another source of unity. I am referring to *the personal prayer of each and every one of us,* whether offered here in a moment of silence or amid the many settings in which our daily life unfolds. "The spiritual life," as the Second Vatican Council reminds us, "is not confined to participation in the liturgy. The Christian is certainly called to pray with others, but he must also enter into his room to pray to the Father in secret; indeed, according to the teaching of the Apostle Paul, he should pray without ceasing" (*Sacrosanctum Concilium,* 12).

How to Pray

2. People always have a great interest in prayer. Like the Apostles, they want *to know how to pray.* The response that Jesus gives is one known to all of us: it is the "Our Father," in which he reveals in a few simple words all the essentials of prayer. The focus is not primarily on ourselves, but on the heavenly Father to whom we commit our lives in faith and trust. Our first concern must be his name, his kingdom, his will. Only then do we ask for our daily bread, for forgiveness, and for deliverance from trials yet to come.

The *"Our Father"* teaches us that our relationship to God is one of dependence. We are his adopted sons and daughters through Christ. All that we are and all that we have comes from him and is destined to return to him. The "Our Father" also presents prayer to us as an expression of our desires. Beset as we are by human weakness, we naturally ask God for many things. Many times we may be tempted to think that he does not hear or answer us. But as St. Augustine wisely reminds us, God already knows what we desire even before we ask. He says that prayer is for our benefit because in praying we "exercise" our desires so that we will grasp what God is preparing to give us. It is an opportunity for us to "widen our hearts" (cf. *Letter to Proba,* Epistle 30).

In other words, God is always listening to us and answering us—but from the perspective of *a love far greater and a knowledge far deeper* than our own. When it appears that he is not fulfilling our desires by granting the things we ask, however unselfish and noble they may be, in reality he is purifying those desires of ours for the sake of a higher good that often surpasses our understanding in this life. The challenge is to "widen our hearts" by hallowing his name, by seeking his kingdom, and by accepting his will. Like Christ in the Garden of Gethsemane we may sometimes pray either for ourselves or others, "Father, you have the power to do all things. Take this cup away!" But also like Christ we must add, "Not my will but your will be done" (cf. Mt 26:39, 42; Mk 14:36; Lk 22:42).

The act of praying is also meant to open us up to God and our neighbor, not only in words but also in action. That is why Christian spirituality, following Jesus himself (cf. Mt 6), associates prayer with *fasting and almsgiving*. A life of self-denial and charity is a sign of conversion to God's way of thinking, to his way of love. By humbling ourselves through penance, we open ourselves to God. By giving in charity, over and above the demands of justice, we open ourselves to our neighbor. St. Peter Chrysologus gives witness to this tradition when he says: "Prayer, fasting, and mercy...give life to one another. What prayer knocks for upon a door, fasting successfully begs and mercy receives. For, fasting is the soul of prayer; and mercy is the life of fasting.... Fasting does not germinate unless watered by mercy" *(Sermon* 43).

Prayer's Tremendous Power

3. Dear brothers and sisters: We must never underestimate the power of prayer to further the Church's redemptive mission and to bring good where there is evil. As I mentioned earlier, we must be united in prayer. We pray not just for ourselves and our loved ones, but also for the needs of *the universal Church and of all mankind:* for the missions and for priestly and religious vocations, for the conversion of sinners and the salvation of all, for the sick and the dying. As members of *the Communion of Saints,* our prayer also embraces the souls of those in Purgatory who, in the loving mercy of God, can still find after death the purification they need to enter into the happiness of heaven. Prayer also makes us realize that sometimes our own troubles and desires are small compared to the needs and to the sufferings of so many of our brothers and sisters throughout the world. There is the spiritual suffering of those who have lost their way in life because of sin or a lack of faith in God. There is the material suffering of millions of people who lack food, clothing, shelter, medicine, and education; of those who are deprived of the most fundamental human rights; of those

who are exiles or refugees because of war and oppression. I know that Miami is no stranger to this kind of suffering. We must act to aleviate it, but we must also pray not only for those who suffer, but also for those who inflict suffering.

Greeting to Hispanics

Dear brothers and sisters: as Pastor of the whole Church I have benefited from the prayers of millions of the faithful throughout the world, and today I express my gratitude to you for the prayers you offer for me, and I ask you to continue. Indeed, with St. Paul I say: "Pray for me that God may put his word on my lips, that I may courageously make known the mystery of the Gospel.... Pray that I may have courage to proclaim it as I ought" (Eph 6:19). And at this moment I am praying in a special way for all of you who make up the household of the faith in this Archdiocese. We are called today and always *to remain united in prayer*—for the glory of the Father, and of the Son, and of the Holy Spirit. Amen.

Strength from Christ's Love

Address at meeting with priests from around the U.S.—St. Martha's Church, Miami, September 10.

Dear brother Priests,

1. Coming here today, I wish to open my heart to you and to *celebrate with you the priesthood* which we all share. I am convinced that there is no better way to start than *to direct our thoughts to that Shepherd whom we all know*—the Good Shepherd, the one High Priest, our Lord and Savior Jesus Christ.

My heart is full of gratitude and praise as *I express my love for the priesthood,* the vocation in which we participate not because we are worthy, but because Christ loves us and has entrusted to us this particular ministry of service. *And I thank God for you, my brother priests.* In the words of St. Paul: "I thank God...whenever I remember you in my prayers—as indeed I do constantly, night and day" (2 Tm 1:3).

I am also grateful to you, my brother priests, for your welcome of fraternal love, expressed personally and through Father McNulty as your representative. I address my words to all of you present here and to all the priests in the United States. To all of you I express my gratitude for your ministry, for your perseverance, for your faith and love, for the fact that you are striving to live the priesthood, close to the people, in truth—the truth of being ministers of Christ the Good Shepherd.

As priests, *we all hold a "treasure in earthen vessels"* (2 Cor 4:7). Through no merit of our own, and with all our human weaknesses, we have been called to proclaim God's word, to celebrate the sacred mysteries, especially the Eucharist, to care for the People of God, and to continue the Lord's ministry of reconciliation. In this way, we are servants both of the Lord and of his people, being ourselves constantly called to conversion, constantly invited to "walk in newness of life" (Rom 6:4).

I have come to the United States, my brother priests, in order to confirm you in your faith, according to the will of Christ (cf. Lk 22:32). I have come to you because I want all distances to be bridged, so that together we may grow and become ever more truly *a communion of faith, hope and love.* I affirm you in the good gifts you have received and in the generous response you have made to the Lord and his people, and I encourage you to become more and more like Jesus Christ—the Eternal High Priest, the Good Shepherd.

St. Paul reminds us as he reminded Timothy, to be fearless in serving Christ: "The Spirit God has given us is no cowardly spirit, but rather one that makes us strong, loving and wise. Therefore, *never be ashamed of your testimony to our Lord,...*but with the strength which comes from God bear your share of the hardship which the Gospel entails" (2 Tm 1:7-8). We know that proclaiming the Gospel and living out our ministry very definitely entail hardship. It would be wrong to reduce priestly life to this one dimension of suffering, but it would also be wrong not to recognize this dimension or to resent it when we encounter it. We are not exempt from the human condition, nor can we ever escape that *emptying of self,* after the example of Jesus, who "was himself tested through what he suffered" (Heb 2:18).

Relationship with Christ

2. It is important that we find satisfaction in our ministry, and that we be clear about the nature of the satisfaction which we can expect. The physical and emotional health of priests is an important factor in their overall human and priestly well-being, and it is necessary to provide for these. I commend your Bishops and you yourselves for giving particular attention to these matters in recent years. Yet, the fulfillment that comes from our ministry does not, in the final analysis, consist in physical or psychological well-being; nor can it ever consist in material comfort and security. *Our fulfillment depends on our relationship with Christ and on the service that we offer to his Body, the Church.* Each of us is most truly himself when he is "for others."

Strength from the Holy Spirit

3. And just here, of course, arises a problem for us in our ministry. So much is asked of us by so many different people, and so often it seems that our response is inade-

quate to their needs. Sometimes this is due to our own human limitations. We can then be tempted to indulge in excessive self-criticism, forgetting that *God can use our weakness as easily as our strength* in order to accomplish his will.

It is a great credit to you, my brothers, that *you are striving to be merciful and gentle and forgiving like the Good Shepherd* whom you know and imitate and love, and to whom you have pledged your fidelity. No other path is possible. Sometimes, however, what is asked of you in the name of compassion may not be in accord with the full truth of God, whose eternal law of love can never contradict the fact that he is always "rich in mercy" (Eph 2:4). True mercy takes into account God's plan for humanity, and this plan—marked by the sign of the Cross—was revealed by a merciful High Priest, who is able "to sympathize with our weakness, ...one who was tempted every way that we are, yet never sinned" (Heb 4:15). If on the other hand, what is claimed to be a gesture of mercy goes contrary to the demands of God's word, it can never be truly compassionate or beneficial to our brothers and sisters in need. Jesus, who was himself the perfect expression of the Father's mercy, was also conscious of being "a sign of contradiction" (Lk 2:34). The Apostle John tells us that, at a certain point in the Lord's ministry, "many of his disciples broke away and would not remain in his company any longer" (Jn 6:66).

And today there are indeed *many sensitive issues* which priests must deal with in their daily ministry. I know from listening to many priests and many Bishops that there are different approaches to such issues. What is seen in one way by some of our brothers is evaluated differently by others. Yes, we all have questions which arise from the exercise of our priesthood—*questions which require* us to seek continually *the light and wisdom that come only from the Holy Spirit.*

In this regard, however, it is important for us to realize that the same Holy Spirit from whom come all the different and wonderful charisms, and who dwells in the hearts of all the faithful, has placed in the Church the specific charism of the Magisterium, through which *he guides the whole community to the fullness of truth.* Through the action of the Holy Spirit the promise of Christ is constantly being fulfilled:

"Know that *I am with you always,* until the end of the world" (Mt 28:20). We know that through the Second Vatican Council the Church has clearly and collegially expressed her teaching on many of the sensitive issues and that much of this teaching has subsequently been reiterated in the different sessions of the Synod of Bishops. By its nature therefore this teaching of the Church is normative for the life of the Church and for all pastoral service. The forthcoming Synod, after extensive consultation and fervent prayer, will consider at length and take a pastoral position on other important issues in the life of the Church.

I am very much aware that *your fidelity to Christ's will for his Church and your pastoral sensitivity demand great sacrifice and generosity of spirit.* As I told the Bishops of the United States, just a few weeks after I was elected Pope: "Like yourselves, I learned as a Bishop to understand firsthand the ministry of priests, the problems affecting their lives, the splendid efforts they are making, the sacrifices that are an integral part of their service to God's people. Like yourselves, I am fully aware of how much Christ depends on his priests in order to fulfill in time his mission of redemption" (November 9, 1978).

Seeking Priestly Vocations

4. In expressing the conviction that Christ needs his priests and wills to associate them with himself in his mission of salvation, we must also emphasize the consequence of this: *the need for new vocations to the priesthood.* It is truly necessary for the whole Church to work and pray for this intention. As Father McNulty stated so well, we priests must personally invite generous young men to give their lives in the service of the Lord; they must truly be attracted by the joy that we project in our own lives and ministry.

There is still one more factor to be considered in evaluating the future of vocations, and it is *the power of Christ's Paschal Mystery.* As the Church of Christ, we are all called to profess his power before the world; to proclaim that he is able, in virtue of his Death and Resurrection, to draw young people to himself, in this generation as in the past; to declare that he is strong enough to attract young men even today to a life of self-sacrifice, pure love and total dedication to the priesthood. As we profess this truth, as we proclaim with faith the power of the Lord of the harvest, we have a right to expect that he will grant the prayers that he himself has commanded to be offered. *The present hour calls for great trust* in him who has overcome the world.

Priests' Indispensable Role

5. The authentic renewal of the Church initiated by the Second Vatican Council has been a great gift of God to his people. Through the action of the Holy Spirit an immense amount of good has been done. We must continue to pray and work that the Holy Spirit will bring his design to fulfillment in us. In this regard *priests have an indispensable role to play in the renewed life of the Church.*

Each day the Church is being renewed by grace as she seeks a deeper and more penetrating understanding of the word of God, as she strives to worship more authentically in spirit and in truth, and as she recognizes and develops the gifts of all her members. These dimensions of renewal require those enduring tasks of priests which give their ministry its unique character: namely, the *ministry of word and Sacrament, the tending of the flock of Christ.*

True renewal presupposes the clear, faithful and effective *proclamation of the word of God.* The Second Vatican Council indicated that this is *the priest's first task (Presbyterorum Ordinis, 4).* Those who preach must do so with dynamic fidelity. This means being ever faithful to what has been handed on in Tradition and Scripture, as taught by the living pastoral authority of the Church, and making every effort to present the Gospel as effectively as possible in its application to new circumstances of life. As often as the word is truly proclaimed, Christ's work of redemption continues. But what is proclaimed must first be lived.

Renewal in Christ greatly depends on the development of *the Church's life of worship.* Because we priests preside at the liturgy, we must come to know and appreciate the rites of the Church through study and prayer. We are called to lead celebrations which are both faithful to the Church's discipline and legitimately adapted, according to her norms, for the good of our people.

Genuine renewal also depends upon the way in which priests exercise their *task of tending the flock of Christ*, especially as they encourage the faithful to use their gifts in the apostolate and in various special forms of service. The Church's *commitment to evangelization*, to proclaiming the word of God, to calling people to holiness of life, cannot be sustained without the tireless efforts and selfless support of priests. In the matter of inviting people, as Jesus did, to conversion—the total conversion of the Gospel—*the example of priests* is extremely important for the authenticity of the Church's life.

This is particularly true in *our own use of the Sacrament of Penance*, through which we are repeatedly converted to the Lord. On this condition rests the full supernatural effectiveness of our "ministry of reconciliation" (2 Cor 5:18) and of our whole priestly lives. The experience of the Church teaches us that "the priest's celebration of the Eucharist and administration of the other Sacraments, his pastoral zeal, his relationship with the faithful, his communion with his brother priests, his collaboration with his Bishop, his life of prayer—in a word, the whole of his priestly existence, suffers an inexorable decline if by negligence or for some other reason he fails to receive the Sacrament of Penance at regular intervals and in a spirit of genuine faith and devotion. If a priest were no longer to go to confession or properly confess his sins, his *priestly being* and his *priestly action* would feel its effects very soon, and this would also be noticed by the community of which he was the pastor" (*Reconciliatio et Paenitentia*, 31).

People expect us to be men of faith and prayer. People look to us for *Christ's truth* and the teaching of his Church. They ask to see *Christ's love* incarnate in our lives. All this reminds us of a very basic truth, that the priest is "another Christ." In a sense, we priests are Christ to all those to whom we minister. This is true of all aspects of our priestly work. But it is particularly true *in the Eucharistic Sacrifice*—from which our priestly identity flows, and in which it is expressed most clearly and effectively. This truth has special relevance also for our service as *ministers of the Sacrament of Reconciliation* through which we render a unique service to the cause of conversion and peace, and to the advancement of God's Kingdom on earth. At this point I would like to repeat those words which I have already addressed to the priests of the Church: "Praise, then, to this silent army of our brothers who have served well and serve each day the cause of reconciliation through the ministry of sacramental penance" *(Reconciliatio et Paenitentia, 29).*

In her *mission to the world,* the Church is renewed as she calls humanity to respond to God's commandment of love, and as she upholds and promotes the values of the Gospel as they affect public life. In doing this she becomes a prophetic voice on matters of truth and justice, mercy and peace. In these tasks involving the world, the leadership of priestly ministry has been and continues to be decisive. Priests who *encourage and support* the laity help them to exercise their own mission to bring the values of the Gospel into public life. Thus, priests and lay people working together can challenge society itself to defend life and all human rights, to protect family life, to work for greater social justice, to promote peace.

Necessity of Personal Prayer

6. One of the notable experiences of priests in the United States in the years since the Council has been *a renewal of their spiritual lives.* Many priests have sought this renewal in groups of fraternal support, through spiritual direction, retreats, and other commendable endeavors. These priests have found their ministry revitalized by a rediscovery of the importance of personal prayer. As you continue to discover Christ both in your prayer and in your ministry, you will experience more deeply that he—the Good Shepherd—is *the very center of your life—the very meaning of your priesthood.*

My brothers: in speaking to you about *prayer* I am not telling you what you do not know, or urging you to do something that you do not practice. Prayer has been part of

your daily lives since your seminary years and even earlier.
But *perseverance in prayer,* as you know, is difficult. Dryness
of spirit, external distractions, the tempting rationalization
that we could be spending our time more usefully—these
things are familiar to anyone who is trying to pray. Inevitably, at one time or another, these elements assail the prayer
life of a priest.

For us priests, prayer is neither a luxury nor an option to
be taken up or put aside as seems convenient. *Prayer is
essential to the pastoral life.* Through prayer we grow in sensitivity to the Spirit of God at work in the Church and in
ourselves. And we are made more aware of others, becoming more "attentive to their needs, to their lives and destiny" *(Holy Thursday Letter to Priests,* 1987, no. 11). Indeed,
through prayer we come to love deeply those whom Jesus
has entrusted to our ministry. Of special importance for our
lives and our ministry is the *great prayer of praise*—the Liturgy
of the Hours—which the Church enjoins on us and which
we pray in her name and in the name of our Lord Jesus
Christ.

Brotherly Support

7. In recent years, priests have often told me of the need
they feel for *support in their ministry.* The challenges of
priestly service today are indeed great, and the demands on
our time and energy seem to increase every day. In such
circumstances how easily we can give in to temptations to
discouragement! But, dear brothers, at these times it is more
important than ever that we heed the advice of the Letter to
the Hebrews: *"Let us keep our eyes fixed on Jesus,* who inspires
and perfects our faith. For the sake of the joy which lay
before him he endured the Cross, heedless of its shame....
Remember how he endured the opposition of sinners; hence
do not grow despondent or abandon the struggle" (Heb
12:2-4).

The encouragement and support that we find *in one
another* is a great gift of God's love—a characteristic of
Christ's priesthood. The increase of mutual support among
brother priests through prayer and sharing is a most encour-

aging sign. The same can be said, on a different level, for the development of presbyteral councils committed to the solidarity of priests with one another and with their Bishop in the mission of the universal Church.

As priests we also need *examples of priestly ministry,* "artists" of pastoral work who both inspire us and intercede for us—priests like Philip Neri, Vincent de Paul, John Vianney, John Bosco, and Maximilian Kolbe. And we can also reflect upon the priestly lives of men whom we have known personally—exemplary priests who inspire us because they have lived the one priestly ministry of Jesus Christ with deep generosity and love.

To persevere in our pastoral ministry we need above all that "one thing only" which Jesus tells us is "required" (cf. Lk 10:42). We need to know the Shepherd very well. We need *a deep personal relationship with Christ,* the source and supreme model of our priesthood—a relationship that requires union in prayer. Our love for Christ, rekindled frequently in prayer—especially prayer before the Blessed Sacrament—is at the foundation of our commitment to celibacy. This love also makes it possible for us, as servants of God's Kingdom, *to love our people freely and chastely and deeply.*

Communion with the Whole Church

8. My brothers: sharing in the one priesthood of Christ, we share the same joys and sorrows. What a joy it is for me to be with you today. I thank you again for the gift of yourselves to Christ and his Church, and I want you to know that I am close to you in your efforts to serve the Lord and his people. You have my gratitude, my prayers, my support and my love. And as I conclude, I express the hope that each of us will always experience the joy of which the Psalmist speaks: "Behold, *how good it is,* and how pleasant, *where brethren dwell at one!''* (Ps 132[133]:1)

Dear brother priests: *Catholic unity is our vocation.* As priests in America you are called to live this Catholic unity in the particular Churches—the dioceses—to which you belong. But all these particular Churches are never more completely themselves, never more faithful to their identity, than when they are living to the full the communion of faith and love of the universal Church. *At the summit of your priestly ministry is this mystery of ecclesial unity,* and you are called to live it in sacrifice and love, in union with Mary the Mother of Jesus.

The protection and tender human love of our Blessed Mother is a great support to all of us priests. Her prayers assist us, her example challenges us, her closeness consoles us. In her presence we experience the joy and hope that we need so much. Is this not the day and the hour, dear brother priests, to turn to her, as we must have done on our ordination day, and *to entrust to her anew ourselves, our people and our sacred ministry?* Why? For the glory of the Father, and of the Son, and of the Holy Spirit.

Dear priests of America, dear brothers: "My love to all of you in Christ Jesus" (1 Cor 16:24).

Shared Responsibility
for Freedom

Address to President and Mrs. Reagan—Viscaya, September 10.

Mr. President,

1. I am grateful for the great courtesy that you extend to me by coming personally to meet me in this city of Miami. Thank you for this gesture of kindness and respect.

On my part I cordially greet you as the elected Chief Executive of the United States of America. In addressing you, I express *my own deep respect for the constitutional structure of this democracy* which you are called to "preserve, protect and defend." In addressing you, Mr. President, I greet once again *all the American people* with their history, their achievements and their great possibilities of serving humanity.

I willingly pay honor to the United States for what she has accomplished for her own people, for all those whom she has embraced in a cultural creativity and welcomed into an indivisible national unity, according to her own motto: *E pluribus unum. I thank America* and all Americans—those of past generations and those of the present—for their generosity to millions of their fellow human beings in need throughout the world. Also today, I wish *to extol* the blessings and gifts that America has received from God and cultivated, and which have become *the true values of the whole American experiment* in the past two centuries.

Bicentennial of U.S. Constitution

2. For all of you this is a special hour in your history: the celebration of *the Bicentennial of your Constitution*. It is a time to recognize the meaning of that document and to reflect on important aspects of the constitutionalism that produced it. It is a time to recall the original American political faith with its appeal to the sovereignty of God. To celebrate the origin of the United States is *to stress those moral and spiritual principles, those ethical concerns that influenced your Founding Fathers* and have been incorporated into the experience of America.

29

Eleven years ago, when your country was celebrating *another great document,* the Declaration of Independence, my predecessor Paul VI spoke to American Congressmen in Rome. His statement is still pertinent today: "At every turn," he said, "your Bicentennial speaks to you of moral principles, religious convictions, inalienable rights given by the Creator." And he added: "We earnestly hope that...this commemoration of your Bicentennial will constitute a rededication to those sound moral principles formulated by your Founding Fathers and enshrined forever in your history" (Address of April 26, 1976).

Freedom—A Gift

3. *Among the many admirable values of this nation* there is one that stands out in particular. It is *freedom.* The concept of freedom is part of the very fabric of this nation as a political community of free people. Freedom is a great gift, a great blessing of God.

From the beginning of America, freedom was directed to forming a well-ordered society and to promoting its peaceful life. Freedom was channeled to the fullness of human life, to the preservation of human dignity and to the safeguarding of all human rights. *An experience in ordered freedom is truly a cherished part of the history of this land.*

This is the freedom that America is called to live and guard and to transmit. She is called to exercise it in such a way that it will also benefit the cause of freedom in other nations and among other peoples. The only true freedom, the only freedom that can truly satisfy, is the freedom to do what we ought as human beings created by God according to his plan. It is *the freedom to live the truth of what we are and who we are* before God, the truth of our identity as children of God, as brothers and sisters in a common humanity. That is why Jesus Christ linked truth and freedom together, stating solemnly: "You will know the truth and the truth will set you free" (Jn 8:32). All people are called to recognize the liberating truth of the sovereignty of God over them both as individuals and as nations.

Freedom and Truth

4. The effort to guard and perfect the gift of freedom must also include the relentless pursuit of truth. In speaking to Americans on another occasion about *the relationship between freedom and truth,* I said that "as a people you have *a shared responsibility for preserving freedom and for purifying it.* Like so many other things of great value, freedom is fragile. St. Peter recognized this when he told the Christians never to use their freedom as a pretext for evil (1 Pt 2:16). Any distortion of truth or dissemination of non-truth is an offense against freedom; any manipulation of public opinion, any abuse of authority or power or, on the other hand, just the omission of vigilance, endangers the heritage of a free people. But even more important, every contribution to promoting truth in charity consolidates freedom and builds up peace. When shared responsibility for freedom is truly accepted by all, a great new force is set at work for the service of humanity" (Address of June 21, 1980).

America's Call to Service

5. *Service to humanity has always been a special part of the vocation of America* and is still relevant today. In continuity with what I said to the President of the United States in 1979, I would now repeat: "Attachment to human values and to ethical concerns, which have been a hallmark of the American people, must be situated, especially in the present context of the growing interdependence of peoples across the globe, within the framework of the view that the common good of society embraces not just the individual nation to which one belongs but the citizens of the whole world.... The present-day relationships between peoples and between nations demand the establishment of greater international cooperation also in the economic field. The more powerful a nation is, the greater becomes its international responsibility, the greater also must be its commitment to the betterment of the lot of those whose very humanity is constantly being threatened by want and need.... America, which in the past decades has demonstrated goodness and generosity in providing food for the hungry of the world, will, I am sure, be

able to match this generosity with an equally convincing contribution to the establishing of a world order that will create the necessary economic and trade conditions for a more just relationship between all the nations of the world, in respect for their dignity and their own personality" (Address at the White House, October 6, 1979).

"New Birth" of Freedom

6. Linked to service, freedom is indeed a great gift of God to this nation. *America needs freedom to be herself and to fulfill her mission* in the world. At a difficult moment in the history of this country, a great American, Abraham Lincoln, spoke of a special need at that time: "that this nation under God shall have a new birth of freedom." *A new birth of freedom is repeatedly necessary:* freedom to exercise responsibility and generosity, freedom to meet the challenge of serving humanity, the freedom necessary to fulfill human destiny, the freedom to live by truth, to defend it against whatever distorts and manipulates it, the freedom to observe God's law—which is the supreme standard of all human liberty, the freedom to live as children of God—secure and happy, *the freedom to be America* in that constitutional democracy which was conceived to be "One Nation under God, indivisible, with liberty and justice for all."

Spiritual Brotherhood

Address at meeting with Jewish leadership—Metro-Dade Cultural Center, September 11.

Dear Friends—Representatives of so many Jewish organizations assembled here from across the United States, My dear Jewish Brothers and Sisters,

1. I am grateful to you for your kind words of greeting. I am indeed pleased to be with you, especially at this time when *the United States tour of the Vatican Judaica Collection begins.* The wonderful material, including illuminated Bibles and Prayerbooks, demonstrates but a small part of the immense spiritual resources of Jewish tradition across the centuries and up to the present time—spiritual resources often used in fruitful cooperation with Christian artists.

It is fitting, at the beginning of our meeting, *to emphasize our faith in the One God,* who chose Abraham, Isaac and Jacob, and made with them a Covenant of eternal love, which was never revoked (cf. Gen 27:13; Rom 11:29). It was rather confirmed by the gift of the *Torah* to Moses, opened by the Prophets to the hope of eternal redemption and to the universal commitment for justice and peace. The Jewish people, the Church and all believers in the *Merciful God*—who is invoked in the Jewish prayers as *'Av Ha-Rakhamîm*—can find in this fundamental Covenant with the Patriarchs *a very substantial starting point for our dialogue and our common witness in the world.*

It is also fitting *to recall God's promise to Abraham and the spiritual fraternity which it established:* "...In your descendants all the nations shall find blessing—all this because you obeyed my command" (Gen 22:18). This spiritual fraternity, linked to obedience to God, requires *a great mutual respect* in humility and confidence.

An objective consideration of our relations during the centuries must take into account this great need.

Shared Principles and Dialogue

2. It is indeed worthy of note that the United States was founded by people who came to these shores, often as religious refugees. They aspired to being treated justly and

33

to being accorded hospitality according to the word of God, as we read in Leviticus: "You shall treat the alien who resides with you no differently than the natives born among you; have the same love for him as for yourself; for you too were once aliens in the land of Egypt. I, the Lord, am your God" (Lev 19:34). Among these millions of immigrants there was a large number of Catholics and Jews. The same *basic religious principles* of freedom and justice, of equality and moral solidarity, affirmed in the *Torah* as well as in the *Gospel,* were in fact reflected in the high human ideals and in the protection of universal rights found in the United States. These in turn exercised a strong positive influence on the history of Europe and other parts of the world. But the paths of the immigrants in their new land were not always easy. Sadly enough, prejudice and discrimination were also known in the New World as well as in the Old. Nevertheless, together, Jews and Catholics have contributed to the success of the American experiment in religious freedom, and, in this unique context, have given to the world *a vigorous form of interreligious dialogue* between our two ancient traditions. For those engaged in this dialogue, so important to the Church and to the Jewish people, I pray: May God bless you and make you strong for his service!

3. At the same time, our common heritage, task and hope do not eliminate *our distinctive identities.* Because of her specific Christian witness, "The Church must preach Jesus Christ to the world" (1974 "Guidelines," I). In so doing we proclaim that "Christ is our peace" (Eph 2:14). As the Apostle Paul said: "All this is from God, who through Christ reconciled us to himself and gave us the ministry of reconciliation" (2 Cor 5:18). At the same time, we recognize and appreciate the spiritual treasures of the Jewish people and their religious witness to God. A fraternal theological dialogue will try to understand, in the light of the mystery of redemption, how differences in faith should not cause enmity but open up the way of *"reconciliation,"* so that in the end "God may be all in all" (1 Cor 15:28).

In this regard I am pleased that the National Conference of Catholic Bishops and the Synagogue Council of America are initiating a consultation between Jewish leaders and

Bishops which should carry forward a dialogue on issues of the greatest interest to the two faith communities.

The Shoah—Never Again!

4. Considering history in the light of the principles of faith in God, we must also reflect on the catastrophic event of the *Shoah*, that ruthless and inhuman attempt to exterminate the Jewish People in Europe, an attempt that resulted in millions of victims—including women and children, the elderly and the sick—*exterminated only because they were Jews*.

Considering this mystery of the suffering of Israel's children, their witness of hope, of faith and of humanity under dehumanizing outrages, the Church experiences ever more deeply her *common bond with the Jewish people* and with their treasure of spiritual riches in the past and in the present.

It is also fitting to recall the strong, unequivocal efforts of the Popes *against anti-Semitism and Nazism* at the height of the persecution against the Jews. Back in 1938, Pius XI declared that "anti-Semitism cannot be admitted" (September 6, 1938), and he declared the total opposition between Christianity and Nazism by stating that the Nazi cross is an "enemy of the Cross of Christ" (Christmas Allocution, 1938). And I am convinced that history will reveal ever more clearly and convincingly how deeply Pius XII felt the tragedy of the Jewish people, and how hard and effectively he worked to assist them during the Second World War.

Speaking in the name of humanity and Christian principles, the Bishops' Conference of the United States denounced the atrocities with a clear statement: "Since the murderous assault on Poland, utterly devoid of every semblance of humanity, there has been a premeditated and systematic extermination of the people of this nation. The same satanic technique is being applied to many other peoples. We feel a deep sense of revulsion against the cruel indignities heaped upon the Jews in conquered countries and upon defenseless peoples not of our faith" (November 14, 1942).

We also remember many others, who, at risk of their own lives, helped persecuted Jews, and are honored by the

Jews with the title of "*Tzaddiqê 'ummôt ha-'olâm*" (Righteous of the Nations).

5. The terrible tragedy of your people has led many *Jewish thinkers* to reflect on the human condition with acute insights. Their vision of man and the roots of this vision in the teachings of the Bible, which we share in our common heritage of the Hebrew Scriptures, offer Jewish and Catholic scholars much useful material for reflection and dialogue.

In order to understand even more deeply *the meaning of the Shoah* and *the historical roots of anti-Semitism* that are related to it, *joint collaboration and studies* by Catholics and Jews on the Shoah should be continued. Such studies have already taken place through many conferences in your country, such as the National Workshops on Christian-Jewish Relations. The religious and historical implications of the Shoah for Christians and Jews will now be taken up formally by the International Catholic-Jewish Liaison Committee, meeting later this year in the United States for the first time. And as was affirmed in the important and very cordial meeting I had with Jewish leaders in Castel Gandolfo on September 1, a Catholic document on the Shoah and anti-Semitism will be forthcoming, resulting from such serious studies.

Similarly, it is to be hoped that common educational programs on our historical and religious relations, which are well developed in your country, will truly promote mutual respect and teach future generations about *the Holocaust* so that never again will such a horror be possible. Never again!

When meeting the leaders of the Polish Jewish community in Warsaw in June of this year, I underscored the fact that through the terrible experience of the Shoah your people have become "a loud warning voice for all of humanity, for all nations, for all the powers of this world, for every system and every individual...a saving warning" (Address of June 14, 1987).

Catholic Respect for Jews

6. It is also desirable that *in every diocese Catholics should implement, under the direction of the Bishops*, the statement of the Second Vatican Council and the subsequent instructions

issued by the Holy See regarding the correct way to preach and teach about Jews and Judaism. I know that a great many efforts in this direction have already been made by Catholics, and I wish to express *my gratitude* to all those who have worked so diligently for this aim.

7. Necessary for any sincere dialogue is the intention of each partner to allow others *to define themselves "in the light of their own religious experience"* (1974 "Guidelines," Introduction). In fidelity to this affirmation, Catholics recognize among the elements of the Jewish experience that Jews have a religious attachment to the Land, which finds its roots in biblical tradition.

After the tragic extermination of the Shoah, the Jewish people began a new period in their history. They have a *right to a homeland*, as does any civil nation, according to international law. "For the Jewish people who live in the State of Israel and who preserve in that land such precious testimonies to their history and their faith, we must ask for the desired security and the due tranquillity that is the prerogative of every nation and condition of life and of progress for every society" *(Redemptionis Anno,* April 20, 1984).

What has been said about the right to a homeland also applies to the Palestinian people, so many of whom remain homeless and refugees. While all concerned must honestly reflect on the past—Muslims no less than Jews and Christians—it is time to forge those solutions which will lead to *a just, complete and lasting peace in that area.* For this peace I earnestly pray.

Common Service to Humanity

8. Finally, as I thank you once again for the warmth of your greeting to me, *I give praise and thanks to the Lord for this fraternal meeting,* for the gift of dialogue between our peoples, and for the new and deeper understanding between us. As our long relationship moves toward its third millennium, it is our great privilege in this generation to be witnesses to this progress.

It is my sincere hope that, as partners in dialogue, as fellow believers in the God who revealed himself, as children of Abraham, we will strive to render *a common service to humanity,* which is so much needed in this our day. We are called to collaborate in service and to unite in a common cause wherever a brother or sister is unattended, forgotten, neglected or suffering in any way; wherever human rights are endangered or human dignity offended; wherever the rights of God are violated or ignored.

With the Psalmist, I now repeat:
"I will hear what God proclaims;
    the Lord—for he proclaims peace
To his people, and to his faithful ones,
    and to those who put in him their hope" (Ps 85:9).

To all of you, dear friends, dear brothers and sisters; to all of you dear Jewish people of America: with great hope I wish you the peace of the Lord. Shalom! Shalom! God bless you on this Sabbath and in this year: *Shabbath Shalom! Shanah Tovah we-Hatimah Tovah!*

The Good Shepherd
Calls Each of Us

Homily at the Miami Eucharist—Tamiani Park, September 11.

"Let the peoples praise you, O God;
Let all the peoples praise you."
"Que todos los pueblos te alaben." (Ps 66[67]:6)

Dear Brothers and Sisters in Christ,

1. The psalm of today's liturgy urges all the peoples and nations of the earth to give glory to God. In the exultant spirit of this exhortation I find myself on American soil, joined with all of you here in Miami, to express and praise the glory of God *through the Sacrifice of Jesus Christ, in the Eucharist.* There is no better way to express God's glory than this Sacrament. *There is no other prayer* which more profoundly unites earth with heaven, or the creature with the Creator, than the Eucharist. There is *no other sacrifice* in which everything that exists, and particularly man, is able to become a gift for the one who has so generously lavished him with gifts.

Dear brothers and sisters in Christ, all of you assembled here today in Southern Florida and all the people of this land—*you, the great nation of the United States,* give glory to God together with me, the Bishop of Rome, the Successor of St. Peter, who is beginning here in Miami his act of papal service. *May God's blessing be upon us!* May the holy fear of God reach the ends of the earth! (cf. Ps 66[67]:8)

Dynamic Growth of Florida Church

2. I am very pleased to be with you in *Florida*, this beautiful land of the sun. I warmly greet you, my brothers and sisters of the Catholic faith, and I extend cordial greetings to those of you who are not members of the Church but are here as welcome friends. I thank you all for coming. I also acknowledge among you the presence of so many ethnic groups, including Cubans, Haitians, Nicaraguans, others

39

from Central America and the Caribbean, together with all the rest who make up the community of the Church. I embrace you all in the love of Christ.

The Church in Florida has a rich and varied history, extending back more than four and a half centuries. Ponce de León discovered this land at Easter time in 1513, and gave it the Spanish name for Easter, *Pascua Florida*. Hence the very name of your state recalls the central mystery of our Christian faith, the Resurrection of our Lord and Savior Jesus Christ. The first settlement and the first parish of North America were established here in the early 1560s, more than fifty years before the Pilgrim Fathers landed at Plymouth Rock.

While Floridians can rightly be proud of their *illustrious history,* they can also boast of *contemporary dynamism and expansion.* Today, Miami is emerging as an international city of ever increasing influence. It is a gateway, *a crossroads of diverse cultures and languages,* a center of communication, travel and commerce, a bridge connecting early and modern American history.

This land of fascinating nature, this home of so many different peoples, this place of tourists and haven for senior citizens, this center of the scientific achievements of Cape Canaveral, this state which is Florida, has also been *a land of rapid growth in building up the Body of Christ.* An indication of this remarkable recent growth is the fact that within just twenty-nine years the Catholic Church in Florida has grown from one diocese to seven. It is indeed a joy for me to be in the midst of this dynamic Church in Florida—a Church which proclaims by word and deed *the Good News of the Easter mystery.*

Jesus, the Good Shepherd

3. *Who is the God whose glory we desire to proclaim by means of the Eucharist?*

He is the God who shows us the way of salvation. Thus the Psalmist, who urges all the nations of the earth to praise the glory of God, at the same time exclaims: "May your ways be known upon earth; among all nations your salvation" (Ps

66[67]:3). Our God shows us the way. He is not the God of intellectual abstraction, but *the God of the Covenant, the God of salvation, the Good Shepherd.*

Christ, the Son of the living God, speaks to us this very day in the Gospel, using *this word* so simple yet so eloquent and rich—*Shepherd!* "I am the Good Shepherd," he says. "I know my sheep and my sheep know me in the same way that the Father knows me and I know the Father" (Jn 10:14-15). In another passage of the Gospel, Christ says to us: "No one knows the Son but the Father, and no one knows the Father but the Son—and anyone to whom the Son wishes to reveal him" (Mt 11:27). *The Son, Jesus Christ,* is the Shepherd precisely *because he reveals the Father to us.* He is the Good Shepherd. And the Father is our Shepherd through the Son, through Christ. And in his Son the Father wants us to have eternal life.

4. Jesus goes on to tell us, in words that speak eloquently of his deep love for us: *"The Good Shepherd lays down his life for the sheep"* (Jn 10:11).

Who is this God whose truth we desire to confess by means of the Eucharist? *He is the Father who in Christ gives life* to us whom he created in his own image and likeness. This *life in God is salvation.* It is liberation from death. It is redemption from our sins. And this God is *Christ,* the Son who is of one substance with the Father, who became man for us and for our salvation—Christ the Good Shepherd who has *given his very own life for the sheep.*

The Eucharist proclaims this truth about God. The Sacrament of the Body and Blood of Christ is offered as a redemptive Sacrifice for the sins of the world. It is the sacrament of the Death and Resurrection of Christ, *in which our new life in God begins.*

This God is Love. The Good Shepherd expresses this truth about God. More than the truth, he expresses the very *reality of God as Love.* Love desires what is good. It desires salvation. It is "gentle and patient," and it "will have no end" (cf. 1 Cor 13:4-8). It will not rest *before it has nourished and given life to all* in the great sheepfold, before it has embraced all. For this reason Jesus says: "I have other sheep that do not belong to this fold. I must lead them, too, and they shall hear my voice. There shall be one flock then, one shepherd" (Jn 10:16).

5. We draw *the image of the flock* and the sheepfold from the text of John's Gospel. At the same time, the reading from the Letter to the Ephesians that we have heard in today's Liturgy enables us to see this image with the eyes of Paul the Apostle. For him *the flock* is *"the body"* of which the head is Christ. And thus it is the Body of Christ. In this context it is not difficult to find the likeness between the Head and the Shepherd.

At the same time however the entire image acquires a new meaning and a new expression. *The Shepherd leads* the flock to the springs of life. *As Head, Christ is the source of life for all* those who make up his Body. Thus all of us, who as one single flock follow Christ the Good Shepherd, are at the same time *called "to build up the Body of Christ"* (Eph 4:12).

According to the Letter to the Ephesians this "building up" has two dimensions: *a personal dimension and a community dimension.* Each person must attain that form of perfection which is Christ come to full stature (cf. Eph 4:13). At the same time, we must all come *to maturity "together" in the community of the Church.* As the whole *People of God* we move toward this fullness in Christ.

Christ gives the Church *a rich variety of charisms* for the purpose of deepening our communion as his Body. He bestows on the Church *a great diversity of vocations,* not just for the well-being of each person but for the good of all. As St. Paul says of Jesus, "It is he who gave apostles, prophets, evangelists, pastors and teachers in roles of service for the faithful *to build up the Body of Christ, till we become one* in faith and in the knowledge of God's Son" (Eph 4:11-13).

Concern for Refugees, Immigrants

6. The Church in the United States, and in a particular way the Church in Miami, experiences this *mystery of unity in diversity* in a very real sense. Yours is a community of compassion, which over and over again has echoed the message inscribed on the Statue of Liberty: "Give me your tired, your

poor, your huddled masses yearning to breathe free." The civic community and the Church in Southern Florida have, time after time, opened their arms to immigrants and refugees. These people were strangers and you welcomed them. And be sure that as often as you did it for them, you did it for Christ (cf. Mt 25:31-46).

I take this occasion to assure you of the Church's particular concern for those who leave their native countries out of suffering and desperation. The frequent repetition of this experience is one of the saddest phenomena of our century. Yet it has often been accompanied by hope and heroism and new life. Here in Miami I know there are many who, in the face of distress have been *faithful to the Gospel and the law of God*. Like others who have remained faithful to Christ and his Church in time of oppression, you must guard and protect your Catholic faith as you now live your lives in freedom.

Fidelity to religious practice requires great personal effort in a complex and industrialized society. It takes maturity of faith and strong conviction to take up the Cross each day and follow in the footsteps of Christ. In today's second reading we hear St. Paul's encouragement: "Let us, then, be children no longer, tossed here and there, carried about by every wind of doctrine that originates in human trickery and skill in proposing error. Rather, let us *profess the truth in love* and *grow to the full maturity of Christ* the head" (Eph 4:14-15).

As I gaze at this great city with its many peoples and cultures, I pray that you will all *help one another with your gifts*. Stay in touch with your own roots, your cultures and your traditions; pass on your heritage to your children; and at the same time, place all these gifts at the service of the whole community. Above all, "Make every effort to preserve the unity which has the Spirit as its origin, and peace as its binding force" (Eph 4:3).

Today's Challenge

7. The work of building up the Body of Christ rests upon all of us in the Church. Certainly there is a vital need today for *evangelization*. And it takes a variety of forms.

There are many ways to serve the Gospel. Despite scientific and technological progress, which truly reflects a form of human cooperation in the creative work of God, faith is challenged and even directly opposed by ideologies and life styles which acknowledge neither God nor the moral law.

Basic human and Christian values are challenged by crime, violence and terrorism. Honesty and justice in *business and public life* are often violated. Throughout the world great sums are spent on armaments while millions of poor people struggle for the basic necessities of life. Alcohol and drug abuse take a heavy toll on *individuals* and on *society.* The commercial exploitation of sex through pornography offends human dignity and endangers the future of *young people.* *Family life* is subjected to powerful pressures; fornication, adultery, divorce and contraception are wrongly regarded as acceptable by many. The unborn are cruelly killed and the lives of the elderly are in serious danger from a mentality that would open the door wide to euthanasia.

In the face of all this, however, faithful Christians must not be discouraged, nor can they conform to the spirit of the world. Instead, they are called upon to acknowledge the supremacy of God and his law, to raise their voices and join their efforts on behalf of moral values, to offer society the example of their own upright conduct, and to help those in need. Christians are called to act with the serene conviction that *grace is more powerful than sin* because of *the victory of Christ's Cross.*

An important part of the mission of evangelization is the task of *reconciliation.* God "has reconciled us to himself through Christ and has given us the ministry of reconciliation" (2 Cor 5:18). For this reason, I am happy that in preparation for my visit to the United States you have made special efforts to promote reconciliation—reconciliation with God, among yourselves and between different races and cultures. In this context too I remind you of Christ's promise in today's Gospel, namely, that when all of us truly listen to his voice, "there shall be *one flock* then, *one shepherd''* (Jn 10:16).

8. Deeply conscious of the truth as it is presented to us in this liturgy by the word of God, let us exclaim once again

with the Psalmist: "God be gracious to us and bless us, *may the light of your face shine upon us"* (Ps 66[67]:2).

Who is this God to whom our prayer is addressed? Who is this God whom our community proclaims and to whom our hearts speak? Let us listen once again to the words of the prophet Zephaniah: "Fear not, O Zion, be not discouraged! *The Lord, your God, is in your midst, a mighty savior"* (Zeph 3:16-17).

The Mighty One!

It is he whom we invoke here, in this land, which in so many ways manifests the strengths and achievements of humanity, of human genius, of intellect, of knowledge and science, of technology and progress.

Who is this God? Once again let us repeat: the Mighty One!

He alone is the Mighty One!

He who *is!* (cf. Ex 3:14).

He in whom "we live and move and have our being!" (Acts 17:28)

"The Alpha and the Omega!" (Rev 1:8)

He alone is the Mighty One! Because he alone is Love.

Here in this land, in this culture of the most advanced progress and affluence, is not the human person at times *insecure and confused* about the ultimate meaning of existence—the ultimate meaning of life? Is not the human person at times very far from Love?

Yet *only Love saves,* and God is Love!

O God of love, O God who saves, "may the light of your face shine upon us!" (Ps 66[67]:2) Amen.

Christ,
Center of the Church

Address to representatives of the Catholic Church in South Carolina—
St. Peter's Church, Columbia, September 11.

"You are the Messiah, the Son of the living God."

(Mt 16:16)

Dear Bishop Unterkoefler,
Dear Brothers and Sisters in Christ,

1. These words, which are recorded in the Gospel of St. Matthew, were spoken by Simon Peter, the first Bishop of Rome. They are full of meaning for everyone who believes in Christ, but they have special meaning for us who are gathered here today in this *Church of St. Peter in Columbia,* which the Successor of Peter is privileged to visit.

It is a great joy for me to come to *the Diocese of Charleston.* I thank you for receiving me with such warmth and fraternal love. Your famous "southern hospitality" makes me feel at home.

As you know, I have come to Columbia to take part in *ecumenical dialogue* with national leaders of other Christian Churches and Ecclesial Communities, and to join with a large gathering of our brothers and sisters in an ecumenical prayer service. Our Lord prayed "that all may be one" (Jn 17:21). We all want to do our part to make this unity come about.

Heart of the Faith

2. *"You are the Messiah, the Son of the living God."*

These words of Peter express *the heart of our faith,* for they reveal the mystery of Christ; they reveal Christ as the Son of the living God, the eternal Word who became man and was born of the Virgin Mary.

Peter was the first of the Apostles, *the first disciple* to make a public declaration of his faith in Jesus the Messiah. The words of Peter's profession of faith were words spoken with real personal conviction, and yet these words did not find their ultimate origin in him. As Jesus told him: "Blest

46

are you, Simon son of Jonah! No mere man has revealed this to you, but my heavenly Father" (Mt 16:17). *Faith in Christ is a gift.* It is not a human achievement. Only God the Father can draw us to Jesus; only he can give us the grace to know Jesus, to accept him as the eternal Son of God, and to profess our faith in him.

3. From that day in the neighborhood of Ceasarea Philippi, Peter's life was radically changed. And not only his life! The other Apostles, the other disciples as well, were granted the gift of faith, and they too became witnesses of the words and deeds of Jesus. A whole new era began in the history of the world—in the history of salvation. And so it has continued down through the ages. People of all centuries, people from all countries have, like Peter, come to know Jesus, to accept him as God's Son—one in being with the Father—to profess their faith in him, and to make his holy Gospel the basis of their Christian lives. *The person of Jesus Christ and his word are forever the center of the Church's life.*

4. But the wonderful gift of faith is not separate from the Cross. Belief in Christ is not free from difficulties. It is not without cost. In fact, our *faith in Jesus Christ is often put to the test.* Peter came to know this only too well. And therefore he writes: "You may for a time have to suffer the distress of many trials; but this is *so that your faith,* which is more precious than the passing splendor of fire-tried gold, *may by its genuineness lead to praise, glory, and honor* when Jesus Christ appears" (1 Pt. 1:6-7).

We recall too the time, after our divine Master spoke of the mystery of the Eucharist, when "many of his disciples broke away and would not remain in his company any longer. Jesus then said to the Twelve, 'Do you want to leave me too?' Simon Peter answered him, '*Lord, to whom shall we go? You have the words of eternal life.* We have come to believe; we are convinced that you are God's holy one'" (Jn 6:66-69).

When our faith is tested, when we are tempted to doubt and turn away, we can find courage and renewed hope in these words of Peter: "Lord, to whom shall we go? You have the words of eternal life." Christ gives us the strength to live according to our faith and to meet all the challenges against it. *From Christ we must learn the way to overcome those sad divisions which still exist today among Christians.* We must be eager to be fully one in faith and love.

South Carolina's Ecumenical Tradition

5. I know that you share this *ecumenical conviction* with me. Indeed, Catholics in South Carolina have long felt the need for ecumenical dialogue and collaboration. First of all because you are a distinct minority—less than three per cent of the population. Moreover, the Catholic Church here has *a long tradition of ecumenical initiative.* Your first *Bishop, John England,* accepted the invitations of other Christians to preach in their churches and to explain the teachings of our faith. And, with the passage of the years, you have never lost this ecumenical spirit.

In more recent times in particular, you have joined with other Christian believers to promote justice and truth, to further mutual understanding and collaboration. This cooperation has been particularly striking in regard to efforts to improve racial relations among citizens of your state. I commend you in these deserving endeavors, so worthwhile and so important.

At the same time, you must never cease to strive for *personal holiness and conversion of heart.* For, as the Second Vatican Council has said: "This change of heart and holiness of life, along with public and private prayer for the unity of Christians, should be regarded as the soul of the whole ecumenical movement" *(Unitatis Redintegratio,* 8).

You Believe and Rejoice

6. Dear friends in Christ, representatives of all the Catholics of the Diocese of Charleston, I thank you for coming to greet me. I wish to assure you of my esteem for all of you who make up this local Church, spread out across this entire state of South Carolina. Know that the Pope admires all the efforts you and your forebears have made to preserve your faith in Jesus Christ, to live this faith and to transmit it to your children.

And now I ask you to take home with you those other words ascribed to Peter—words which explain so well what it means to believe in Christ, the Son of the living God. He wrote: *"Although you have never seen him, you love him,* and without seeing *you now believe in him,* and rejoice with inexpressible joy touched with glory because you are achieving *faith's goal, your salvation"* (1 Pt 1:8-9).

Dear Catholic people of this Diocese of Charleston, never forget that faith in Jesus Christ brings you to salvation and eternal life!

The Challenge of Truth

Greeting to the President and students of the University of South Carolina—Columbia, September 11.

Dear Dr. Holderman,

Dear Friends,

1. Thank you for your thoughtful words of greeting and for the cordial welcome which you have extended to me. I am most grateful. For many months I have looked forward to my visit to South Carolina. It is a great joy for me finally to be here.

At the same time, I come to this state in response to *a solemn duty*. Indeed, is it not the duty of every follower of Christ to work for the unity of all Christians? To desire anything else would be not only a scandal, but a betrayal—a betrayal of the Lord who himself prayed that his disciples would be one, and who died on the Cross in order *"to gather into one* all the dispersed children of God" (Jn 11:52). I pray that the ecumenical initiative which we are undertaking today will be pleasing in God's sight and bring us all closer to the full union of faith and love in our Savior.

2. It is a pleasure for me to come to the campus of this major university. As you know, I myself have had a long and happy association with *the university world* in my homeland. I know how important universities are for *the advancement of research and for the development of knowledge and culture.* I offer all of you my personal encouragement for the educational program which you carry out here in Columbia and for the contribution that you are making to the future of society. To place human knowledge at the service of humanity is a great task.

3. I wish to add a special word of greeting and support *for the students* of the University of South Carolina. Before you lies the wonderful *world of knowledge and the immense challenge of truth.* Here you can come to a much greater understanding of yourself and of the universe. You can delve into the wealth of literature handed down from the past. You can explore the vast fields of the sciences and the arts. You can engage in research and future planning. Here in this

center of higher education, you must prepare yourselves to make your own contribution to society.

My special hope for you is this: that you will always have *a great love for truth*—the truth about God, the truth about man and the truth about the world. I pray that through truth you will serve humanity and experience real freedom. In the words of Jesus Christ: "You will know the truth and the truth will set you free" (Jn 8:32).

May God, the source of life and truth, bless all of you at the University of South Carolina.

The Soul of Ecumenism

Address to thirty Protestant leaders in a closed meeting at the University of South Carolina—Columbia, September 11.

Dear Friends, dear Brothers and Sisters,

1. I praise "the God and Father of our Lord Jesus Christ who has bestowed on us in Christ every spiritual blessing in the heavens!" (Eph 1:3) In particular I give thanks to him today for granting me the opportunity of this meeting with you, representatives of Christian Churches and Ecclesial Communities in the United States. I believe that our meeting is important not only in itself, for the reflections and Christian experience that we share with each other, but also as an outspoken testimony on our part that *we are definitively committed* to treading the path which the Holy Spirit has opened before us—the path of repentance for our divisions, and of working and praying for that perfect unity which the Lord himself wishes for his followers.

I am grateful to you for your presence, and for the statement with which you have wished to open this meeting. And in a wider perspective, I wish *to thank you for the ecumenical contacts and collaboration* in which you so willingly engage here in the United States with the National Conference of Bishops and the Catholic Dioceses. Indeed I am grateful for all the earnest ecumenical activity carried out in this country.

Koinonia

2. In recent decades, especially under the impulse of the Second Vatican Council, the Catholic Church has placed renewed emphasis on the term "communion" *(koinonia)* as an especially appropriate way of describing the profound divine and human reality of the Church, the Body of Christ—*the unity of the baptized in the Father, the Son and the Holy Spirit.* Our communion is primarily with the Triune God, but it intimately unites us among ourselves.

This communion is increased in us as we share in the gifts with which Christ has endowed his Church. Some of these are eminently spiritual in nature, such as the life of grace; faith, hope and charity; and other interior gifts of the Holy Spirit (cf. *Unitatis Redintegratio*, 3). In addition, there are exterior gifts, which include the word of God in Sacred Scripture, Baptism and the other Sacraments, as well as the ministries and charisms which serve ecclesial life.

Although we are not yet in agreement as to how each of our Churches and Ecclesial Communities relates to the fullness of life and mission which flow from God's redemptive act through the Cross and Resurrection of Jesus Christ, it is no small achievement of the ecumenical movement that after centuries of mistrust, we humbly and sincerely *recognize in each other's communities the presence and fruitfulness of Christ's gifts at work*. For this divine action in the lives of all of us, we offer thanks to God.

Interior Renewal

3. I wish to note in particular the reference made in the opening statement to the sense of spiritual yearning among Christians in this country—a yearning which in part manifests itself in an increasing interest in the life of prayer, in spirituality and in ecumenism. In a word, it is *a yearning for deeper insights into our Christian identity* and, consequently, for *a renewal of our ecclesial life*. This important phenomenon can be found to a greater or lesser degree in all Ecclesial Communities, not only in the United States but throughout the world. Surely it is a sign of the action of the Holy Spirit in the People of God. As leaders in our respective communions, we have the awesome task and privilege of collaborating to ensure that this grace will not be received by us in vain (cf. 2 Cor 6:1).

From the Catholic perspective, a primary factor relating to ecumenical involvement with other Christian bodies has been, from the outset, *the purification and renewal of Catholic life itself*. The Second Vatican Council's Decree on Ecumenism indicated: "In ecumenical work, Catholics must assuredly be concerned for their separated brethren, praying for them, keeping them informed about the Church, making the first approaches toward them. But their primary duty is to make an honest and careful appraisal of whatever needs to be renewed and achieved in the Catholic household itself" (*Unitatis Redintegratio*, 4).

It is not difficult to see how the internal renewal and purification of the ecclesial life of all of us is essential to any progress we may make toward unity. For *Christ's call to unity is at the same time a call to holiness and a call to greater love.* It is a call for us to render our witness more authentic. Only by becoming more faithful disciples of Jesus Christ can we hope to travel the path of unity under the guidance of the Holy Spirit and in the strength of his grace. Only by fully accepting Jesus Christ as the Lord of our lives can we empty ourselves of any negative thinking about each other.

It is important for all of us to realize how much conversion of heart depends on prayer, and how much prayer contributes to unity. The Second Vatican Council spoke about a *"spiritual ecumenism"* which it described as "the soul of the whole ecumenical movement," and which it identified as "a change of heart and holiness of life, coupled with public and private prayer for the unity of Christians" (*Unitatis Redintegratio*, 8).

Clarifying Relationships

4. In speaking of the priority of internal renewal and prayer in the ecumenical task, I do not intend in any way to minimize other important factors such as our *common Christian service* to those in need, or our *common study* carried out in theological dialogues.

In the case of *dialogues,* the results reached in them thus far merit the most serious consideration and gratitude from all of us. They tend to increase mutual understanding in ways that have already greatly changed our relationship for the better. Our meeting here today is itself a testimony of this.

Further, these dialogues continue to uncover the deep sources of our common faith and the extent to which that faith, even while we remain apart, is truly shared by our

Churches and Ecclesial Communities. In doing so, such exchanges help us *to face our remaining differences in a more intelligible context*. It is the task of dialogue to face these differences and to work toward the time when it will be possible for Christians to confess together the one faith and to celebrate together the one Eucharist.

On the international level, the response of the Catholic Church to the document *Baptism, Eucharist and Ministry*, which has now been sent to the Commission on Faith and Order, is an effort to contribute to this process directed toward confessing the one faith together. I am convinced that the Lord will give us the light and strength to pursue this course together for the glory of his name.

Indispensable as the work of dialogue is, and even though the act of dialogue itself begins to improve relations between us, our ultimate purpose goes beyond the statements and reports of ecumenical commissions. Those statements must be properly evaluated by our respective Churches and Ecclesial Communities in order to determine the level of ecclesial communion that actually exists, so that it may be *properly reflected in the lifestream of ecclesial life*. We must greatly rejoice in discovering the extent to which we are already united, while we respectfully and serenely acknowledge the factors that still divide us.

Seeking Ways of Collaboration

5. In regard to *our common service and collaboration*, the statement you have presented puts before all of us important questions. How may we collaborate to promote justice, exercise compassion, search for peace, bring the witness of the Gospel to unbelievers, and manifest our *koinonia?* These issues challenge all of us. Together we must seek to discover the concrete ways in which we may respond in common.

You rightly designate these questions as "points of conversation" among us. As an initial approach, an introduction to our conversation, I would like to make the following brief remarks. First, we are all convinced that the deepest lessons a Christian can learn in this life are learned at the foot of the

Cross. When our Churches and Ecclesial Communities address one another and the whole human family, we must do so *from the foot of the Cross of Jesus Christ*—the wellspring of wisdom and the source of our witness. From the Cross we learn the qualities required in our ecumenical search for unity. "For it is from newness of attitudes (cf. Eph 4:23), from self-denial and unstinted love that yearnings for unity take their rise and grow toward maturity" *(Unitatis Redintegratio,* 7). Ecumenism is not a matter of power and human "tactics." It is *a service of truth in love and humble submission to God.*

Similarly, our collaboration in the important areas you list is not a matter of measured calculation. We do not collaborate simply for the sake of efficiency, or for reasons of mere strategy, or for advantage and influence. *We collaborate for the sake of Christ,* who urges us to be one in him and in the Father, so that the world may believe (cf. Jn 17:21).

Christ in Our Midst

6. The ecumenical community has now welcomed me twice to this country. I in turn have had the joyful opportunity of welcoming many of you to Rome, the City of the Apostles and Martyrs, Peter and Paul. I believe that these and other cordial meetings have the effect, with God's grace, of breaking down the barriers of misunderstanding that have plagued us for centuries. How often we read in the Scriptures of encounters being occasions of grace, either encounters of the Lord with his disciples, or encounters of the disciples with others to whom they are bringing the word. I believe that in meetings such as these, where two or three or more of us are gathered in his name, *Christ is here in our midst* asking from each of us a greater depth of commitment to service in his name, and therefore, a greater degree of unity among ourselves.

I join my prayer to yours that the Christian communities of the United States may continue *to meet with each other, to work with each other, and to pray with each other* so that the Father will be glorified in the fulfillment of Christ's prayer:

"That their unity may be complete.
So shall the world know that you sent me,
and that you loved them as you loved me" (Jn 17:23).

So be it.

The Family's Crisis—
A Call to All Christians

Address given during an ecumenical service at Williams-Brice Stadium— Columbia, September 11.

Praised be Jesus Christ!

Dear Brothers and Sisters,

1. I greet each one of you in our Lord and Savior Jesus Christ. It is indeed the "Lord of both the dead and the living" (Rom 14:9) who has brought us together in this holy assembly of Christian people, a joy-filled gathering of different Ecclesial Communions: Orthodox, Anglicans, Methodists, Baptists, Lutherans, Presbyterians, members of the United Church of Christ and of other Reformed Churches, Disciples of Christ, members of the Peace Churches, Pentecostals, members of the Polish National Catholic Church and Catholics.

We stand side by side *to confess Jesus Christ,* "the one mediator between God and man" (1 Tm 2:5), for "at Jesus' name every knee must bend in the heavens, on the earth and under the earth, and every tongue proclaim to the glory of God the Father: *Jesus Christ is Lord!''* (Phil 2:10)

We have come here to pray, and in doing so we are following the example of all the saints from the beginning— especially the Apostles—who, in awaiting the Holy Spirit, "devoted themselves to prayer, together with the women and Mary the Mother of Jesus, and with his brethren" (Acts 1:14). Together we are renewing our common faith in the eternal redemption which we have obtained through the Cross of Jesus Christ (cf. Heb 9:12), and our hope that, just as Jesus rose from the dead, so too we shall rise to eternal life (cf. Phil 3:11). In fact, through our *Baptism in the name of the Father and of the Son and of the Holy Spirit,* we have been buried with Christ "so that, just as Christ was raised from the dead by the glory of the Father, we too might live a new life" (Rom 6:4). Living a new life in the Spirit, we are *a pilgrim people,* pressing forward amid the persecutions of the world and the consolations of God, announcing the death of the Lord until he comes (cf. 1 Cor 11:26; *Lumen Gentium,* 8).

Brothers and sisters: we are divided in many ways in our faith and discipleship. But we are here together today as sons and daughters of *the one Father,* calling upon *the one Lord Jesus Christ,* in the love which *the same Holy Spirit* pours forth into our hearts. Let us give thanks to God and let us rejoice in this fellowship! And let us commit ourselves further to the great task which Jesus himself urges upon us: to go forward along the path of Christian reconciliation and unity "without obstructing the ways of divine Providence and without prejudging the future inspiration of the Holy Spirit" *(Unitatis Redintegratio,* 24).

2. In this service of Christian witness we have listened together to the word of God given to us in the Holy Scriptures. *The Scriptures are dear to all of us. They are one of the greatest treasures we share.* In the Sacred Scriptures and in the deeds of divine mercy which they narrate, God our Father, out of the abundance of his love, speaks to us as his children and lives among us. The Bible is holy because in its inspired and unalterable words the voice of the Holy Spirit lives and is heard among us, sounding again and again in the Church from age to age and from generation to generation (cf. *Dei Verbum,* 21).

Marriage in Christ

3. Today this stadium has resounded with passages from Holy Scripture bearing on the reality of *the family.* We have heard the plea and promise made by the young widow, Ruth: "wherever you go I will go, wherever you lodge I will lodge, your people shall be my people, and your God my God. Wherever you die I will die and there be buried" (Ru 1:16-17). To hear these words is to be moved with a deep feeling for *the strength of family ties:* stronger than the fear of hardships to be faced; stronger than the fear of exile in an unfamiliar land; stronger than the fear of possible rejection. The bond that unites a family is not only a matter of natural kinship or of shared life and experience. It is essentially a holy and religious bond. *Marriage and the family are sacred realities.*

The sacredness of Christian marriage consists in the fact that in God's plan the marriage covenant between a man and a woman becomes *the image and symbol of the covenant which unites God and his people* (cf. Hos 2:21; Jer 3:6-13; Is 54:5-10). It is the sign of Christ's love for his Church (cf. Eph 5:32). Because God's love is faithful and irrevocable, so those who have been married "in Christ" are called to remain faithful to each other forever. Did not Jesus himself say to us: "What therefore God has joined together, let no man put asunder" (cf. Mt 19:6)?

Contemporary society has a special need of the witness of couples who persevere in their union, as an eloquent (even if sometimes suffering) "sign" in our human condition of the steadfastness of God's love. Day after day *Christian married couples are called to open their hearts ever more to the Holy Spirit whose power never fails,* and who enables them to love each other as Christ has loved us. And, as St. Paul writes to the Galatians, "the fruit of the Spirit is love, joy, peace, patient endurance, kindness, generosity, faith, mildness and chastity" (Gal 5:22-23). All of this constitutes the rule of life and the program of personal development of Christian couples. And each Christian community has a great responsibility to sustain couples in their love.

A "Church in Miniature"

4. From such love Christian families are born. In them *children are welcomed as a splendid gift of God's goodness,* and they are educated in the essential values of human life, learning above all that "man is more precious for what he is than for what he has" (cf. *Gaudium et Spes*, 35). The entire family endeavors to practice respect for the dignity of every individual and to offer disinterested service to those in need (cf. *Familiaris Consortio*, 37).

Christian families exist to form *a communion of persons in love*. As such, the Church and the family are, each in its own way, living representations in human history of the eternal loving communion of the Three Persons of the Most Holy Trinity. In fact, the family is called the Church in miniature, "the domestic church," a particular expression of the Church through the human experience of love and common life (cf. *Familiaris Consortio*, 49). Like the Church, the family ought to be a place where the Gospel is transmitted and *from which the Gospel radiates to other families and to the whole of society.*

Cultural Pressures on Family Life

5. In America and throughout the world, *the family is being shaken* to its roots. The consequences for individuals and society in personal and collective instability and unhappiness are incalculable. Yet, it is heartening to know that in the face of this extraordinary challenge many Christians are committing themselves to the defense and support of family life. In recent years the Catholic Church, especially on the occasion of the 1980 Synod of the world's Bishops, has been involved in an extensive reflection on the role of the Christian family in the modern world. This is a field in which there must be the maximum collaboration among all who confess Jesus Christ.

So often the pressures of modern living separate husbands and wives from one another, threatening their lifelong *interdependence in love and fidelity.* Can we also not be concerned about the impact of cultural pressures upon *relations between the generations,* upon parental authority and the transmission of sacred values? Our Christian conscience should be deeply concerned about the way in which *sins against love and against life* are often presented as examples of "progress" and emancipation. Most often, are they not but the age-old forms of selfishness dressed up in a new language and presented in a new cultural framework?

6. Many of these problems are the result of *a false notion of individual freedom at work in our culture,* as if one could be free only when rejecting every objective norm of conduct, refusing to assume responsibility or even refusing to put curbs on instincts and passions! Instead, *true freedom* implies that we are capable of choosing a good without constraint. This is the truly human way of proceeding in the choices— big and small—which life puts before us. The fact that we are also able to choose *not* to act as we see we should is a necessary condition of our moral freedom. But in that case we must account for the good that we fail to do and for the

evil that we commit. This sense of moral accountability needs to be reawakened if society is to survive as a civilization of justice and solidarity.

It is true that our freedom is weakened and conditioned in many ways, not least as a consequence of the mysterious and dramatic history of mankind's original rebellion against the Creator's will, as indicated in the opening pages of the Book of Genesis. But *we remain free and responsible beings* who have been redeemed by Jesus Christ, and we must *educate our freedom* to recognize and choose what is right and good, and to reject what does not conform to the original truth concerning our nature and our destiny as God's creatures. *Truth*—beginning with the truth of our redemption through the Cross and Resurrection of Jesus Christ—*is the root and rule of freedom, the foundation and measure of all liberating action* (cf. *Instruction on Christian Freedom and Liberation*, 3).

Right Choices

7. It would be a great tragedy for the entire human family if the United States, which prides itself on its consecration to freedom, were to lose sight of the true meaning of that noble word. America: you cannot insist on the right to choose without also insisting *on the duty to choose well, the duty to choose the truth*. Already there is much breakdown and pain in your own society because fundamental values, essential to the well-being of individuals, families and the entire nation, are being emptied of their real content.

And yet, at the same time, throughout this land there is *a great stirring*, an awareness of *the urgent need to recapture the ultimate meaning of life and its fundamental values*. Surely by now we must be convinced that only by recognizing the primacy of moral values can we use the immense possibilities offered by science and material progress to bring about the true advancement of the human person in truth, freedom and dignity. As Christians, our specific contribution is *to bring the wisdom of God's word to bear on the problems of modern living* in such a way that modern culture will be led to a more profoundly restored covenant with divine Wisdom itself (cf. *Familiaris Consortio*, 8). As we heard proclaimed in the Gospel reading, Jesus indicates that the supreme norm of our behavior and our relationships, including our relationship with him, is always obedience to the will of the Creator: "Whoever does the will of my heavenly Father is brother and sister and mother to me" (Mt 12:50).

The Churches and Families

8. Brothers and sisters: to the extent that God grants us to *grow in Christian unity let us work together to offer strength and support to families* on whom the well-being of society depends, and on whom our Churches and Ecclesial Communities depend. May the families of America live with grateful hearts, giving thanks to the Lord for his blessings, praying for one another, bearing one another's burdens, welcoming one another as Christ has welcomed them.

My prayer for all of you at the end of this second day of my visit echoes the words of Paul to the Thessalonians: "May the God of peace make you perfect in holiness.... May the grace of our Lord Jesus Christ be with you" (1 Thes 5:23, 28).

Sharers
in the Divine Communion

Address given to priests and religious during a prayer service held at St. Louis Cathedral—New Orleans, September 12.

"The grace of the Lord Jesus Christ, and the love of God, and the fellowship of the Holy Spirit be with you all!"

(2 Cor 13:14)

Dear Archbishop Hannan,
Dear Brothers and Sisters,

1. From this Cathedral of St. Louis I am happy to greet, in the name of the Most Holy Trinity, the whole Church in New Orleans—all those who make up her membership, all those who work together to fulfill her mission. In particular today I greet all of you, dear priests and religious of Louisiana. Here in this mother Church of the Archdiocese, *I give thanks and praise to the living God* for your lives of dedicated service to Christ and his Church.

This temple of God, this house of prayer and gate of heaven stands as the *central point of the city of New Orleans,* and from this place all distances are measured. Here Christ dwells in your midst, present in word and Sacrament, making this a place of grace and blessing for all the People of God. Here God the Father is adored in spirit and truth (cf. Jn 4:23), and here the Holy Spirit is always at work in the hearts of the faithful, preparing them for the glory of the heavenly Jerusalem.

And just as this Cathedral of St. Louis is the focal point of the city of New Orleans, so too *Christ is the very center of your lives.* Christ is for you "the beginning and the end" (Rv 21:6); he is for you "the way, and the truth, and the life" (Jn 14:6). So closely are you identified with Christ that each of you can say, as did St. Paul: "The life I live now is not my own; Christ is living in me. I still live my human life, but it is a life of faith in the Son of God, who loved me and gave himself for me" (Gal 2:20). And together with St. Paul you must proclaim: "Nothing will be able to separate us from the love of God that comes to us in Christ Jesus, our Lord" (Rom 8:39).

The Church in Louisiana owes a great debt of gratitude to the many priests and religious who have labored here from the beginning. That tradition of heroic dedication in proclaiming the Gospel of Christ by word and deed continues today in the service that you render to the People of God. Always remember that the supernatural effectiveness of your service within the Church is linked to *the witness of your life lived in union with Christ.* You are therefore called to conform your lives more and more to the person and message of Jesus Christ. And never forget that the precise goal of all apostolic service is to lead all people to communion with the Most Holy Trinity.

The Church and the Triune God

2. Our lives as Christians find their origin and destiny in *the mystery of the Most Holy Trinity,* the fundamental mystery of our Christian faith. The one God whom we worship is a unity of Three Divine Persons, "equal in majesty, undivided in splendor, yet one Lord, one God, ever to be adored" (Preface of the Most Holy Trinity). The Father and the Son and the Holy Spirit exist in an eternal communion of life and love with one another. In the Church we are privileged *to participate now and forever in the communion of life and love,* which is the mystery of God, One in Three.

The Second Vatican Council teaches that "it is from the mission of the Son and the mission of the Holy Spirit that the Church takes her origin, in accordance with the decree of God the Father" *(Ad Gentes,* 2). Thus as members of the Church we benefit from *the mission of the Son* and *the mission of the Holy Spirit* which flow from "'that fountain of love' or charity within God the Father" *(ibid.).* It is from the Father, "who is 'origin without origin,' that the Son is begotten and the Holy Spirit proceeds through the Son" *(ibid.).*

In revealing to us the mystery of the Father *the Son carries out the Father's will and brings about our salvation.* And in describing the mission of the Holy Spirit, the Council says: "When the work which the Father had given the Son to do on earth (cf. Jn 17:4) was accomplished, the Holy Spirit was sent on the day of Pentecost in order that he might forever sanctify the Church, and thus all believers would have access to the Father through Christ in the one Spirit (cf. Eph 2:18)" *(Lumen Gentium, 4)*.

3. In St. John's Gospel we read: "No one has ever seen God. It is God the only Son, ever at the Father's side who revealed him" (Jn 1:18). Although the Old Testament contained elements that prepared us for the revelation of Jesus, it did not unveil this profound mystery of God: the mystery of the Father, the intimate life of God, the communion of the Three Divine Persons. *Only the Son of God made man bears witness to the truth about the Trinity; only he reveals it.*

The truth about the divine Sonship of Jesus and the Trinitarian mystery of the Father and the Son and the Holy Spirit are alluded to at the time of the Annunciation, as well as during the baptism of Jesus in the Jordan. Moreover, during his public ministry Jesus speaks about his Father and the Holy Spirit. In the Gospel of John we find many affirmations by Jesus about the intimate union that he shares with the Father. But it is during his discourse *at the Last Supper that Jesus discloses in a definitive way the truth about the Holy Spirit* and the relationship which the Spirit has with the Father and the Son.

We can say that throughout his teaching, Jesus "has opened up vistas closed to human reason" *(Gaudium et Spes,* 24) concerning the life of the One God in the Trinity of divine Persons. When he had completed his Messianic mission and he was taking leave of his Apostles on the day of his Ascension, Jesus announced to them: "Go, therefore, and make disciples of all nations. Baptize them in the name of the Father, and of the Son, and of the Holy Spirit" (Mt 28:19). Thus with these last words *Jesus solemnly entrusts to them the supreme truth of the undivided Unity of the Most Holy Trinity.*

Religious and God's Love

4. Dear brothers and sisters: your life of service dedicated to Christ and his Church bears witness to *the reality of God's love for his people.* You joyfully proclaim the Good News of faith, that "God is love" (1 Jn 4:8). In Jesus' conversation

with Nicodemus, we hear those words: "Yes, God so loved the world that he gave his only Son, that whoever believes in him may not die but may have eternal life" (Jn 3:16). The Father so loved the world that he sent us his only Son, and through his Son he sent the Holy Spirit. Today and each day of our lives we celebrate the love of God the Father for each of us—the love revealed in the Word made flesh and in the gift of the Holy Spirit. Moreover, we proclaim that God sent his only Son into the world *not to condemn the world,* but that the world might be saved through him. Yes, we proclaim to the world *God's everlasting love.*

May the prayers of the Blessed Virgin Mary, Our Lady of Prompt Succor and Mother of Divine Love, help you and the whole Church in New Orleans and throughout Louisiana to bear witness to the merciful love of the Father, and the Son, and the Holy Spirit.

The Church and
the Black Community

Address given at a meeting with Black Catholic leadership—Superdome, New Orleans, September 12.

Dear Brothers and Sisters in Christ,

1. "Go into the whole world and *proclaim the Good News* to all creation" (Mk 16:15). With these words, our Lord Jesus Christ directed the Church to speak his own message of life to the whole human family. The apostles first responded to the Savior's call and travelled throughout the known world, sharing with every one who would listen what they had seen and heard (cf. 1 Jn 1:3), speaking about God's Kingdom and about reconciliation in Christ.

Today, almost two thousand years later, the Church still seeks to respond generously to Christ's command. The world we must serve today is much bigger, and the people who long to hear the word of life are numerous indeed. While the words of the Lord remain true, "The harvest is good but laborers are scarce" (Mt 9:37), still we rejoice that the Holy Spirit has enriched the Church with many hands for the harvest. There are worthy laborers in every corner of the earth, people of every culture, who are eager *to live the Gospel and to proclaim it by word and example.*

I am especially happy to meet with you who make up the black Catholic leadership in the United States. Your great concern, both as blacks and as Catholics, is—and must always be—that all your black brothers and sisters throughout America may hear and embrace the saving and uplifting Gospel of Jesus Christ. I willingly join my voice to those of the Bishops of your country who are encouraging you *to give priority to the great task of evangelization,* to be missionaries of Christ's love and truth within your own black community. To all the members of the black community throughout the United States, I send my greetings of respect and esteem.

All Are Called to Evangelize

2. My dear brother Bishops, who share with me the burdens and joys of the episcopacy: I am pleased that the universality of the Gospel and the cultural diversity of your nation are increasingly mirrored in the composition of the American hierarchy. While your apostolic ministry draws you to serve all the faithful of your respective dioceses—and in collegial unity the whole Body of Christ—it is fitting for many reasons that your own black brothers and sisters should have a special right to your pastoral love and service. United with the Successor of Peter *in the College of Bishops, you are a sign of the unity and universality of the Church* and of her mission. As Bishops, we are entrusted with the task of preserving in its integrity the Good News of salvation and of presenting it as effectively as possible to our people, so that they may all discover in Jesus Christ "the way, and the truth, and the life" (Jn 14:6).

Our brothers in *the priesthood,* ministering in the person of Christ and in union with us, transmit the teaching of the faith and celebrate the sacred mysteries of salvation. How fruitful it is for the mission of the Church in America when so many priests from different racial and ethnic groups proclaim together Christ's liberating Gospel and thus bear witness to the fact that it rightfully belongs to everyone.

The Church in the United States is distinguished by its large number of *deacons,* among whom are several hundred from the black Catholic community. As heralds of the Gospel and servant ministers of Christ, dear brothers, you complete the threefold ministry of the Sacrament of Orders. In the Church you are called to the service of the word, of the Eucharist and of charity. Your generous response is a clear indication of the growing maturity of the black Catholic community, a maturity emphasized by the black bishops of your country in their Pastoral Letter "What We Have Seen and Heard."

Even in those days—by the grace of God now long past—when your people struggled under the terrible burden of slavery, brave spirits within the community embraced the evangelical counsels and dedicated themselves to *the religious life.* Thus they bore eloquent witness to the power of the

Holy Spirit accomplishing the work of spiritual freedom even in the moment of physical oppression. Black religious today offer a comparable witness to the Church and society, proclaiming God's kingdom to a world shackled by consumerism, mindless pleasure-seeking and irresponsible individualism—shackles of the spirit which are *even more destructive than the chains of physical slavery.*

I am close to the whole black community in the great mission and responsibility of encouraging more and more young Americans of their race to respond to the Lord's invitation to religious life and the priesthood. I urge you to be faithful to prayer and to do all you can to ensure that those who are called will find the support and the assistance which they need in order to pursue these vocations and to persevere in them.

3. The Church's work of evangelization finds entry into the human community in a special way through the lives of *lay people.* As my predecessor Paul VI pointed out, the laity's "own field of evangelizing activity is the vast and complicated world of politics, society and economics, but also the world of culture, of the sciences and the arts, of international life, of the mass media" *(Evangelii Nuntiandi,* 70). By fulfilling worthily the broad range of their temporal involvement, lay men and women bear witness in a unique way to *the universal call to holiness.* The witness of their faithful lives speaks an uplifting message to the world.

I express *my deep love and esteem for the black Catholic community in the United States.* Its vitality is a sign of hope for society. Composed as you are of many lifelong Catholics, and many who have more recently embraced the faith, together with a growing immigrant community, you reflect the Church's ability to bring together a diversity of people united in faith, hope and love, sharing a communion with Christ in the Holy Spirit. I urge you to keep alive and active *your rich cultural gifts.* Always profess proudly before the whole Church and the whole world *your love for God's word;* it is a special blessing which you must forever treasure as a part of your heritage. Help us all to remember that *authentic freedom* comes from accepting the truth and from living one's life in accordance with it—and the full truth is found only in

Christ Jesus. Continue to inspire us by your desire to forgive—as Jesus forgave—and by your *desire to be reconciled* with all the people of this nation, even those who would unjustly deny you the full exercise of your human rights.

The Family and Evangelization

4. I am sure that you share with me a special concern for that most basic human community, *the family.* Your faithful Christian families are a source of comfort in the face of the extraordinary pressures affecting society. Today, you must *rediscover the spirit of family life* which refuses to be destroyed in the face of even the most oppressive forces. Surely that spirit can be found in exploring your spiritual and cultural heritage. The inspiration you draw from the great men and women of your past will then allow your young people to see the value of a strong family life. Know that the Pope stands united with the black community as it rises to embrace its full dignity and lofty destiny.

The family is *the first setting of evangelization,* the place where the Good News of Christ is first received, and then, in simple yet profound ways, handed on from generation to generation. At the same time, families in our time vitally depend upon the Church to defend their rights and to teach the obligations and responsibilities which lead to the fullness of joy and life. Thus, I urge all of you, especially the clergy and religious, to work for the promotion of family values within the local community. And I remind those responsible for making and administering laws and public policies that social problems are never solved, but only worsened, by positions which weaken or destroy the family.

Solidarity with the Oppressed

5. Even in this wealthy nation, committed by its Founding Fathers to the dignity and equality of all persons, the black community suffers a disproportionate share of economic deprivation. Far too many of your young people receive less than an equal opportunity for a quality education and for gainful employment. The Church must continue to

join her efforts with the efforts of others who are working to correct all imbalances and disorders of a social nature. Indeed, *the Church can never remain silent in the face of injustice*, wherever it is clearly present.

In the most difficult hours of your struggle for civil rights amidst discrimination and oppression, God himself guided your steps along the way of peace. Before the witness of history *the response of non-violence stands, in the memory of this nation, as a monument of honor to the black community* of the United States. Today as we recall those who with Christian vision opted for non-violence as the only truly effective approach for ensuring and safeguarding human dignity, we cannot but think of the Reverend Dr. Martin Luther King, Jr. and of the providential role he played in contributing to the rightful human betterment of black Americans and therefore to the improvement of American society itself.

My dear brothers and sisters of the black community: it is the hour to give thanks to God for his liberating action in your history and in your lives. This liberating action is *a sign and expression of Christ's Paschal Mystery*, which in every age is effective in helping God's people to pass from bondage into their glorious vocation of full Christian freedom. And as you offer your prayer of thanksgiving, you must not fail to concern yourselves with the plight of your brothers and sisters in other places throughout the world. *Black Americans must offer their own special solidarity of Christian love to all people who bear the heavy burden of oppression*, whatever its physical or moral nature.

Mutual Enrichment

6. The Catholic Church has made a profound contribution to the lives of many members of the black community in this land through the gift of education received in *Catholic schools*. Because of the splendid commitment of dioceses and parishes, many of you here today have joined us at the Table of unity and faith: a result of the evangelization carried out in these institutions. Catholic schools have a special place in the work of spreading the Gospel of Christ. They are a great

gift from God. Keep your Catholic schools strong and active. Their uncompromising *Catholic identity and Catholic witness* at every level must continue to enrich the black communities of this nation.

7. In addition to the schools, other means of evangelization should also be given priority. Among these *the means of social communication* deserve special attention. The mass media are also a great gift of God's Providence and should be fully utilized in the service of the Gospel of our Lord Jesus Christ. They can be of immense service to the millions of black people who long to hear the Good News of salvation proclaimed in ways that speak to their own heritage and traditions.

While remaining faithful to her doctrine and discipline, *the Church esteems and honors all cultures;* she respects them in all her evangelizing efforts among the various peoples. At the first Pentecost, those present heard the Apostles speaking in their own languages (cf. Acts 2:4f.). With the guidance of the Holy Spirit, we try in every age to bring the Gospel convincingly and understandably to people of all races, languages and cultures. It is important to realize that there is no black Church, no white Church, no American Church; but there is and must be, in the one Church of Jesus Christ, a home for blacks, whites, Americans, every culture and race. What I said on another occasion, I willingly repeat: "The Church is catholic...because she is able to present in every human context the revealed truth, preserved by her intact in its divine content, in such a way as to bring it into contact with the lofty thoughts and just expectations of every individual and every people" *(Slavorum Apostoli,* 18).

Dear brothers and sisters: *your black cultural heritage enriches the Church* and makes her witness of universality more complete. In a real way *the Church needs you, just as you need the Church,* for you are part of the Church and the Church is part of you. As you continue to place this heritage at the service of the whole Church for the spread of the Gospel, the Holy Spirit himself will continue through you his work of evangelization. With a joyful and a hopeful heart, I entrust you and the whole black community to the loving care of Mary, Mother of our Savior. May she, who both listened to the word and believed in it, guide your lives and those of future generations of black Catholics within the one People of God, the one Mystical Body of Christ. Through her intercession may grace be to all of you "who love our Lord Jesus Christ with unfailing love" (Eph 6:23).

Molding the Human Person

Address given to 1,800 leaders in Catholic elementary, secondary and religious education—Superdome, New Orleans, September 12.

Dear Brothers and Sisters,

1. I thank all of you for your warm welcome and I praise our Lord and Savior Jesus Christ who gives me this opportunity to meet with you, *the representatives of Catholic Elementary and Secondary Schools and leaders in Religious Education.* My first word to you is one of esteem and encouragement: I wish to assure you that I fully appreciate the extraordinary importance of your commitment to Catholic education. I commend you for your concern for the vitality and Catholic identity of the educational centers in which you work, throughout the length and breadth of the United States. I encourage you to continue to fulfill *your special role within the Church and within society* in a spirit of generous responsibility, intelligent creativity and the pursuit of excellence.

American Freedom and Catholic Education

2. It is fitting that we should be meeting in this historic city, itself the meeting-point of several rich cultures, where the Capuchin Fathers and the Ursuline Sisters founded schools at the very dawn of your emergence as a nation. You are preparing to observe *the 200th Anniversary of the signing of the Constitution of the United States.* There is no doubt that the guarantee of religious freedom enshrined in the Bill of Rights has helped make possible the marvelous growth of Catholic education in this country.

Over the years much has been attempted and much has been achieved by Catholics in the United States to make available for their children the best education possible. Much has been done in the specific area of bringing the wealth of our Catholic faith to children and adults in the home, in schools and through religious education programs. The presence of the Church in the field of education is wonderfully manifested in the vast and dynamic network of schools and educational programs extending from the preschool through the adult years. *The entire ecclesial community*—Bishops, priests, religious, the laity—the Church in all her parts, *is called to value ever more deeply the importance of this task and mission, and to continue to give it full and enthusiastic support.*

Religious, Lay Teachers and Parents

3. In the beginning and for a long time afterwards, women and men Religious bore the chief organizational and teaching responsibilities in Catholic education in this country. As pioneers they met that challenge splendidly, and they continue to meet it today. The Church and—I am certain— the nation will forever feel a debt of gratitude toward them. The importance of *the presence of committed Religious, and of religious communities, in the educational apostolate has not diminished with time.* It is my heartfelt prayer that the Lord will continue to call many young people to the religious life, and that their witness to the Gospel will remain a central element in Catholic education.

4. In recent years, thousands of *lay people* have come forward as administrators and teachers in the Church's schools and educational programs. By accepting and developing the legacy of Catholic thought and educational experience which they have inherited, they take their place as *full partners in the Church's mission* of educating the whole person and of transmitting the Good News of salvation in Jesus Christ to successive generations of young Americans. Even if they do not "teach religion," their service in a Catholic school or educational program is part of the Church's unceasing endeavor to lead all to "profess the truth in love and grow to the full maturity of Christ the head" (Eph 4:15).

I am aware that not all questions relating to the organization, financing and administration of Catholic schools in an increasingly complex society have been resolved to the satisfaction of all. We hope that such matters will be settled with justice and fairness for all. In this regard it is important to proceed in a proper perspective. For a Catholic educator, the Church should not be looked upon merely as an employer. The Church is the Body of Christ, carrying on the mission of the Redeemer throughout history. *It is our privilege to share in that mission,* to which we are called by the grace of God and in which we are engaged together.

5. Permit me, brothers and sisters, to mention briefly something that is of special concern to the Church. I refer to *the rights and duties of parents in the education of their children.* The Second Vatican Council clearly enunciated the Church's position: "Since parents have conferred life on their children, they have a most solemn obligation to educate their offspring. Hence, parents must be acknowledged as the first and foremost educators of their children" (*Gravissimum Educationis,* 3). In comparison with the educational role of all others, their role is primary; it is also *irreplaceable and inalienable.* It would be wrong for anyone to attempt to usurp that unique responsibility (cf. *Familiaris Consortio,* 36). Nor should parents in any way be penalized for choosing for their children an education according to their beliefs.

Parents need to ensure that their own homes are places where spiritual and moral values are lived. They are right to insist that their children's faith be respected and fostered. As educators you correctly see your role as cooperating with parents in their primary responsibility. Your efforts to involve them in the whole educational process are commendable. This is an area in which pastors and other priests can be especially supportive. To these I wish to say: try to make every effort to ensure that religious education programs and, where possible, parish schools are *an important part of your ministry;* support and encourage teachers, administrators and parents in their work. Few efforts are more important for the present and future well-being of the Church and of the nation than efforts extended in the work of education.

The Service of Catholic Schools

6. *Catholic schools* in the United States have always enjoyed *a reputation for academic excellence and community service.* Very often they serve large numbers of poor children and young people, and are attentive to the needs of minority groups. I heartily encourage you to continue to provide quality Catholic education for the poor of all races and

national backgrounds, even at the cost of great sacrifice. We cannot doubt that such is part of God's call to the Church in the United States. It is a responsibility that is deeply inscribed in the history of Catholic education in this country.

On another occasion, speaking to the Bishops of the United States, I mentioned that the Catholic school "has contributed immensely to the spreading of God's word and has enabled the faithful 'to relate human affairs and activities with religious values in a single living synthesis' *(Sapientia Christiana,* 1). In the community formed by the Catholic school, the power of the Gospel has been brought to bear on thought patterns, standards of judgment and norms of behavior. As an institution, the Catholic school has to be judged extremely favorably if we apply the sound criterion: 'You will know them by their deeds' (Mt 7:16), and again, 'You can tell a tree by its fruit' (Mt 7:20)" (Address of October 28, 1983).

At this point I cannot fail to praise *the financial sacrifices of American Catholics* as well as the substantial contributions of individual benefactors, foundations, organizations and business to Catholic education in the United States. The heroic sacrifices of generations of Catholic parents in building up and supporting parochial and diocesan schools must never be forgotten. Rising costs may call for new approaches, new forms of partnership and sharing, new uses of financial resources, but I am sure that all concerned will face the challenge of Catholic schools with courage and dedication, and not doubt the value of the sacrifices to be made.

Aims and Goals

7. But there is another challenge facing all those who are concerned with Catholic education. It is the pressing challenge of clearly identifying *the aims of Catholic education,* and applying proper methods in Catholic elementary and secondary education and religious education programs. It is the challenge of fully understanding the educational enterprise, of properly evaluating its content, and *of transmitting the full truth concerning the human person,* created in God's image and called to life in Christ through the Holy Spirit.

The *content of the individual courses* in Catholic education is important both in religious teaching and in all the other subjects that go to make-up the total instruction of human persons and to prepare them for their life's work and their eternal destiny. It is fitting that teachers should be constantly challenged by *high professional standards in preparing and teaching their courses.* In regard to the content of religion courses, the essential criterion is fidelity to the teaching of the Church.

Educators are likewise in a splendid position to inculcate into young people *right ethical attitudes.* These include attitudes toward material things and their proper use. The whole life style of students will reflect the attitudes that they form during their years of formal education.

In these tasks you will find guidance in many documents of the Church. Your own Bishops, applying the universal teaching of the Church, have helped point the way for you, notably in their pastoral letter *To Teach as Jesus Did* and in the National Catechetical Directory. I would also remind you of the Holy See's documents on *The Catholic School* and *Lay Catholics in Schools: Witnesses to Faith.* There we are reminded that it is the school's task to cultivate the intellectual, creative and esthetic faculties of the individual; to develop in students the ability to make correct use of their judgment, will and affectivity; to promote in them a sense of values; to encourage just attitudes and prudent behavior; to introduce them to the cultural patrimony handed down from previous generations; to prepare them for their working lives, and to encourage the friendly interchange among students of diverse cultures and backgrounds that will lead to mutual understanding and love.

8. *The ultimate goal of all Catholic education is salvation in Jesus Christ.* Catholic educators effectively work for the coming of Christ's Kingdom; this work includes transmitting clearly and in full the message of salvation, which elicits the response of faith. In faith we know God, and the hidden purpose of his will (cf. Eph 1:9). In faith we truly come to know ourselves. *By sharing our faith we communicate a complete vision of the whole of reality and a commitment to truth and goodness.* This vision and this commitment draw the strands

of life into a purposeful pattern. By enriching your students' lives with the fullness of Christ's message and by inviting them to accept with all their hearts Christ's work, which is the Church, you promote most effectively their integral human development, and you help them to build a community of faith, hope and love.

This Christian message is the more urgent for those young ones who come from broken homes and who, often with only one parent to encourage them, must draw support and direction from their teachers in school.

In your apostolate of helping to bring Christ's message into the lives of your students, the whole Church supports you and stands with you. The Synod of Bishops, in particular, has recognized the importance of your task and the difficulties you face. For these reasons it has called for concerted efforts to compose a universal catechism. This project will not eliminate the great challenge of a need for creativity in methodology, nor will it minimize the continued need for the inculturation of the Gospel, but it will assist all the local Churches in effectively presenting in its integrity the content of Catholic teaching. In the Church in America, an important part of the truly *glorious chapter of Catholic education* has been the transmitting of Christ's message through *religious education programs* designed for children and young people outside Catholic schools. For this too I give thanks to God, recalling all those who throughout the history of this nation have so generously collaborated in this "work of faith and labor of love" (1 Thes 1:3).

Building Community

9. *Community is at the heart of all Catholic education,* not simply as a concept to be taught, but as a reality to be lived. In its deepest Christian sense the community is a sharing in the life of the Blessed Trinity. Your students will learn to understand and appreciate the value of community *as they experience love, trust and loyalty in your schools and educational programs,* and as they learn to treat all persons as brothers and sisters created by God and redeemed by Christ. Help them to grasp this sense of community by active participa-

tion in the life of the parish and the diocese and especially by receiving the Sacraments of Penance and the Eucharist. The Second Vatican Council explicitly includes learning to adore God in spirit and in truth among the aims of all Christian education (cf. *Gravissimum Educationis*, 2).

A sense of community implies *openness to the wider community*. Often, today, Catholic education takes place in changing neighborhoods; it requires respect for cultural diversity, love for those of different ethnic backgrounds, service to those in need, without discrimination. Help your students to see themselves as members of the universal Church and the world community. Help them to understand the implications of justice and mercy. Foster in your students *a social consciousness* which will move them to meet the needs of their neighbors, and to discern and seek to remove the sources of injustice in society. No human anxiety or sorrow should leave the disciples of Jesus Christ indifferent.

Jesus—Model, Guide and Strength

10. The world needs more than just social reformers. It needs saints. Holiness is not the privilege of a few; it is a gift offered to all. *The call to holiness is addressed also to you and to your students.* To doubt this is to misjudge Christ's intentions: for "each of us has received God's favor in the measure in which Christ bestowed it" (Eph 4:7).

Brothers and sisters: take Jesus Christ the Teacher as the model of your service, as your guide and source of strength. He himself has told us: *"You address me as 'Teacher' and 'Lord,' and fittingly enough, for that is what I am"* (Jn 13:13-14). He taught in word and deed, and his teaching cannot be separated from his life and being. In the Apostolic Exhortation on Catechesis I stated: "The whole of Christ's life was a continual teaching: his silence, his miracles, his gestures, his prayer, his love for people, his special affection for the little and the poor, his acceptance of the total sacrifice on the Cross for the redemption of the world, and his Resurrection.... Hence for Christians the crucifix is one of the most sublime and popular images of Christ the Teacher" *(Catechesi Tradendae,* 9).

11. Dear friends, Jesus shares with you his teaching ministry. Only in close communion with him can you respond adequately. This is my hope; this is my prayer: *that you will be totally open to Christ*. That he will give you an ever greater love for your students and an ever stronger commitment to your vocation as Catholic educators. If you continue to be faithful to this ministry today, as you have been in the past, you will be doing much in shaping a peaceful, just and hope-filled world for the future. *Yours is a great gift to the Church, a great gift to your nation.*

Follow Jesus with Open Hearts

Address prepared for delivery at the youth rally held in the Superdome— New Orleans, September 12. (The actual talk to the 88,000 young people was condensed due to the lack of time.)

PART I

Dear Young People of New Orleans,
Dear Young People of America,

1. Listening to what you are telling me by your presence and through your representatives, I know that you are *very much conscious of having a special mission in this world,* of being partners in the mission of the Church.

I also know that in fulfilling your mission you are willing to give, you are willing to share, and you are willing to serve. And you are willing to do all this *together,* not alone! In this you are like Jesus: Jesus *gave* and he *served* and he was never alone. He tells us: "The one who sent me is with me. He has not left me alone" (Jn 8:29).

Yes, dear young people, I too want *to speak about your mission,* the reason for your life on earth, *the truth of your lives.* It is extremely vital for you to have a clear idea of your mission, in order to avoid being confused or deceived. In speaking to the Christians of his time, St. Paul explicitly urged them: "Let no one deceive you in any way" (2 Thes 2:3). And today I say the same to you, young people of America: "Let no one deceive you in any way"—about your mission, about the truth, about where you are going. *Let no one deceive you about the truth of your lives.*

The Truth Frees Us

2. But what is the opposite of deception? Where can you turn to find answers that satisfy, answers that will last? The opposite of deception is truth—the person who *tells* the truth, the person who *is* the truth. Yes, *the opposite of deception is Jesus Christ,* who tells us: "I am the way, and *the truth,* and the life" (Jn 14:6). Jesus Christ is the Son of God. He reveals the truth of God. But he is also man. He shares in

our humanity and came into the world to teach us about ourselves, to help us discover ourselves.

You young people are proud to live in a free country and you should be grateful to God for *your freedom*. But even though you can come and go as you like, and do what you want, you are not really free if you are living under the power of error or falsehood, deceit or sin. Only Jesus Christ can make you fully free through his truth. And that is why he said: "You will know the truth, and the truth will set you free." And that is why he added, "If the Son frees you, you will really be free" (Jn 8:32, 36). Dear young people: the whole message of Jesus in the Gospels and through his Church helps you to discover who you really are, to discover all the dimensions of your lives.

Youth's Responsibilities

3. Each of us is *an individual*, a person, a creature of God, one of his children, someone very special whom God loves and for whom Christ died. This identity of ours determines the way we must live, the way we must act, the way we must view our mission in the world. We come from God, we depend on God, *God has a plan for us*—a plan for our lives, for our bodies, for our souls, for our future. This plan for us is extremely important—so important that God became man to explain it to us.

In God's plan we are individuals, yes, but we are also part of a *community*. The Second Vatican Council emphasized the fact that God did not call us to share his life merely as unrelated individuals. Rather he wanted to mold us into a people as his sons and daughters (cf. *Ad Gentes*, 2). This aspect of our being a community, of our sharing God's life as a people, is part of our identity: who we are, what we are, where we are going.

Right away we can see that as persons we have responsibilities and that *these responsibilities are part of our freedom*. The Vatican Council went so far as to say that "man is defined first of all by his responsibilities toward his brothers and sisters and toward history" (*Gaudium et Spes*, 55).

To understand ourselves as members of a community, as individuals linked together to make up the People of God, *as persons responsible for others,* is a great insight—an insight that is necessary for fulfilling our mission properly.

4. As Christians you have these insights and Christ today wants to reinforce them in you. You speak about "being partners," of sharing and serving and working together. And all of this is linked to God's plan, according to which we are brothers and sisters in Christ—brothers and sisters who belong to the People of God and who are made to live in community, to think about others, to help others. Dear young people of America: in the Church there are many different gifts. There is room for many different cultures and ways of doing things. *But there is no room in the Church for selfishness.* There is no room in the world for selfishness. It destroys the meaning of life; it destroys the meaning of love; it reduces the human person to a subhuman level.

When we speak about the need of being open to others, of taking into account the community, of fulfilling our responsibilities to all our brothers and sisters, we are actually talking about *the whole world.* Your mission as young people today is to the whole world. In what sense? You can never forget the interdependence of human beings wherever they are. When Jesus tells us to love our neighbor, he does not set a geographical limit. What is needed today is a solidarity between all the young people of the world—a solidarity especially with the poor and all those in need. You young people must change society *by your lives* of justice and fraternal love. It is not just a question of your own country, but of the whole world. This is certainly your mission, dear young people. You are partners with each other, partners with the whole Church, *partners with Christ.*

5. In order, however, to accomplish this great work, to be in a condition to change the world in the name of Jesus, you yourselves must actually be living according to your own identity—*according to God's plan for your lives.* Once again it is the word of Jesus that directs your lives and tells you what that plan is. You remember how much Jesus insisted on the commandment of love, how much he insisted

on living according to certain norms called the Beatitudes: "Blessed are the meek.... Blessed are the merciful.... Blessed are the clean of heart.... Blessed are the peacemakers." All of this is part of the plan.

When St. Paul says, "Let no one deceive you," he is in effect saying: Do not believe anyone who contradicts Jesus or his message which is transmitted to you by the Church. Jesus speaks to you, young people, and tells you the value of meekness, mercy and humility. Other voices in the world will immediately shout out: "weakness!" In the Gospel Jesus emphasizes the value of honesty, uprightness, justice, and fairness. But when you practice these virtues, you are liable to be accused of being "naive." Jesus and his Church hold up to you God's plan for human love, telling you that sex is a great gift of God that is reserved for marriage. At this point the voices of the world will try to deceive you, with powerful slogans, claiming that you are "unrealistic," "out of it," "backward," even "reactionary." But the message of Jesus is clear: purity means true love, and it is the total opposite of selfishness and escape.

"Yes" to God's Plan

6. Jesus' message applies to all the areas of life. He reveals to us the truth of our lives and all aspects of this truth. Jesus tells us that *the purpose of our freedom is to say "yes" to God's plan for our lives.* What makes our "yes" so important is that we say it freely; we are able to say "no." Jesus teaches us that we are accountable to God, that we must follow our consciences, but that our consciences must be formed according to God's plan for our lives. In all our relationships to other people and to the world, Jesus teaches us what we must do, how we must live in order not to be deceived, in order to walk in truth. And today, dear young people, I proclaim to you again Jesus Christ: *the way,* and the truth and the life—your way, *your truth* and your life.

What is in accord with the truth of Jesus is fulfillment, joy and peace, even if it means effort and discipline. What is not in accord with his truth means disorder, and when done deliberately it means sin. Deliberate or not, it eventually means unhappiness and frustration.

Hold on to the Truth

7. It is with the truth of Jesus, dear young people, that you must face the great questions in your lives, as well as the practical problems. The world will try to deceive you about many things that matter: about your faith, about pleasure and material things, about the dangers of drugs. And at one stage or another the false voices of the world will try to exploit your human weakness by telling you that life has no meaning at all for you. *The supreme theft in your lives would be if they succeeded in robbing you of hope.* They will try, but they will not succeed if you hold fast to Jesus and his truth.

The truth of Jesus is capable of reinforcing all your energies. It will unify your lives and consolidate your sense of mission. You may still be vulnerable to attack from the pressures of the world, from the forces of evil, from the power of the devil. *But you will be invincible in hope:* "in Christ Jesus our hope" (1 Tm 1:1).

Dear young people, *the word of Jesus and his truth* and his promises of fulfillment and life *are the Church's response* to the culture of death, to the onslaughts of doubt and to the cancer of despair.

Let me just add two practical thoughts from the Second Vatican Council. The Council tells us that we must avoid thinking that we have at hand the solutions to all the *particular* problems of life (cf. *Gaudium et Spes*, 33). But at the same time the Church knows that *she possesses the light* in which the solutions to the problems of humanity *can be discovered* (*ibid.*, 12). What is this light? What can it be? Only *the truth of Jesus Christ!*

PART II

Dear Young People,

8. I would like to add something else to what I have already said to you. I would like to speak to you briefly about *prayer,* about communion with God, a communion that is deeply personal between ourselves and God.

In prayer we express to God our feelings, our thoughts, our sentiments. We wish to love and be loved, to be understood and to understand. Only God loves us perfectly, with an everlasting love. In prayer, we open our hearts and our minds to this God of love. And it is prayer that makes us one with the Lord. Through prayer we come to share more deeply in God's life and in his love.

Jesus Prayed

9. One of the most striking things about *Jesus* was *his habit of prayer*. In the midst of an active public ministry, we find him going away by himself to be alone in silence and communion with his Father in heaven. On the sabbath, he made it a practice to go to the synagogue and pray with others in common. When he was together with his disciples, or when he was by himself, he prayed to the Father whom he dearly loved.

St. Mark's Gospel describes an evening in Capernaum when Jesus cured many who were sick and expelled many demons. After giving us this description of Christ's generous care for others, St. Mark adds, "Rising early the next morning, he went off to a lonely place in the desert; there *he was absorbed in prayer*" (Mk 1:35).

And St. Luke informs us that, before Jesus selected the Twelve to be his Apostles, *"he went out to the mountain to pray, spending the night in communion with God"* (Lk 6:12). In fact, it seems that it was his example of prayer that *prompted his disciples to want to pray:* "One day he was praying in a certain place," Luke tells us, and "when he had finished, one of his disciples asked him, 'Lord, teach us to pray'" (Lk 11:1). That was the occasion when Jesus taught them the prayer that we call the "Lord's prayer," or the "Our Father."

We Must Keep Praying

10. If you really wish to follow Christ, if you want your love for him to grow and last, then you must be *faithful to prayer*. It is *the key to the vitality of your life in Christ*. Without prayer, your faith and love will die. If you are constant in

daily prayer and in the Sunday celebration of Mass, your love for Jesus will increase. And your heart will know deep joy and peace, such as the world could never give.

But many young people tell me that they do not know *how to pray,* or they wonder if they are praying in a way that is correct. Here again, you must look to the example of Christ. How did Jesus himself pray?

First of all, we know that his prayer is marked by a spirit of joy and praise. *"Jesus rejoiced in the Holy Spirit* and said: 'I offer you praise, O Father, Lord of heaven and earth'" (Lk 10:21). In addition, he entrusted to the Church at the Last Supper the celebration of the Eucharist, which remains for all ages the most perfect means of offering to the Father glory and thanksgiving and praise.

Yet, there were also times of suffering when, in great pain and struggle, Jesus poured out his heart to God, seeking to find in his Father both comfort and support. For example, in the Garden of Gethsemane, when the inner struggle became even more difficult, then, *"in his anguish he prayed with all the greater intensity,* and his sweat became like drops of blood falling to the ground" (Lk 22:44). "He prayed with all the greater intensity"—what an example for us when we find life difficult, when we face a painful decision or when we struggle with temptation. At times like these, Jesus prayed with all the greater intensity. We must do the same!

When it is difficult therefore to pray, the *most important thing* is *not to stop praying,* not to give up the effort. At these times, *turn to the Bible* and to *the Church's liturgy.* Meditate on the life and teachings of Jesus as recorded in the Gospels. Ponder the wisdom and counsel of the Apostles and the challenging messages of the Prophets. Try to make your own the beautiful prayers of the Psalms. You will find in the inspired word of God the spiritual food you need. Above all, your soul will be refreshed when you take part wholeheartedly with the community in the celebration of the Eucharist, the Church's greatest prayer.

11. Do you recall the story of Jesus and his Mother Mary at the wedding feast of Cana? At a certain point in the feast, when they had run out of wine, Mary told those waiting on

table, *"Do whatever he tells you"* (Jn 2:5). When the waiters followed Mary's advice, Jesus rewarded their faith and changed water into wine, a wine that far surpassed the quality of what had been served before. And Mary's advice still holds true today. For the true success of our lives consists in *knowing and doing the will of Jesus,* in doing whatever Jesus tells us. When you pray, you must realize that prayer is not just asking God for something or seeking special help, even though prayers of petition are true ways of praying. But prayer should also be characterized by *thanksgiving and praise,* by *adoration and attentive listening,* by *asking God's pardon* and forgiveness. If you follow Jesus' advice, and pray to God constantly, then you will learn to pray well. God himself will teach you.

Prayer can truly change your life. For it turns your attention away from yourself and directs your mind and your heart toward the Lord. If we look only at ourselves, with our own limitations and sins, we quickly give way to sadness and discouragement. But if we keep *our eyes fixed on the Lord,* then our hearts are filled with hope, our minds are washed in the light of truth, and we come to know the fullness of the Gospel with all its promise and life.

Prayer and the Holy Spirit

12. Prayer also helps us *to be open to the Holy Spirit,* the Spirit of truth and love, the Spirit who was given to the Church so that she could fulfill her mission in the world. It is the Holy Spirit who gives us the strength to resist evil and do good, to do our part in building up the Kingdom of God.

It is significant that the symbol of the Holy Spirit on Pentecost was *tongues of fire.* In fact, fire is often the symbol that the Bible uses to speak of the action of God in our lives. For the Holy Spirit truly inflames our hearts, engendering in them enthusiasm for the works of God. And when we pray, the Holy Spirit stirs up within us love of God and love of our neighbor.

The Holy Spirit brings us joy and peace. The modern technological world can offer us many pleasures, many comforts of life. It can even offer us temporary escapes from life. But what the world can never offer is lasting joy and peace. These are the gifts which only the Holy Spirit can give. And these are the gifts that I ask for you, so that you may be strong in hope and persevering in love. But *the condition for all of this is prayer*, which means contact with Christ, communion with God. Dear young people: my message to you is not new. I have given it before and, with God's grace, I will give it again. And so, as long as the memory of this visit lasts, may it be recorded that I, John Paul II, came to America *to call you to Christ, to invite you to pray!*

We All Must Forgive

Homily at the New Orleans Eucharist—Lakefront Arena, September 12.

"My Lord, be patient with me and I will pay you back in full." (Mt 18:26; cf. v. 29)

Dear Brothers and Sisters in Christ,

1. This plea is heard twice in *the Gospel parable*. The first time it is made by the servant who owes his master ten thousand talents—an astonishingly high sum according to the value of money in New Testament times. Shortly afterwards the plea is repeated by another servant of the same master. He too is in debt, not to his master, but to his fellow servant. And his debt is only a tiny fraction of the debt that his fellow servant had been forgiven.

The point of the parable is the fact that the servant with the greater debt receives understanding from the master to whom he owes much money. The Gospel tells us that "the master let the official go and wrote off the debt" (Mt 18:27). Yet that same servant would not listen to the plea of his fellow servant who owed him money. He had *no pity* on him, but "had him put in jail until he paid back what he owed" (Mt 18:30).

Jesus often used parables like this one in his teaching; they are *a special method of proclaiming the Good News*. They enable the listener to grasp more easily the "Divine Reality" which Jesus came to reveal. In today's parable, we sense almost immediately that it is a prelude to the words which Jesus commands us to use when we pray to our heavenly Father: *"forgive us our debts, as we forgive our debtors"* (Mt 6:12).

These words from the "Our Father" also have something very important to teach us. If we want God to hear us when we plead like the servant—"Have patience with me"—then we must be equally willing to listen to our neighbor when he pleads: "Give me time and I will pay you back in full." *Otherwise we cannot expect pardon from God,* but punishment instead. In the parable the servant is punished because, though a debtor himself, he is intolerant as a creditor toward his fellow servant.

Christ is very clear. When we ourselves are without sympathy or mercy, when we are guided by *"blind" justice* alone, then we cannot count on the mercy of that "Great Creditor" who is God—God, before whom we are all debtors.

God's Merciful Love

2. In the parable we find two different standards or ways of measuring, *God's standard and man's standard.* The divine standard is one in which justice is totally permeated by *merciful love.* The human standard is inclined to stop at justice alone—justice which is without mercy, and which in a sense is "blind" with regard to man.

Indeed, human justice is often governed by *hatred and revenge,* as the first reading from the Book of Sirach reminds us. It reads—and the words of the Old Testament are strong—"Should a man nourish anger against his fellows and expect healing from the Lord?... If he who is but flesh cherishes wrath, who will forgive his sins?... Remember your last days, set enmity aside.... Think of the command-ments, hate not your neighbor.... Should a man refuse mercy to his fellows, yet seek pardon for his own sins?" (Sir 28:3, 5-7, 4)

The exhortations in the Book of Sirach and in the Gospel move in the same direction. The human way of measuring— the measure of justice alone—which is often "blind" or "blinded" by hatred, *must accept God's standard.* Otherwise, justice by itself easily becomes injustice, as we see expressed in the Latin saying: *summum ius, summa iniuria.* The rigor-ous application of the law can sometimes be the height of injustice.

As I said in my Encyclical Letter on the Mercy of God: "In every sphere of interpersonal relationships justice must, so to speak, be *"corrected"* to a considerable extent by that love which, as St. Paul proclaims, 'is patient and kind' or, in other words, possesses the characteristics of that merciful love which is so much of the essence of the Gospel and Christianity" (*Dives in Misericordia,* 14).

"Seventy Times Seven"

3. Merciful love is also the basis of the Lord's answer to
Peter's question: "When my brother wrongs me, how often
must I forgive him? Seven times?" "No," Jesus replied, "not
seven times; I say, *seventy times seven times*" (Mt 18:21-22). In
the symbolic language of the Bible, this means that we must
be able to forgive everyone every time. Surely this is one of
the most difficult and *radical* commands of the Gospel. Yet
how much suffering and anguish, how much futility, destruction and violence would be avoided, if only we put into
practice in all our human relationships the Lord's answer to
Peter.

Merciful love is absolutely necessary, in particular, for
people who are close to one another: for husbands and wives,
parents and children, and among friends (cf. *Dives in Misericordia*, 14). At a time when family life is under such great
stress, when a high number of divorces and broken homes
are a sad fact of life, we must ask ourselves whether human
relationships are being based—as they should be—on the
merciful love and forgiveness revealed by God in Jesus
Christ. We must examine our own heart and see how willing
we are to forgive and to accept forgiveness in this world as
well as in the next.

No relationship as intense and close as marriage and the
family can survive without forgiveness "seventy times seven
times." If couples cannot forgive with the tenderness and
sensitivity that mercy brings, then they will inevitably begin
to see their relationship only in terms of justice, of what is
mine and what is yours—emotionally, spiritually and
materially—and in terms of real or perceived injustices. This
can lead to *estrangement and divorce*, and often develops into a
bitter dispute about property and, more tragically, about
children. The plight of the children alone should make us
realize that the refusal to forgive is not in keeping with the
true nature of marriage as God established it and as he
wants it to be lived. No doubt some people will object that
Christ's teaching about the indissolubility of marriage, as it
is upheld by the Church, is lacking in compassion. But what
must be seen is the ineffectiveness of divorce (and its ready

availability in modern society) to bring mercy and forgiveness and healing to so many couples and their children—in whose troubled lives there remain a brokenness and a suffering that will not go away. The words of the merciful Christ, who fully understands the human heart, remain forever: "What therefore God has joined together, let no man put asunder" (Mt 19:6).

At the same time, merciful love and forgiveness are never meant to cancel out *a person's right to justice*, even in marriage. In the encyclical to which I referred a moment ago I said that "properly understood, justice constitutes...the goal of forgiveness. In no passage of the Gospel message does forgiveness or mercy...mean indulgence toward evil, scandals, injury or insult.... Reparation for evil and scandal, compensation for injury, and satisfaction for insult are conditions for forgiveness" *(Dives in Misericordia,* 14). All forgiveness requires repentant love.

This also applies in the wider context of *social, political, cultural and economic life* within and among nations and peoples. May we not hope for what Pope Paul VI described as the "civilization of love" instead of "an eye for an eye and a tooth for a tooth," the attitude which ravages the face of the earth and scars the family of mankind? As I have said, this love, based on the forgiveness which Jesus described to Peter, does not mean that the objective demands of justice, which people legitimately seek, are thereby canceled out. Sometimes those demands, however, are very complex.

A case with special urgency today is *the international debt question.* As you know, many developing countries are heavily in debt to industrialized nations; and for a variety of reasons are finding it harder and harder to repay their loans. "Blind" justice alone cannot solve this problem in an ethical way that promotes the human good of all parties. Merciful love calls for mutual understanding and a recognition of human priorities and needs above and beyond the "blind" justice of financial mechanisms. We must arrive at solutions that truly reflect both complete justice and mercy (cf. *At the Service of the Human Community: An Ethical Approach to the International Debt Question,* Pontifical Commission "Iustilia et Pax," 1986).

The nature of the Church's concern in these matters is reflected in the Pastoral message on the American Economy issued by the Bishops of the United States. They say: "We write...as heirs of the biblical prophets who summon us 'to do justice, to love kindness and to walk humbly with our God' (Mi 6:8).... We speak as moral teachers, not economic technicians. We seek...to lift up the human and ethical dimensions of economic life..." (nn. 4, 7). *To do justice, yes—but also to love.* This is at the heart of Christ's message. It is the only way to reach that "civilization of love" that ensures peace for ourselves and for the world.

All Debtors to God

4. "Forgive us...as we forgive."

The Eucharist which we are celebrating and in which we are taking part is linked to the deepest truth of these words. Each time we participate in the Eucharist, we must *translate,* as it were, the parable of today's Gospel into the reality of that sacrament which is the "great mystery of faith." When we gather together, we must be aware of how much we are *debtors to God the Creator, God the Redeemer.* Debtors—first for our Creation, and then for our Redemption. The Psalmist exclaims:

"Bless the Lord, O my soul,
    and all my being, bless his holy name.
Bless...and forget not all his benefits" (Ps 102[103]:1-2).

This exhortation is directed to each one of us, and at the same time to the whole community of believers. Forget not ...the gift of God. Forget not...that you have received his bounty: *in Creation*—that is to say, in your existence and in all that is in and around you; *in Redemption*—in that grace of adoption as sons and daughters of God in Christ, at the price of his Cross.

When we receive a gift we are a debtor. Indeed we are more than a debtor because it is not possible to repay a gift adequately. And yet we must try. *We must give a gift in return for a gift.* God's generous gift must be repaid by our gift. And our gift, reflecting as it does our great limitations, must aim at imitating the divine generosity, the divine standard of giving. In Christ our gift must be transformed, so as to unite us with God. The Eucharist is the sacrament of such a *transformation*. Christ himself makes us "an everlasting gift to the Father." Truly this is the great mystery of faith and love.

5. "Forgive us our debts, as we forgive our debtors."

With these words from the prayer taught to us by the Son of God, I address all those gathered here in *New Orleans* in the spirit of the Gospel—all those who make up the Eucharistic assemblies of the local Churches of this region. I greet you as the proud heirs of *a rich and diverse cultural history,* as people who can therefore appreciate the need for merciful love among individuals and groups. Here we have represented the cultures of France and other European nations, of black people, Hispanics, and more recently Vietnamese. Today this region continues to be the home of various races and cultures now united in one nation, the United States.

All of those races and cultures have enriched the life of your local Church within the distinctively French heritage that men like Robert Cavelier, Sieur de la Salle, and Jean Baptiste Le Moyne, Sieur de Bienville conferred upon this land centuries ago. You are also a people who have only to look about you to see the many *wonderful gifts* conferred by the mighty Mississippi River and its fertile delta, and by the riches of the sea. All this comes to you as a gift from God. By wise stewardship and the responsible use of these resources, you can find dignity in your work as you seek to provide for yourselves and your families. May you continue to work in harmony for the good of the society you belong to, always keeping in mind the words of Christ's prayer: "Forgive us our debts, as we forgive our debtors."

Modern man easily forgets the proportion, or rather, the lack of proportion between what he has received and what he is obliged to give. He has grown so much in his own eyes, and is so sure that everything is the work of his own genius and of his own "industry," that he no longer sees the One who is the Alpha and the Omega, the Beginning and the End—the One who is the First Source of all that is, as well as its Final End—the One in whom all that exists finds its proper meaning.

Modern man easily *forgets that he has received a great gift.* Yet, at the base of all that he is and of all that the world is, there is the gift—the free gift of Love. As man loses this awareness, he also *forgets the debt* and the fact that he is a debtor. He loses his *consciousness of sin.* Many people today, especially those caught up in a civilization of affluence and pleasure, live as though sin did not exist and as if God did not exist.

For this reason we need to listen with special attention to the Letter to the Romans: "None of us lives as his own master and none of us dies as his own master. While we live we are responsible to the Lord, and when we die we die as his servants. Both in life and in death we are the Lord's. That is why Christ died and came to life again, that he might be Lord of both the dead and the living" (14:7-9). We must *listen carefully* to these words of St. Paul and *remember* them well.

"My Lord, *be patient with me* and I will pay you back in full."

"Love is patient; love is kind.... Love does not rejoice in what is wrong but rejoices with the truth.... Love never fails" (1 Cor 13:4, 6, 8). Yes, love is supreme. Amen.

The Gospel Purifies Culture

Address to representatives of Catholic higher education—Xavier University, New Orleans, September 12.

Dear Friends,

Dear Leaders in Catholic Higher Education,

1. At the end of this day dedicated to *the prayerful celebration of Catholic education in the United States*, I greet you and all those whom you represent, with esteem and with affection in our Lord Jesus Christ. I thank the Association of Catholic Colleges and Universities for having arranged this meeting. I express my gratitude to Dr. Norman Francis and to all at Xavier University for their hospitality at this Institution, which, in so many ways, serves the cause of Catholic higher education.

"I will bless the Lord at all times;
his praise shall be ever in my mouth.
Glorify the Lord with me,
let us together extol his name" (Ps 34:2, 4).

Yes, let us join *in thanking God* for the many good things that he, the Father of Wisdom, has accomplished through Catholic colleges and universities. In doing so, let us be thankful for the special strengths of your schools—for their Catholic identity, for their service of truth, and for their role in helping to make the Church's presence felt in the world of culture and science. And let us be thankful *above all for the men and women committed to this mission*—those of the past and those of today—who have made and are making Catholic higher education the great reality that it is.

The Past Challenges the Present

2. The United States is unique in its *network of more than two hundred and thirty-five colleges and universities* which identify themselves as Catholic. The number and diversity of your institutions are in fact without parallel; they exercise an influence not only within the United States but also throughout the universal Church, and they bear a responsibility for her good.

Two years from now you will celebrate the two hundredth anniversary of the founding by John Carroll of Georgetown University, the first Catholic University in the United States. After Georgetown, through the leadership of religious Congregations and farseeing Bishops, and with the generous support of the Catholic people, other colleges and universities have been established in different parts of this vast country. For two centuries these institutions have contributed much to *the emergence of a Catholic laity*, which today is intimately and extensively involved in industry, government, the professions, arts and all forms of public and private endeavor—all those activities that constitute the characteristic dynamism and vitality of this land.

Amidst changing circumstances, Catholic universities and colleges are challenged to retain *a lively sense of their Catholic identity* and to fulfill their specific *responsibilities to the Church and to society*. It is precisely in doing so that they make their distinctive contribution to the wider field of higher education.

The Catholic identity of your institutions is a complex and vitally important matter. This identity depends upon *the explicit profession of Catholicity* on the part of the university as an institution, and also upon *the personal conviction and sense of mission* on the part of its professors and administrators.

3. During my pastoral visit to this country in 1979, I spoke of various elements that contribute to the mission of Catholic higher education. It is useful once again to stress the importance of *research into questions vital for the Church and society*—a research carried out "with a just sense of history, together with the concern to show the full meaning of the human person regenerated in Christ"; to emphasize the need for *educating men and women of outstanding knowledge* who, "having made a personal synthesis between faith and culture, will be both capable and willing to assume tasks in the service of the community and of society in general, and to bear witness to their faith before the world"; and finally, to pursue the establishment of *a living community of faith*, "where sincere commitment to scientific research and study goes together with a deep commitment to authentic Chris-

tian living" (Address at Catholic University, Washington, DC, October 7, 1979, No. 3).

Faith and Learning

4. To appreciate fully the value of your heritage, we need to recall the origins of Catholic university life. The university as we know it began in close association with the Church. This was no accident. *Faith and love of learning have a close relationship.* For the Fathers of the Church and the thinkers and academics of the Middle Ages, the search for truth was associated with the search for God. According to Catholic teaching—as expressed also in the First Vatican Council—the mind is capable not only of searching for the truth but also of grasping it, however imperfectly.

Religious *faith itself calls for intellectual inquiry;* and the confidence that there can be no contradiction between faith and reason is a distinctive feature of the Catholic humanistic tradition, as it existed in the past and as it exists in our own day.

Catholic higher education is called to exercise, through the grace of God, an extraordinary "share in the work of truth" (3 Jn 8). The Catholic university is dedicated to the service of the truth, as is every university. In its research and teaching, however, it proceeds from the vision and perspective of faith and is thus enriched in a specific way.

From this point of view one sees that there is an intimate relationship between the Catholic university and the teaching office of the Church. The Bishops of the Church, as *Doctores et Magistri Fidei,* should be seen not as external agents but as participants in the life of the Catholic university in its privileged role as protagonist in *the encounter between faith and science and between revealed truth and culture.*

Modern culture reflects many tensions and contradictions. We live in an age of great technological triumphs but also of great human anxieties. Too often today, the individual's vision of reality is fragmented. At times experience is mediated by forces over which people have no control; sometimes there is not even an awareness of these forces. The temptation grows to relativize moral principles and to privilege process over truth. This has grave consequences for the moral life as well as for the intellectual life of individuals and of society. The Catholic university must address all these issues from the perspective of faith and out of its rich heritage.

Toward Truly Human Culture

5. Modern culture is marked by a pluralism of attitudes, points of view and insights. This situation rightly requires mutual understanding; it means that society and groups within society must respect those who have a different outlook from their own. But *pluralism* does not exist for its own sake; it *is directed to the fullness of truth.* In the academic context, the respect for persons which pluralism rightly envisions does not justify the view that ultimate questions about human life and destiny have no final answers or that all beliefs are of equal value, provided that none is asserted as absolutely true and normative. Truth is not served in this way.

It is true, of course, that the culture of every age contains certain ambiguities which reflect the inner tensions of the human heart—the struggle between good and evil. Hence the Gospel, in its continuing encounter with culture, must always *challenge the accomplishments and assumptions of the age* (cf. Rom 12:2). Since, in our day, the implications of this ambiguity are often so destructive to the community, so hostile to human dignity, it is crucial that *the Gospel should purify culture, uplift it, and orient it to the service of what is authentically human.* Humanity's very survival may depend on it. And here, as leaders in Catholic education in the United States, you have an extremely important contribution to make.

Today there exists an increasingly evident need for philosophical reflection concerning the truth about the human person. A metaphysical approach is needed as an antidote to intellectual and moral relativism. But what is required even more is *fidelity to the word of God,* to ensure that human progress takes into account the entire revealed truth of the eternal act of love in which the universe and especially the human person acquire ultimate meaning. The more one seeks to unravel the mystery of the human person, the more open one becomes to the mystery of transcendence. The more deeply one penetrates the divine mystery, the more one discovers the true greatness and dignity of human beings.

The Mission of Theology

6. In your institutions, which are privileged settings for the encounter between faith and culture, *theological science has a special role* and deserves a prominent place in the curriculum of studies and in the allocation of research resources. But theology, as the Church understands it, is much more than an academic discipline. Its data are the data of God's Revelation entrusted to the Church. The deeper understanding of the mystery of Christ, the understanding which theological reflection seeks, is ultimately *a gift of the Holy Spirit given for the common good of the whole Church.* Theology is truly a search to understand ever more clearly the heritage of faith preserved, transmitted and made explicit by the Church's teaching office. And theological instruction serves the community of faith by helping new generations to understand and to integrate into their lives the truth of God, which is so vital to the fundamental issues of the modern world.

7. *Theology is at the service of the whole ecclesial community.* The work of theology involves an interaction among the various members of the community of faith. The Bishops, united with the Pope, have the mission of authentically teaching the message of Christ; as Pastors, they are called to sustain the unity in faith and Christian living of the entire People of God. For this they need the assistance of Catholic theologians, who perform an inestimable service to the Church. But theologians also need the charism entrusted by Christ to the Bishops and, in the first place, to the Bishop of Rome. The fruits of their work, in order to enrich the lifestream of the ecclesial community, must ultimately be tested and validated by the Magisterium. In effect, therefore, *the ecclesial context of Catholic theology gives it a special character and value, even when theology exists in an academic setting.*

Here, the words of St. Paul concerning the spiritual gifts should be a source of light and harmony for us all: "There are different gifts but the same Spirit; there are different ministries but the same Lord; there are different works but the same God who accomplishes all of them in everyone. To each person the manifestation of the Spirit is given for the common good" (1 Cor 12:4-7). In the different offices and functions in the Church, it is not some power and dominion that is being divided up, but rather *the same service of the Body of Christ that is shared according to the vocation of each.* It is a question of *unity in the work of service.* In this spirit I wish to express cordial support for the humble, generous and patient work of theological research and education being carried out in your universities and colleges in accordance with the Church's mission to proclaim and teach the saving wisdom of God (cf. 1 Cor 1:21).

Religious and Moral Development

8. My own university experience impels me to mention another related matter of supreme importance in the Catholic college and university, namely, *the religious and moral education of students and their pastoral care.* I am confident that you too take this special service very seriously, and that you count it among your most pressing and most satisfying responsibilities. One cannot meet with college and university students anywhere in the world without hearing their questions and sensing their anxieties. In their hearts your students have many questions about faith, religious practice and holiness of life. Each one arrives on your campuses with a family background, a personal history, and an acquired culture. They all want to be accepted, loved and supported by *a Christian educational community* which shows friendship and authentic spiritual commitment.

It is your *privilege to serve your students in faith and love;* to help them deepen their friendship with Christ; to make available to them the opportunities for prayer and liturgical celebration, including the possibility to know the forgiveness and love of Jesus Christ in the Sacraments of Penance and the Eucharist. You are able, as Catholic educators, to introduce your students to *a powerful experience of community* and to *a very serious involvement in social concerns* that will enlarge their horizons, challenge their life-styles and offer them authentic human fulfillment.

University students, for example, are in a splendid position to take to heart the Gospel invitation to go out of themselves, to reject introversion and to concentrate on the needs of others. Students with the opportunities of higher education can readily grasp *the relevance for today of Christ's parable of the rich man and Lazarus* (cf. Lk 16:19ff.), with all of its consequences for humanity. What is at stake is not only the rectitude of individual human hearts but also the whole social order as it touches the spheres of economics, politics and human rights and relations.

Here in the Catholic university centers of this nation, vivified by the inspiration of the Gospel, must be drawn up *the blueprints for the reform of attitudes and structures* that will influence the whole dynamic of peace and justice in the world, as it affects East and West, North and South. It is not enough to offer to the disadvantaged of the world crumbs of freedom, crumbs of truth and crumbs of bread. The Gospel calls for much more. The parable of the rich man and the poor man is directed to the conscience of humanity, and, today in particular, to the conscience of America. But that conscience often passes through the halls of Academe, through nights of study and hours of prayer, finally to reach and embrace the whole prophetic message of the Gospel. "Keep your attention closely fixed on it," we are told in the Second Letter of Peter, "as you would on a lamp shining in a dark place until the first streaks of dawn appear and the morning star rises in your hearts" (2 Pt 1:19).

Strengthen Your Catholic Commitment

9. Dear brothers and sisters, as leaders in Catholic university and college education, you have inherited a tradition of service and academic excellence, the cumulative effort of so many who have worked so hard and sacrificed so much for Catholic education in this country. Now there lies before you the wide horizon of the third century of the nation's

constitutional existence, and the third century of Catholic institutions of higher learning serving the people of this land. The challenges that confront you are just as testing as those your forefathers faced in establishing the network of institutions over which you now preside. Undoubtedly, the greatest challenge is, and will remain, that of *preserving and strengthening the Catholic character of your colleges and universities*—that institutional commitment to the word of God as proclaimed by the Catholic Church. This commitment is both an expression of spiritual consistency and a specific contribution to the cultural dialogue proper to American life. As you strive to make the presence of the Church in the world of modern culture more luminous, may you listen once again to Christ's prayer to his Father for his disciples: *"Consecrate them by means of truth—'Your word is truth'"* (Jn 17:17).

May the Holy Spirit, the Counselor and Spirit of Truth, who has enlivened and enlightened the Church of Christ from the beginning, give you great confidence in the Father's word, and sustain you in the service that you render to the truth through Catholic higher education in the United States of America.

We Need God's Forgiveness

Homily at San Antonio Eucharist—Westover Hills, September 13.

"My soul, give thanks to the Lord;
    all my being, bless his holy name" (Ps 102[103]:1).

Dear Brothers and Sisters,
Dear Friends, Citizens of San Antonio and of the State of Texas,

1. It gives me an immense joy to be with you on this Sunday morning and to invoke God's blessings upon this vast state and upon the whole Church in this region.

Texas! The name immediately brings to mind *the rich history and cultural development* of this part of the United States. In this marvelous setting, overlooking the *city of San Antonio,* I cannot but reverently evoke the memory of the Franciscan Father Massanet who, on the feast of St. Anthony of Padua, June 13, 1691, celebrated Mass along the banks of the San Antonio River for the members of an early Spanish expedition and a group of local Indian people.

Since then, people of many different origins have come here, so that today yours is *a multicultural society* striving for the fullness of harmony and collaboration among all. I express my cordial gratitude to the representatives of the state of Texas and the city of San Antonio who have wished to be present at this moment of prayer. I also greet the members of the various Christian Communions who join us in praising the name of our Lord Jesus Christ. A special word of thanks to Archbishop Flores and to the Bishops, priests, deacons, religious, and all the Catholic faithful of Texas. The peace of Christ be with you all!

2. *Today is Sunday:* the Lord's Day. Today is like the "seventh day" about which the Book of Genesis says that "God rested from all the work he had undertaken" (Gn 2:2). Having completed the work of creation, he "rested." God rejoiced in his work; he "looked at everything that he had made, and he found it very good" (Gn 1:31). *"So God blessed the seventh day and made it holy"* (Gn 2:3).

On this day we are called to reflect more deeply on the mystery of creation, and therefore of our own lives. We are called to "rest" in God, the Creator of the universe. Our

duty is to praise him: "My soul, give thanks to the Lord....
Give thanks to the Lord *and never forget all his blessings*" (Ps
102[103]:1-2). This is a task for each human being. Only the
human person, created in the image and likeness of God, is
capable of raising a hymn of praise and thanksgiving to the
Creator. The earth, with all its creatures, and the entire
universe, call on man to be their voice. Only the human
person is capable of releasing from the depths of his or her
being that hymn of praise, proclaimed without words by all
creation: "My soul, give thanks to the Lord; *all my being,*
bless his holy name" (v. 1).

The Message of the Liturgy

3. What is the message of today's liturgy? To us gathered here in San Antonio, in the state of Texas, and taking
part in the Eucharistic Sacrifice of our Lord and Savior Jesus
Christ, St. Paul addresses these words: *"None of us lives as
his own master, and none of us dies as his own master.* While we
live we are responsible to the Lord and when we die we die
as his servants. Both in life and death *we are the Lord's"*
(Rom 14:7-8).

These words are *concise, but filled with a moving message.*
"We live" and "we die." We live in this material world that
surrounds us, limited by the horizons of our earthly journey
through time. We live in this world, *with the inevitable prospect
of death*, right from the moment of conception and of birth.
And yet, we must look beyond the material aspect of our
earthly existence. Certainly, bodily death is a necessary passage for us all; but it is also true that what from its very
beginning has borne in itself the image and likeness of God
cannot be completely given back to the corruptible matter of
the universe. This is a fundamental truth and attitude of our
Christian faith. In St. Paul's terms: "While we live we are
responsible to the Lord, and when we die we die as his
servants." We live *for* the Lord, and our dying too is life in
the Lord.

Today, on this Lord's Day, I wish to invite all those who
are listening to my words, not to forget our immortal destiny: life after death—the eternal happiness of heaven, or the

awful possibility of eternal punishment, eternal separation from God, in what the Christian tradition has called hell (cf. Mt 25:41; 22:13; 25:30). *There can be no truly Christian living without an openness to this transcendent dimension of our lives.* "Both in life and death we are the Lord's" (Rom 14:8).

Death and Life

4. The Eucharist that we celebrate constantly confirms our living and dying "in the Lord": *"Dying you destroyed our death, rising you restored our life."* In fact, St. Paul wrote: "We are the Lord's. That is why Christ died and came to life again, that he might be Lord of both the dead and the living" (Rom 14:8-9). Yes, *Christ is the Lord!*

The Paschal Mystery has transformed our human existence, so that it is no longer under the dominion of death. In Jesus Christ, our Redeemer, "we live for the Lord" and "we die for the Lord." Through him and with him and in him, *we belong to God* in life and in death. We exist not only "for death" but "for God." For this reason, on this day "made by the Lord" (Ps 118[119]:24), the Church *all over the world* speaks her blessing from the very depths of the Paschal Mystery of Christ: "My soul, give thanks to the Lord; all my being bless his holy name. Give thanks...*and never forget all his blessings"* (Ps 102[103]:1-2).

"Never forget!" Today's reading from the Gospel according to St. Matthew gives us an example of a man who has forgotten (cf. 18:21-35). He has forgotten the favors given by his lord—and consequently he has shown himself to be cruel and heartless in regard to his fellow human being. In this way the liturgy *introduces us to the experience of sin* as it has developed from the beginning of the history of man alongside the experience of death.

We die in the physical body when all the energies of life are extinguished. *We die through sin when love dies in us. Outside of love there is no life.* If man opposes love and lives without love, death takes root in his soul and grows. For this reason Christ cries out: "I give you a new commandment: Love one another. Such as my love has been for you, so must your love be for each other" (Jn 13:34). The cry for love is the cry for life, for the victory of the soul over sin and death. The source of this victory is *the Cross of Jesus Christ: his Death and his Resurrection.*

The Ministry of Reconciliation

5. Again, in the Eucharist, our lives are touched by *Christ's own radical victory over sin—sin which is the death of the soul,* and—ultimately—the reason for bodily death. "That is why Christ died and came to life again, that he might be Lord of the dead" (cf. Rom 14:9)—that he might give life again to those who are dead in sin or because of sin.

And so, the Eucharist begins with *the penitential rite.* We confess our sins in order to obtain forgiveness through the Cross of Christ, and so receive a part in his Resurrection from the dead. But if our conscience reproaches us with *mortal sin,* our taking part in the Mass can be fully fruitful only if beforehand we receive absolution *in the Sacrament of Penance.*

The *ministry of reconciliation* is a fundamental part of the Church's life and mission. Without overlooking any of the many ways in which Christ's victory over sin becomes a reality in the life of the Church and of the world, it is important for me to emphasize that it is above all *in the Sacrament of forgiveness and reconciliation that the power of the redeeming blood of Christ is made effective in our personal lives.*

6. In different parts of the world there is *a great neglect of the Sacrament of Penance.* This is sometimes linked to an obscuring of the religious and moral conscience, a loss of the sense of sin, or a lack of adequate instruction on the importance of this sacrament in the life of Christ's Church. At times the neglect occurs because we fail to take seriously our lack of love and justice, and God's corresponding offer of reconciling mercy. Sometimes there is a hesitation or an unwillingness to accept maturely and responsibly the consequences of the objective truths of faith. For these reasons it is necessary to emphasize once again that *"with regard to the substance of the sacrament* there has always remained firm and unchanged in the consciousness of the Church *the certainty* that, by the will of Christ, forgiveness is offered to each

individual by means of sacramental absolution given by the ministers of Penance" *(Reconciliatio et Paenitentia,* 30).

Again, I ask all my brother Bishops and priests to do everything possible to make the administration of this sacrament *a primary aspect* of their service to God's people. There can be no substitute for the means of grace which Christ himself has placed in our hands. The Second Vatican Council never intended that this Sacrament of Penance be less practiced; what the Council expressly asked for was that the faithful might more easily understand the sacramental signs and more eagerly and *frequently* have recourse to the sacraments (cf. *Sacrosanctum Concilium,* 59). And just as sin deeply touches the individual conscience, so we understand why the absolution of sins must be individual and not collective, except in extraordinary circumstances as approved by the Church.

I ask you, dear Catholic brothers and sisters, not to see Confession as a mere attempt at psychological liberation— however legitimate this too might be—but as a sacrament, a liturgical act. *Confession* is an act of honesty and courage—*an act of entrusting ourselves,* beyond sin, *to the mercy of a loving and forgiving God.* It is an act of the prodigal son who returns to his Father and is welcomed by him with the kiss of peace. It is easy, therefore, to understand why "every confessional is a special and blessed place from which there is born new and uncontaminated a reconciled individual—a reconciled world!" *(Reconciliatio et Paenitentia,* 31, V; cf. III)

The potential for *an authentic and vibrant renewal of the whole Catholic Church* through the more faithful use of the Sacrament of Penance is immeasurable. It flows directly from the loving heart of God himself! This is a certainty of faith which I offer to each one of you and to the entire Church in the United States.

To those who have been far away from the Sacrament of Reconciliation and forgiving love I make this appeal: *come back to this source of grace; do not be afraid!* Christ himself is waiting for you. He will heal you, and you will be at peace with God!

To all the young people of the Church, I extend a special invitation to receive Christ's forgiveness and his strength in

the Sacrament of Penance. It is *a mark of greatness* to be able
to say: I have made a mistake; I have sinned, Father; I have
offended you, my God; I am sorry; I ask for pardon; I will
try again, because I rely on your strength and I believe in
your love. And I know that the power of your Son's Paschal
Mystery—the Death and Resurrection of our Lord Jesus
Christ—is *greater than my weaknesses and all the sins of the
world.* I will come and confess my sins and be healed, and I
will live in your love!

A Meeting of Cultures

7. In Jesus Christ the world has truly known the mystery of forgiveness, mercy and reconciliation, which is proclaimed by God's word this day. At the same time, God's
inexhaustible mercy to us obliges us *to be reconciled among
ourselves.* This makes practical demands on the Church in
Texas and the Southwest of the United States. It means
bringing *hope and love wherever there is division and alienation.*

Your history registers *a meeting of cultures,* indigenous
and immigrant, sometimes marked by tensions and con-
flicts, yet *constantly moving toward reconciliation and harmony.*
People of different races and languages, colors and customs,
have come to this land to make it their home. Together with
the indigenous peoples of these territories, there are the
descendants of those who came from almost every country
in Europe: from Spain and France, from Germany and
Belgium, from Italy, Hungary and Czechoslovakia, from
Ireland, England and Scotland. And even from my own
native Poland—for it was to Texas, and Panna Maria, that the
first Polish immigrants came to the United States. There are
descendants of those who came in chains from Africa; those
from Lebanon, the Philippines and Vietnam, and from every
Latin American country, especially from Mexico.

This land is a crossroads, standing at the border of two
great nations, and experiencing both the enrichment and the
complications which arise from this circumstance. You are
thus a symbol and a kind of laboratory testing America's
commitment to her founding moral principles and human
values. These principles and values are now being reaf-

firmed by America as she celebrates the Bicentennial of her Constitution, and speaks once more about justice and freedom, and about the acceptance of diversity within a fundamental unity—a unity arising from a shared vision of the dignity of every human person, and a shared responsibility for the welfare of all, especially of the needy and the persecuted.

The Hispanic Community

8. Against this background one may speak of a current phenomenon here and elsewhere—*the movement of people northwards,* not only from Mexico but from other southern neighbors of the United States. On this matter also there is work of reconciliation to be done. Among you there are people of great courage and generosity who have been doing much on behalf of suffering brothers and sisters arriving from the south. They have sought to show compassion in the face of complex human, social and political realities. *Here* human needs, both spiritual and material, continue to call out to the Church with thousands of voices, and the whole Church must respond by the proclamation of God's word and by selfless deeds of service. Here too there is ample space for continuing and growing collaboration among members of the various Christian Communions.

In all of this *the Hispanic community itself faces the greatest challenge.* Those of you of Hispanic descent—so numerous, so long present in this land, so well equipped to respond—are called to hear the word of Christ and take it to heart: "I give you a new commandment: love one another. Such as my love has been for you, so must your love be for each other" (Jn 13:34). And Jesus specified that this love embraces the entire range of human needs from the least to the greatest: "I promise you that whoever gives a cup of cold water to one of these lowly ones...will not want for his reward" (Mt 10:42). The Hispanic community also has to respond to its own needs, and to show generous and effective solidarity among its own members. I urge you to hold fast to your Christian faith and traditions, especially in defense of the family. And I pray that the Lord may provide many more vocations to the priesthood and to the religious life among your young people.

May you who have received so much from God *hear the call to a renewal of your Christian life and to fidelity to the faith of your fathers.* May you respond in the spirit of Mary, the Virgin Mother whom the Church sees "maternally present and sharing in the many complicated problems which today beset the lives of individuals, families and nations...helping the Christian people in the constant struggle between good and evil, to ensure that it 'does not fall,' or if it has fallen, that it 'rises again'" *(Redemptoris Mater,* 52).

Journey in Hope

9. Today's liturgy helps us to reflect deeply *on life and death,* on the victory of life over death. On this earth, in the visible world of creation, *man exists "for death"*; and yet, in Christ, he is called to communion with God, with *the living God who "gives life."* He is called to this communion precisely through the death of Christ—the death which "gives life."

Today, all over the world, countless people—people of many countries and continents, languages and races, are sharing sacramentally in the death of Christ. *We, here in Texas, journey together with them* toward the fulfillment of the Paschal Mystery in life. We journey, conscious of being sinners, conscious of being mortal. But we journey on *in hope,* in union with the Sacrifice of Christ, through Eucharistic communion with him and *with love* for each other. *We live for the Lord! We die for the Lord! We belong to the Lord! Come, Lord Jesus!* (cf. Rv 22:20) Amen.

The Gift of Grace

Angelus message following the Eucharistic Celebration—Westover Hills, Texas, September 13.

1. At the end of this Eucharistic Celebration, I invite you to join me in praying the *Angelus*.

Whenever we turn to *Mary* the Mother of God in prayer, we are reminded that she is *"full of grace."* This is how the Angel Gabriel greeted her at the time of the Annunciation: "Hail, full of grace, the Lord is with you" (Lk 1:28). And indeed these words of the angel are true. Of all the people God has created, she alone was always free from sin. From the first moment of her existence she was in communion with the Father, and the Son and the Holy Spirit. *Mary responded to this great gift of God* with openness and generosity: "Let it be done to me," she said, "according to your word" (Lk 1:38).

2. Like Mary, *we too have been given the gift of God's grace,* even though we have not received its fullness. Like Mary, we are called to respond, to be open to God's word, to be generous in saying *yes* to God. For us this means doing God's will, living according to his commandments, serving our neighbor, avoiding sin. In other words, *with Mary we must respond with love to God's love.*

Let us turn then to Mary whom we honor under many titles, but here today in San Antonio under her special title of *Our Lady of Guadalupe.*

Human Worth, Human Development

Address to representatives of Catholic Charities, USA, and other Catholic and ecumenical social service agencies—Municipal Auditorium, San Antonio, September 13.

Dear Brothers and Sisters,

I am grateful for your presentation of the vast network of Christian love and human solidarity in which you are engaged. May the Lord sustain you in your zeal. "May mercy, peace and love be yours in ever greater measure" (Jude 1).

1. Catholic Charities is a title that speaks wonderfully well of the generous commitment of the Catholic people of the United States to the cause of human solidarity and Christian love. It gives me great joy to be among you, members of Catholic Charities, USA, your associated agencies and your colleague organizations in social ministry. Through your efforts you help *to make the loving compassion of our Lord and Savior Jesus Christ present to human needs.*

Jesus Christ was born poor, lived poor, and died poor. He loved the poor. In his kingdom the poor have a special place. The Church cannot be any different. She must be ever more fully aware of her fundamental duty to reflect in her life and action the very love with which God loves his creatures. For what is at stake is the mystery of God's love as explained in the First Letter of John: "We, for our part, love because he *first loved us*" (1 Jn 4:19). *All service has its first moment in God.*

God Rescues the Oppressed

2. You carry on a tradition and you live out a teaching grounded in Sacred Scripture, proclaimed by the Church and relevant to every age. *Service to the needy* not only builds up social harmony, it *reveals God, our Father, the rescuer of the oppressed.* In the Old Testament it was God's love for his people that decreed a special concern for the stranger, the widow and the orphan. As God had treated his people, so were they to treat others. The year of jubilee and the sabbatical year restored economic balance: slaves were set free, land

was returned to its original owners, debts were cancelled (cf. Ex 21ff.; Lv 25). Justice and mercy alike were served. The Prophets repeatedly drew attention to the inner qualities of heart that must animate the exercise of justice and service: "Not as man sees does God see, because man sees the appearance but the Lord looks into the heart" (1 Sm 16:7).

In the New Testament the mystery of God's love is further revealed: "God so loved the world that he gave his only Son" (Jn 3:16). *Through the heart of Jesus the fullness of God's infinite mercy appeared in the world.* Marveling at the Incarnation of God's Son, Mary exclaims that through this child the lowly shall be lifted up, their hunger shall be satisfied, and God's mercy shall be extended to all (cf. Lk 1:46-55). Years later, in announcing his own ministry, Jesus sums up his life's program in the words of Isaiah: "to bring glad tidings to the poor, to proclaim liberty to captives, recovery of sight to the blind and release to prisoners, to announce a year of favor from the Lord" (Lk 4:18-19). Jesus identifies himself with the poor and the defenseless: what we do for them is done for him, the service we fail to render them is service denied to him (cf. Mt 25:31-46).

Gross disparities of wealth between nations, classes and persons *re-enact the Gospel parable of the rich man and the poor man Lazarus.* And with the same dire consequences of which the Gospel speaks: "My child, replied Abraham, remember that you were well off in your lifetime, while Lazarus was in misery. Now he has found consolation here, but you have found torment" (Lk 16:25). The warning is as valid today as it was two thousand years ago.

Call to Compassion

3. From the beginning the Church has worked to carry out this teaching in her ministry. It is not necessary here to trace the extremely varied history of Christian service. The Church has always sought to respond to the stranger, the widow and the orphan; she has founded countless schools, hospitals, hospices, child-care facilities, and shelters. In our own times the Second Vatican Council has forcefully re-affirmed *the Church's vocation*—in fidelity to her Lord—*to love*

all those who are afflicted in any way: to recognize in the poor and the suffering the likeness of her poor and suffering Founder; to do all she can to relieve their needs, striving to serve Christ in them (cf. *Lumen Gentium,* 8). Twenty years after the Council, the Christian community is more than ever aware that the poor, the hungry, the oppressed, the sick and the handicapped share in a special way in the Cross of Christ and therefore need the Church's ministry.

Works of mercy, justice and compassion are basic to the history of the Church in the United States. The two American women who have been numbered among the saints, Frances Xavier Cabrini and Elizabeth Ann Seton, have been thus honored principally because of their work for their poorer brothers and sisters. The initiatives of Catholic Charities in the United States go back to before the Declaration of Independence. Countless institutions and structures have been established to assist the orphan, the immigrant, the ethnic groups, all persons in need—of every race and creed. Countless Americans of all extractions have made the compassionate service of their fellow human beings the whole purpose and method of their lives. In particular, generations of Religious, women and men, have consumed themselves in selfless service, under the sign of love.

Preference for the Poor

4. The Church has always proclaimed a love of preference for the poor. Perhaps the language is new, but the reality is not. Nor has the Church taken a narrow view of poverty and the poor. *Poverty,* certainly, is often a matter of *material deprivation.* But it is also a matter of *spiritual impoverishment, the lack of human liberties,* and the result of *any violation of human rights and human dignity.* There is a very special and pitiable form of poverty: *the poverty of selfishness,* the poverty of those who have and will not share, of those who could be rich by giving but choose to be poor by keeping everything they have. These people too need help.

The Christian view is that human beings are to be valued for what they are, not for what they have. In loving the poor and serving those in whatever need, the Church seeks above all to respect and heal their human dignity. *The aim of Christian solidarity and service is to defend and promote, in the name of Jesus Christ, the dignity and fundamental human rights of every person.* The Church "bears witness to the fact that this dignity cannot be destroyed, whatever the situation of poverty, scorn, rejection or powerlessness to which a human being has been reduced. She shows her solidarity with those who do not count in a society by which they are rejected spiritually and sometimes even physically. She is particularly drawn with maternal affection toward those children who, through human wickedness, will never be brought forth from the womb to the light of day, as also for the elderly, alone and abandoned. The special option for the poor, far from being a sign of particularism or sectarianism, manifests the universality of the Church's being and mission" *(Instruction on Christian Freedom and Liberation, 68).*

For "the poor in spirit" the Church has a very special love. She has inherited it from Christ, who called them "blest" (Mt 5:3). On the one hand the Church knows, from the words of Christ, that despite all human efforts the poor will always be with us (cf. Mt 26:11). On the other hand, in all her efforts to uplift the poor she knows and proclaims the ambivalence of possessions. Indeed, where the pursuit of wealth is treated as the supreme good, human beings become imprisoned in the hardening of their hearts and in the closing of their minds (cf. *Populorum Progressio, 19).* For this reason too, the Church, in the very act of serving the poor and relieving their sufferings, must also continue to proclaim and serve their higher needs—those of the spirit.

Individual Love and Initiative

5. Service to those in need must take the form of direct action to relieve their anxieties and to remove their burdens, and at the same time lead them to the dignity of self-reliance. In this respect I wish to express *the Church's immense gratitude to the many Americans* who are working to help their fellow human beings, in all the different forms which relief and development take in today's world. And I solemnly thank the American people for the generous way

in which they respond to the appeal for financial support for the many splendid programs of assistance carried out in their name. In the case of the many programs run by the Catholic Church, I wish to invite all who have responsibility for them to ensure that they will always be, and be seen to be, in full accord with Catholic principles of truth and justice.

The organizational and institutional response to needs, whether in the Church or in society, is extremely necessary but it is not sufficient in itself. In this regard I would repeat a concern I mentioned in my Apostolic Letter on Human Suffering: "Institutions are very important and indispensable; nevertheless, *no institution can, by itself, replace the human heart, human compassion, human love or human initiative when it is a question* of dealing with the sufferings of another. This refers to physical sufferings, but it is even more true when it is a question of the many kinds of moral suffering and when it is primarily the soul that is suffering" *(Salvifici Doloris,* 29).

Furthermore, in the necessary organizational and institutional response to needs, it is essential to avoid reducing human beings to mere units or categories of political or social planning and action. Such a process leads to new and other unjust forms of anonymity and alienation.

Social Sin

6. Service to the poor also involves speaking up for them, and trying *to reform structures which cause or perpetuate their oppression.* As committed Catholics involved in helping to meet people's many concrete needs, you are still called to reflect on another dimension of a worldwide problem: *the relationship between rich societies and poor societies,* rich nations and poor nations. Your insights must be prayerfully joined to those of many other people to see what can be done as soon as possible to purify the social structures of all society in this regard.

In the final analysis, however, we must realize that social injustice and unjust social structures exist only because individuals and groups of individuals deliberately maintain or tolerate them. It is these *personal choices,* operating through structures, that breed and propagate situations of poverty, oppression and misery. For this reason, overcoming "social" sin and reforming the social order itself must begin with *the conversion of our hearts*. As the American Bishops have said: "The Gospel confers on each Christian the vocation to love God and neighbor in ways that bear fruit in the life of society. That vocation consists above all in a change of heart: a conversion expressed in praise of God and in concrete deeds of justice and service" *(Economic Justice for All: Catholic Social Teaching and the U.S. Economy,* 327).

To many people, mercy and conversion may seem like poor tools for solving social problems. Some are tempted to accept ideologies that use force to carry out their programs and impose their vision. Such means sometimes produce what appear to be successes. But these successes are not real. Force and manipulation have nothing to do with true human development and the defense of human dignity. Catholic social teaching is totally different, not only as re-gards goals, but also as regards the means to be used. For the Christian, *putting right human ills must necessarily take into account the reality of Creation and Redemption.* It means *treating every human being as a unique child of God,* a brother or sister of Jesus Christ. The path of human solidarity is the path of service; and true service means selfless love, open to the needs of all, without distinction of persons, with the explicit purpose of reinforcing each person's sense of God-given dignity.

Transformation of Society

7. *Solidarity and service are above all a duty of Christian love* which must involve the whole community. When we are tempted to congratulate ourselves on what we have done, we must soberly bear in mind the words of Jesus: "When you have done all you have been commanded to do, say, 'We are useless servants. We have done no more than our duty'" (Lk 17:10). When we are faced with the vastness of this duty of love, with the boundless needs of the poor in America and throughout the world, when we are disappointed by slowness and setbacks in the reform of structures and in our

own conversion, let us not lose heart, and let us not settle for what has already been accomplished. *Love can overcome great obstacles, and God's love can totally transform the world.*

As the Church tries to express Christian solidarity in generous service, she also wishes to draw attention to *the importance of worship and prayer and their relationship to service.* In looking to the example of Christ, the Church can never forget that all Christ's actions were accompanied by prayer. It is in prayer that the Church develops and evaluates her social consciousness and unceasingly discovers anew her vocation to serve the needy of the world, as Jesus did. Addressing a group of American Bishops during their last *ad limina* visit, I spoke of this specifically Christian and ecclesial dimension of all social and charitable action: "Only a worshiping and praying Church can show herself sufficiently sensitive to the needs of the sick, the suffering, the lonely— especially in the great urban centers—and the poor everywhere. The Church as *a community of service* has first to feel the weight of the burden carried by so many individuals and families, and then strive to help alleviate these burdens. The discipleship that the Church discovers in prayer she expresses in deep interest for Christ's brethren in the modern world and for their many different needs. Her concern, manifested in various ways, embraces—among others—the areas of housing, education, health care, unemployment, the administration of justice, the special needs of the aged and the handicapped. In prayer, the Church is confirmed in her solidarity with the weak who are oppressed, the vulnerable who are manipulated, the children who are exploited, and everyone who is in any way discriminated against" (Address of December 3, 1983, No. 6).

8. *Catholic Charities and related organizations exist essentially to spread Christian love.* It is especially through charitable activities at the parish level that the entire Church in the United States joins in the tasks of mercy, justice and love. We have seen today how Catholic Charities and all its colleague associations have lent God their own flesh—their hands and feet and hearts—so that his work may be done in our world. For your long and persevering service—creative and courageous, and blind to distinctions of race or

religion—you will certainly hear Jesus' words of gratitude: *"You did it for me"* (Mt 25:40).

Gather, transform and serve! When done in the name of Jesus Christ, this is the spirit of Catholic Charities and of all who work in this cause, because it is the faithful following of the One who did "not come to be served but to serve" (Mk 10:45). By working for a society which fosters the dignity of every human person, not only are you serving the poor, but you are renewing *the founding vision of this nation under God!* And may God reward you abundantly!

Dialogue with Christ

Address given to seminarians and men and women preparing for religious life—San Fernando Cathedral, San Antonio, September 13. (The Spanish version of this address will be found in the Appendix.)

"Remove the sandals from your feet, for *the place where you stand is holy ground.*" (Ex 3:5)

1. These words of God marked the beginning of a new way of life for Moses. The place where he was standing was holy ground, for he was standing in *the awesome presence of Almighty God.* And on that holy ground, he heard a voice calling him to a special mission of service to the People of God. From that moment forward, Moses' life would be radically altered. He would henceforth place his life at the service of the God of Abraham, Isaac and Jacob. No longer would his life be his own. He would lead the Chosen People out of slavery in Egypt toward freedom in the Promised Land. In meeting God on holy ground, speaking with him there, and hearing his summons to service, Moses came to a new understanding of himself and entered into a deeper commitment to God and his people. *The mission of Moses began under the sign of God's holiness.*

Dear brothers and sisters in the Lord: it is a deep joy for me to be with you today in this historic *Cathedral of San Fernando,* the oldest cathedral sanctuary in the United States. It is with great gratitude to God that I meet with you who are preparing to serve the Lord as priests and religious, you who in a singular and remarkable way have, like Moses, heard the voice of God calling you to *that "holy ground" of a special vocation in the Church.* You have stood in the awesome presence of the Lord and heard him call you by name. And listening to his voice with prayerful discernment you have joyfully begun your formation for the priesthood or the religious life.

Lifelong Dialogue of Love

2. From the human point of view, a vocation in the Church *begins with a discovery,* with finding the pearl of great price. You discover Jesus: his person, his message, his call.

In the Gospel which we have heard today, we reflect on the call of Jesus to the first disciples. The first thing that Andrew did after meeting Jesus was to seek out his brother Simon and tell him: *"We have found the Messiah!"* Then Philip, in a similar way, sought out Nathanael and told him: *"We have found* the one Moses spoke of in the law—the prophets too—*Jesus,* son of Joseph, from Nazareth" (cf. Jn 1:35-51).

After the initial discovery, a dialogue in prayer ensues, a dialogue between Jesus and the one called, *a dialogue which goes beyond words* and expresses itself in love.

Questions are an important part of this dialogue. For example, in the Gospel account of the call of the disciples, we are told that "when Jesus turned around and noticed them following him, he asked them, *'What are you looking for?'* They said to him, 'Rabbi' (which means teacher), 'where do you stay?' *'Come and see,'* he answered" (Jn 1:38-39).

What begins as a discovery of Jesus moves to a greater understanding and commitment through *a prayerful process of questions and discernment.* In this process, our motives are purified. We come face to face with pointed questions such as, "What are you looking for?" And we even find ourselves asking questions of Jesus, as Nathanael did: *"How do you know me?"* (Jn 1:48) It is only when we have reflected candidly and honestly in the silence of our hearts that we begin to be convinced that the Lord is truly calling us.

Yet, even then, the process of discernment is not over. Jesus says to us as he said to Nathanael: *"You will see much greater things than that"* (Jn 1:50). Throughout our lives, after we have made a sacred and permanent commitment and after our active service of the Lord has begun, we still need the dialogue of prayer that will continually deepen our knowledge and love of our Lord Jesus Christ.

Dear students for the priesthood and candidates for the religious life: you stand in *a long line of people who have given themselves totally* for the sake of the Kingdom of God, and who have shared our Lord's sacrifice and entered into his Paschal victory. For generations many of the generous priests and religious who have served the Church in Texas have come with immigrants from other lands, or as missionaries from other places. I wish to express my gratitude to God for the contribution which they have made to establishing the Church here. At the same time I praise the Lord of the harvest for all of you and for the growing number of native-born vocations, and I fervently pray that this increase continues.

Like all those who have gone before you, you will have trials. Your fidelity will be ensured only when you invoke the strength of the Lord, only when you rely on Christ's grace. But if Christ is the center of your lives, the one for whom you live and die, then your generous service to your brothers and sisters will know no limits. You will love those who are difficult to love, and you will *enrich the world with the Gospel* of Jesus Christ.

The Priestly Vocation

3. I would now like to speak *to the seminarians*. Dear brothers in Christ, as men preparing for priestly ordination, it is important for you to have *a clear understanding of the vocation* to which you feel called, so that your promise of lifelong fidelity may be maturely made and faithfully kept. Your life in the priesthood will closely join you with the Eucharist; you will be ministers of the mysteries of God; you will be expected to preach and teach in the name of the Church.

The Eucharist is the principal reason for the ordained priesthood. As I said in my 1980 Holy Thursday Letter: "Through our ordination...we priests are united in a singular and exceptional way to the Eucharist. In a certain way we derive *from* it and exist *for it"* (No. 2). No work we do as priests is so important. The celebration of the Eucharist is the way that we best serve our brothers and sisters in the world, because it is the source and center of the dynamism of their Christian lives.

How crucial it is then, for our own happiness and for the sake of a fruitful ministry, that we *cultivate a deep love for the Eucharist.* During your seminary days, a thorough theological study of the nature of the Eucharistic mystery and an accurate knowledge of liturgical norms will prepare you well to foster the full, conscious and active participation of the community in the liturgy. The future priest is called to reflect and to profess with the Second Vatican Council that "the other sacraments, as well as every ministry of the Church and every work of the apostolate, are linked with the Holy Eucharist and are directed toward it. For the most Blessed Eucharist contains the Church's entire spiritual wealth, that is, Christ himself" *(Presbyterorum Ordinis, 5)*.

The task of *preaching the Gospel* is of supreme importance in the priesthood. And since, as St. Paul says, "faith comes through hearing, and what is heard is the word of Christ" (Rom 10:17), seminary formation must aim at fostering *a deep understanding of the word of God* as it is lived and proclaimed by the Church. Always remember the words of the Prophet Jeremiah: "When I found your words, I devoured them; they became my joy and the happiness of my heart, because I bore your name, O Lord" (Jer 15:16).

In order for your preaching to bear fruit in the lives of those whom you will serve, you will have to nourish in your own mind and heart *a real internal adherence to the Magisterium* of the Church. For, as the Council reminded us, "the task of priests is not to teach their own wisdom but God's word, and to summon all people urgently to conversion and to holiness" *(Presbyterorum Ordinis, 4)*.

The priest needs to know the real living conditions of the people he serves, and he must live among them as a true brother in Christ. He can never be separated from the community. But there is a real sense in which, like the Apostle Paul, he is—in the very words of Scripture—*"set apart to proclaim the Gospel of God"* (Rom 1:1). In his priestly identity he is commissioned for a special service—a unique service—to the Body of Christ. For this reason, the Second Vatican Council spoke in this way: "By their vocation and ordination, priests of the New Testament are indeed set apart in a certain sense within the midst of God's people. But this is so, not that they may be separated from this people or from any man, but that they may be totally dedicated to the work for which the Lord raised them up. They cannot be ministers of Christ unless they are witnesses and dispensers of a life other than this earthly one" *(ibid., 3)*.

Each one of you is called to embrace freely a celibate life

for the sake of Jesus and his Kingdom, in order to become a
"man for others." If it is modeled on the generous divine
and human love of Jesus for his Father and for every man,
woman and child, your celibacy will mean an enhancement
of your life, *a greater closeness to God's people*, an eagerness to
give yourself without reserve. By embracing celibacy in the
context of the priesthood, you are committing yourself to a
deeper and more universal love. Above all, *celibacy means the
gift of yourself to God*. It will be the response, in Christ and
the Church, to the gifts of Creation and Redemption. It will
be part of your sharing, at the deepest level of human
freedom and generosity, in the Death and Resurrection of
Jesus. Humanly speaking this sacrifice is difficult because of
our human weaknesses; without prayer it is impossible. It
will also require discipline and effort and persevering love
on your part. But in your gift of celibacy to Christ and his
Church, even the world will be able to see the meaning of
the Lord's grace and the power of his Paschal Mystery. This
victory must always be visible in your joy.

The Council stressed the *essential difference* between the
ordained priesthood and the priesthood of all the baptized,
and prescribed a priestly formation in seminaries which is
distinct from other forms of formation (cf. *Lumen Gentium,*
10; *Optatam Totius,* 4). At the heart of this essential difference
is the truth that Jesus entrusted the Twelve with the authority to proclaim the Gospel, celebrate the Eucharist, forgive
sins and provide for the pastoral care of the community. This
authority is given for a truly specific purpose and through
ordination is shared by the successors of the Apostles and
their collaborators in the ordained priesthood. It is given for
a particular ministry of service to be carried out in imitation of
the Son of Man, who came to serve. The ministry of the
ordained priest is essential to the life and development of
the Church; it is an essential service to the rest of the
Church. It is clear that those who are preparing for this
specific ministry will have *special needs and requirements* that
differ from those of the rest of the community.

All the members of the Church are summoned to share
in her mission by reason of their Baptism and Confirmation.
Priests can best assist and encourage others in the service of

the Gospel by being faithful themselves to their priestly ministry in the Church. "Hence, whether engaged in prayer and adoration, preaching the word, offering the Eucharistic Sacrifice, and ministering the other sacraments or performing any of the works of the ministry for people, priests are contributing to the extension of God's glory as well as to the development of divine life in people" *(Presbyterorum Ordinis,* 2).

The Religious Vocation

4. And now I turn to you, my brothers and sisters who are preparing for the *religious life.* Yours too is a great and specific gift of God's love. To each of you, as to the first disciples, Jesus has said: *"Come and see"* (Jn 1:39). There is no force or coercion on the part of Christ, but rather an invitation, extended simply and personally, to come and stay in his house, to be in his presence, and with him to praise his Father in the unity of the Holy Spirit.

A religious vocation is *a gift,* freely given and freely received. It is a profound expression of *the love of God* for you and, on your part, it requires in turn *a total love for Christ.* Thus, the whole life of a religious is aimed at strengthening the bond of love which was first forged in the *Sacrament of Baptism.* You are called to do this in religious consecration through the profession of the evangelical counsels of chastity, poverty and obedience (cf. Can. 573, §§1-2).

During your years of preparation, the Church is eager that you receive a formation that will prepare you to live your religious consecration in fidelity and joy, a formation that is both deeply human and Christian, a formation that will help you to accept ever more generously *the radical demands of the Gospel* and bear public witness to them. Your very life is meant to be a confident and convincing affirmation that Jesus is "the Way, and the Truth, and the Life" (Jn 14:6).

What you must develop, first and foremost, is *the habit and discipline of prayer.* For who you *are* is more fundamental than any service you perform. In this regard, the Second Vatican Council said that religious should "seek God before all things" and "combine contemplation with apostolic love" *(Perfectae Caritatis,* 5). This is no easy task, for prayer has many dimensions and forms. It is both personal and communal, liturgical and private. It deepens our union with God and fosters our apostolic love. A climate of silence is needed as well as a personal life-style that is simple and ready for sacrifice.

The liturgical life of the community greatly influences the personal prayer of all the members. The *Eucharist* will always be the source and summit of your life in Christ. It is the Sacrament through which *the worship of your whole existence is presented to God in union with Christ* (cf. Can. 607, §1). The Eucharist is the point where the offering of your chastity, poverty and obedience is made one with the Sacrifice of Christ.

In your religious consecration, *the Sacrament of Penance* is a constant reminder to you of the call of Jesus to conversion and newness of life. Precisely because you are called by your religious profession to bear witness to the holiness of God, you must help the People of God *never to lose their sense of sin.* To be authentic in following Christ in the perfection of charity, you must be the first to recognize sin in your hearts, to repent and glorify God's grace and mercy. Conversion is a lifelong process, requiring repentant love. The Sacrament of Penance is the Sacrament in which our weakness meets God's holiness in the mercy of Christ.

In a thousand ways the Church will call you into service in her mission for the Kingdom of God. She needs your talents, your availability to come and go according to the needs of the hour, which are often the needs of the poor. She needs your collaboration in the cause of faith and justice. *She needs your work* and everything that you can do for the Gospel. But, above all, the Church needs what you are; *she needs you:* men and women consecrated to God, living in union with Christ, living in union with his Church, striving after the perfection of love. Why? *Because of the holiness of God!* Dear brothers and sisters, *what you do is important, but what you are is even more important*—more important for the world, more important for the Church, more important for Christ.

In Mary, the Mother of Christ and the Church, you will understand the identity of your own life. She showed throughout her life the meaning of the evangelical counsels, to which your religious consecration is directed. Her words to the angel—"I am the servant of the Lord. Let it be done to me as you say" (Lk 1:38)—show the obedient, total surrender which our consecration to God requires and which your vows express.

The Mission of the Laity

5. Of course, *the call to holiness* is a *universal* call. All members of the Church, without exception, are summoned by God to grow in personal sanctity and to share in the mission of the Church. A heightened awareness of this truth has been one of the fruits of the Second Vatican Council. And it has helped foster a clearer awareness of *the role of the laity* in building up the Kingdom, as well as a closer collaboration of the laity with the clergy and religious. As persons preparing for the priesthood and religious life, it will be your privilege to help explore still more effective forms of collaboration in the future. But even more importantly, you will be in a position to encourage the lay people to fulfill *that mission which is uniquely their own* in those situations and places in which the Church can be the salt of the earth only through them.

The Council spoke very clearly about their special mission. Among other things, it stated: "The laity, by their very vocation, seek the Kingdom of God by engaging in temporal affairs and by ordering them according to the plan of God. They live in the world, that is, in each and in all of the secular professions and occupations. They live in the ordinary circumstances of family and social life, from which the very web of their existence is woven" (*Lumen Gentium*, 31). This activity of the laity constitutes a specific contribution to the Body of Christ. Yours is another charism, a different gift to be lived differently, so that, *in true diversity*, there may be real unity in the work of service.

Gratitude and Appeal

6. On this occasion, I cannot fail to express my special gratitude and encouragement to those of you who are responsible for the formation of candidates for the priesthood

and religious life. Be assured that all your efforts, work and sacrifice are deeply appreciated by the Church and by me personally. Your task is a vital one for the future of the Church, and your contribution to the life of the People of God is a lasting one. Certainly it is crucial that you yourselves be steeped in sound doctrine, pastoral experience and holiness of life. Of great importance is your attitude of faith, and particularly your personal example of *filial love for the Church*, as well as *your loyal adherence to her authentic ordinary Magisterium* (cf. *Lumen Gentium*, 25). St. Paul tells us: "Christ loved the Church. He gave himself up for her to make her holy" (Eph 5:25-26). I pray that your own lives will always be animated by this kind of sacrificial love.

I wish to add a word of deep appreciation to all those parents who sustain and encourage their children in the following of Christ. The prayerful support, understanding and love that you give them is of immense value.

7. At this time I wish to appeal to the Church in the United States for *vocations* to the priesthood and religious life. The duty of fostering such vocations rests on the whole Christian community, and certainly families have traditionally made the greatest contribution. We must always remember too the impact on vocations that can be made by zealous priests and religious, by their example of generous service, by the witness of their charity, their goodness and their joy. Above all, *the key to vocations is persevering prayer,* as Jesus himself commanded: "The harvest is good but laborers are scarce. Beg the harvest master to send out laborers to gather his harvest" (Mt 9:37-38).

Dear brothers and sisters, you have come to know the Lord Jesus. You have *heard his voice, discovered his love,* and *answered his call.* May he, the Lord Jesus, who has begun this good work in you, bring it to completion for the glory of his Father and by the power of his Spirit. Remember always: "The place where you stand is holy ground" (Ex 3:5).

And may the Blessed Virgin Mary help you by her prayers, and by the example of her love.

The Parish and the Family

Address to Hispanics at Our Lady of Guadalupe Plaza—San Antonio, September 13.

Dear Brothers and Sisters in Christ,

1. This is a moment of great joy for me. I have looked forward to this meeting with you, *members of the Hispanic community* of San Antonio, present here as representatives of all your Hispanic brothers and sisters in the United States. You are here too as *a parish community*, and through you therefore my words are addressed to every parish community throughout the United States.

I greet each one of you with love in our Lord and Redeemer Jesus Christ. I am particularly happy to speak to you in the beautiful Spanish language, in this square named in honor of Our Lady of Guadalupe. Our gathering here is a vivid reminder, in the current Marian Year, of *the special place of the Mother of the Redeemer in the mystery of Christ and of the Church*. It speaks to us of how dear our Blessed Mother has always been to you people of Hispanic culture and how important she continues to be today in your lives of faith and devotion. Marian shrines and places of pilgrimage are a kind of "geography" of faith by which we seek to meet the Mother of God in order to find a strengthening of our Christian life (cf. *Redemptoris Mater,* 28). Popular devotion to the Blessed Virgin Mary is rooted in sound doctrine, and authentic religious experience is appropriate and important in the lives of all Christ's followers.

Missionaries to One Another

2. *The Hispanic heritage of San Antonio and the Southwest is very important for the Church.* Spanish was the language of the first evangelizers of this continent, precisely in this region. The missions here in San Antonio and throughout the Southwest are visible signs of the many years of evangelization and service carried out by the first missionaries. Their preaching of salvation in Jesus Christ was authenticated by their own integrity of life and by the spiritual and corporal works of mercy and love which they performed. Following

133

their example, thousands of dedicated priests, religious and lay people have labored to build up the Church here. Today it is your turn, in fidelity to the Gospel of Jesus Christ, to build your lives on the rock of your Christian faith. It is your turn to be evangelizers of each other and of all those whose faith is weak or who have not yet given themselves to the Lord. May you be no less zealous in evangelization and in Christian service than your forebears!

The Parish—"Family of Families"

3. Today I wish to speak to you about *your parish*, which is the place and community in which you nourish and express your Christian life. I wish to speak of the parish as *the family of families*, for parish life is especially related to the strengths and weaknesses and needs of the families that make it up. There are of course many things that could be said about parish life; today it is only possible for me to emphasize certain aspects.

It is useful to begin with a well-known passage from the New Testament which helps us to keep in mind just why the members of a Catholic parish come together in the name of Jesus. In the Acts of the Apostles we read about the early Christians: "They devoted themselves to the apostles' instruction and the communal life, to the breaking of bread and prayers" (2:42). *Instruction in the faith of the Apostles, the building up of a living community, the Eucharist and the other sacraments, and the life of prayer*—these are essential factors of the life of every parish.

Transmitting the Faith

4. First, instruction or *catechesis*. Everyone needs to be instructed in the faith. St. Paul summarizes it this way: "Everyone who calls on the name of the Lord will be saved. But how shall they call on him in whom they have not believed? And how can they believe unless they have heard of him? And *how can they hear unless there is someone to preach?*" (Rom 10:13-14) In a parish *the faith is proclaimed and transmitted* in many ways: through the liturgy, especially the

Eucharist with its appropriate homilies; through religious instruction in schools and catechetical programs; through adult religious education; through prayer-groups and associations for pastoral activity; through the Catholic press.

There are two things that I wish to emphasize about transmitting the faith. *Catechesis has an objective content.* We cannot invent the faith as we go along. We must receive it *in* and *from* the universal community of faith, the Church to whom Christ himself has entrusted a teaching office under the guidance of the Spirit of Truth. Every catechist must sincerely and reverently be able to apply to himself or herself the words of Jesus: "My doctrine is not my own, it comes from him who sent me" (Jn 7:16; cf. *Catechesi Tradendae*, 6). Likewise, *every baptized person,* precisely by reason of being baptized, has *the right to receive the authentic teaching of the Church* regarding doctrinal and moral aspects of Christian life (cf. Can. 229; *Catechesi Tradendae*, 14).

The other point I wish to make about instruction in the faith is that *family catechesis precedes, accompanies and enriches all other forms of catechesis* (cf. *Catechesi Tradendae*, 68). This means that the parish, in considering its catechetical programs, should give particular attention to its families. But above all it means that the family itself is the first and most appropriate place for teaching the truths of the faith, the practice of Christian virtues and the essential values of human life.

Service to the Family

5. The second aspect of parish life that is contained in the text from the Acts of the Apostles concerns *the parish's task of building up a living community.* I have already said that every parish is *a family of families.* The vitality of a parish greatly depends on the spiritual vigor, commitment and involvement of its families. The family in fact is the basic unit of society and of the Church. It is "the domestic church." Families are those living cells which come together to form the very substance of parish life. Some are healthy and filled with the love of God which is poured forth into our hearts through the Holy Spirit who has been given to us

(cf. Rom 5:5). In some there is little energy for the life of the Spirit. Some have broken down altogether. The priests and their collaborators in a parish must try to be very close to all families in their need for pastoral care, and to provide the support and spiritual nourishment they require.

The pastoral care of families is a vast and complex field of the Church's ministry, but it is a most urgent and pressing service. Each parish must be fully committed to it, especially in the face of so much breakdown and undermining of family life in society. I appeal to all priests—pastors, associates and all concerned—to the permanent deacons, and to the religious and lay leaders to do everything possible, working together, *to serve the family* as effectively as possible. *This involves proclaiming the whole truth about marriage and family life:* the exclusive nature of conjugal love, the indissolubility of marriage; the Church's full teaching on the transmission of life and the respect due to human life from the moment of conception until natural death; the rights and duties of parents with regard to the education of their children, especially their religious and moral education, including proper sex education. *Parents and family members must, moreover, be helped and sustained in their struggle to live by the sacred truths of faith.* The Church must furnish families with the spiritual means of persevering in their sublime vocation and of growing in the special holiness to which Christ calls them.

Apostolic Families

6. *Just as the parish is responsible for the family, so the family must be aware of its obligations to the parish,* which is the larger family. Today, Catholic couples and families must think especially of the service which they have a duty to render to other couples and families, especially those who experience problems. This apostolate of couple to couple and family to family can be carried out in many ways: prayer, good example, formal or informal instruction or counseling and material assistance of many sorts (cf. *Familiaris Consortio,* 71). I appeal to you, the Catholic families of the United States: *be true families*—united, reconciled and loving; and *be true Catholic families*—prayerful communities living the Catholic faith,

open to the needs of others, taking part fully in the life of the parish and of the Church at large.

The Sacramental Life

7. Another fundamental aspect of parish life is *the worthy celebration of the Sacraments,* including sacramental marriage. This Sacrament forms *the stable basis of the whole Christian community.* Without it, Christ's design for human love is not fulfilled, his plan for the family is not followed. It is precisely because Christ established marriage as a Sacrament and willed it to be a sign of his own permanent and faithful love for the Church that the parish must explain to the faithful why all trial marriages, merely civil marriages, free unions, and divorces do not correspond to Christ's plan.

The sacramental life of the Church is centered above all in the Eucharist, which celebrates and brings about the unity of the Christian community—unity with God and unity with one another. *In the Mass, the Sacrifice of the Cross is perpetuated* throughout the centuries until Christ comes again. *The Body and Blood of the Lord are given to us as our spiritual food.* The parish community has no greater task or privilege than to gather, like Christ's first disciples, for "the breaking of the bread" (Acts 2:42).

I now repeat especially to all parishes the invitation already addressed to the whole Church: to promote and foster *public and private devotion to the Holy Eucharist also outside of Mass* (cf. *Inaestimabile Donum,* 20ff.). For, in the words of the Second Vatican Council: "The most blessed Eucharist contains the Church's entire spiritual wealth, that is, Christ himself" *(Presbyterorum Ordinis,* 5).

The sacramental life of a parish extends also to the other sacraments which mark the important moments of the life of individuals and families, and of the entire parochial community. I wish to mention in particular *the Sacrament of Penance* and the *important need for Catholics to confess their sins regularly.* In recent years, many have grown neglectful of this wonderful gift by which we obtain Christ's forgiveness of our sins. The state of the Sacrament of Penance in each parish and in each local Church is a good indicator of the authentic maturity of the faith of the priests and people. It is necessary that Catholic families instill in their members a deep love of this beautiful means of reconciliation with our heavenly Father, with the Church and with our neighbor. Parents, more by example than by words, should encourage their children to go to Confession regularly. Parishes need to encourage families to do this; they need to support them through proper catechesis. Needless to say, priests, who are the ministers of God's grace in this Sacrament, should make certain that the Sacrament is conveniently available in its authorized forms.

The Life of Prayer

8. Finally, I refer briefly to *the life of prayer* as it manifests itself within the Christian community. This is an area in which the interaction between the family and the parish is especially clear and profound. *Prayer begins in the home.* The prayers that serve us well in life are often those learned at home when we were children. But prayer in the home also serves to introduce the children to the liturgical prayer of the whole Church; it helps all to apply the Church's prayer to everyday events and to the special moments of a family's experience (cf. *Familiaris Consortio,* 61).

Everyone involved in parish life should be concerned to encourage and support *family prayer* by every means available; and families themselves should be making efforts to engage in family prayer and to integrate that prayer into the prayer-life of the wider ecclesial community.

I am happy to know that the number of Hispanic priests and men and women religious is growing. But many more are needed. Young Hispanics: is Christ calling you? Hispanic families: are you willing to give your sons and daughters to the Church's service? *Do you ask the Lord to send laborers into his harvest?* Christ needs Hispanic laborers for the great harvest of the Hispanic community and the whole Church.

Outreach to the Needy

9. And finally I wish to encourage all families and parishes not to be inward-looking, not to dwell on themselves. *Jesus commands us to serve our neighbor,* to reach out to those in need. And I ask you especially to reach out to those brothers and sisters in the faith who have drifted away because of indifference or who have been hurt in some way. I invite all you who are unsure about the Church or who doubt that you will be welcome *to come home to the family of families, to come home to your parish.* You belong there! It is your family in the Church, and the Church is the household of God in which there are no strangers or aliens (cf. Eph 2:19).

We are gathered in front of a parish which is dedicated to *Our Lady of Guadalupe,* Mother of Jesus, Mother of the Church, Mother of the Americas, and in particular of Mexico. When Jesus died on the Cross, he entrusted his Mother to his beloved disciple, John. The Gospel tells us that from that moment the disciple took her into his home (cf. Jn 19:27). What better way is there for you to celebrate this Marian Year than by taking Mary, the Mother of the Redeemer into your homes! This means *imitating her faith and discipleship;* it means keeping her present in your family prayers, especially the family rosary; turning to her, asking her intercession for the grace of conversion and renewal; entrusting yourselves and your families to her maternal care.

May God bless each and every one of you.

May he bless every family and parish.

May the Blessed Virgin of Guadalupe love and protect the Hispanic people of the land.

Viva la Virgen de Guadalupe!

Developing the Whole Person

Address to the people of Phoenix at the plaza of St. Mary's Basilica—September 14.

Dear Friends,

1. With fraternal esteem, I extend to all of you—the people of *Phoenix and the American Southwest*—my greetings of joy and peace! You have welcomed me with open arms. I thank you for your most cordial hospitality.

In particular today, I wish to greet our *Spanish-speaking* brothers and sisters. Your hospitality is a reminder of the great strength, vitality and generosity which the Hispanic community has brought to the United States. I ask you to grow ever closer to your Church and to enrich her with the profession and faithful practice of your faith—the faith of pioneers, missionaries and martyrs. Long live Our Lady of Guadalupe!

"God Enriches"

2. By a happy act of providence, my visit to Arizona coincides with *the Seventy-fifth Anniversary of Arizona's Statehood*. On this happy occasion, I offer to all of you my best wishes and congratulations.

Like all of America's Southwest, Arizona faces challenges of *amazing growth*. I am told that the motto of your state is *"Ditat Deus,"* "God enriches." And indeed you have all around you ample proof of this enrichment: in the majesty and beauty of your landscape, and especially in the diversity and giftedness of your people. Your state and the ever-growing number of its citizens have been greatly blessed and enriched by God. In the past forty years, in particular, you have experienced *remarkable progress and development*. And this brings with it increased obligations and responsibilities.

Genuine Human Development

3. My visit to Arizona also coincides with another anniversary. *Twenty years* have passed since Pope Paul VI published his important Encyclical *Populorum Progressio*, which

was a document of great insight on the topic of true human development as seen in the light of the Gospel of Jesus Christ. Although two decades have passed since the Encyclical first appeared, its message remains today, as then, both challenging and prophetic.

A fundamental principle put forth by Pope Paul is that development, in order to be truly authentic, must *contribute to the good of the whole person* (cf. *Populorum Progressio*, 14). Thus, development can never be reduced to economic expansion alone or to values that are strictly temporal. What is ultimately at stake is the well-being of persons in all *the spiritual and physical dimensions* of their humanity, including the moral, social, cultural and economic aspects.

Efforts aimed at promoting development need to be accompanied by the search for *a transcendent humanism*, a humanism which is oriented toward God. Your Arizona state motto expresses well the reason for this: *God enriches*. Yes, God alone is the source of all that is good. God alone is the Creator of all things. As the Apostle St. Paul once said: "It is he (God) who gives to all life and breath and everything else.... In him we live and move and have our being" (Acts 17:25-28). In order to be genuine, development must aim at improving people's living conditions and at the same time promote a transcendent humanism which acknowledges the sovereignty of God.

Fraternal Solidarity

4. By its very nature, true human advancement is *necessarily outgoing*; it cannot be concentrated on itself. It must reach out to include more and more people in its influence. Any progress which would secure the betterment of a select few at the expense of the greater human family would be an erroneous and distorted progress. It would be an outrage against the demands of justice and an affront to the dignity of every human being.

In this regard, the following words of Pope Paul VI ring true: "Both for nations and for individuals, avarice is the most evident form of moral underdevelopment" (*Populorum Progressio*, 19). And that is why he insisted on the need for a *spirit of human solidarity* to accompany all efforts for development. The temptation toward avarice is certainly not restricted to any one nation or group of people. In fact, it is part and parcel of our common human condition, which stands in need of constant conversion. Yet, does not the temptation present itself more forcefully to those who have received a larger. share of the material goods of the earth?

The Second Vatican Council of the Catholic Church stated unequivocally: "Advanced nations have a very heavy obligation to help the developing peoples" (*Gaudium et Spes,* 86). These words apply with special relevance to the people of Arizona and of all the United States, whom God has so richly blessed. As you look with gratitude upon the high standard of living that many of you enjoy, at least in comparison to the rest of the world, *may your hearts go out to the less fortunate.* May your hearts and hands be open to the poor, both within your own society and in developing nations of the world. Just as God enriches you, so may you be channels of enrichment for others.

Jesus Has Shown the Way

5. Those of us who are Christians draw inspiration to take up this task from the words and example of *our Lord Jesus Christ.* Although he is God, he humbled himself and assumed our humanity, becoming one like us in all things but sin (cf. Phil 2:5-11; Heb 4:15). Thus, he forged a bond of *unbreakable solidarity with every human being.* In him our humanity is sacred and forever linked with God.

In his public ministry we see how *Jesus came to serve and not to be served.* One of the signs of his mission was that he preached the Gospel to the poor (cf. Mt 11:2-5), and he showed in daily life a special love for the poor and suffering. We are convinced, therefore, that if we follow the teaching and example of our beloved Lord, we shall find ourselves more closely united with one another, especially the needy, and we shall experience that transcendent dimension of life which can only be attained in union with God.

Dear friends: I have spoken with you today about development because I am convinced, as was Pope Paul VI, that in our highly technological age *"the new name for peace is development"* (cf. *Populorum Progressio,* 87). If we wish then to promote the tranquillity of order in our world, we must be deeply committed to that authentic development which contributes to the good of every person everywhere, in all the dimensions of human life. For this reason *my appeal to America is for human solidarity throughout this land and far beyond its borders.* This is the culmination of true progress; this is the measure of true greatness; this is the condition of true and lasting peace for America and for the world!

God bless Arizona! God bless you all! *Ditat Deus!*

Extending
Jesus' Healing Mission

Address to 2,000 health care persons—Convention Center, Phoenix, September 14.

Dear Brothers and Sisters,
Leaders in Catholic Health Care,

1. In the joy and peace of our Lord Jesus Christ I greet you and thank you for your warm welcome. This meeting gives us the opportunity to honor and give thanks to God for one of the most extensive and fundamental works of the Catholic Church in the United States—all that is embraced in the term "Catholic health care." I am pleased to be able to express to you who represent so many of your country's health care organizations *the esteem, support and solidarity of the whole Church.* In you, Jesus Christ continues his healing ministry, "curing the people of every disease and illness" (cf. Mt 4:23).

This is the high dignity to which you and your colleagues are called. This is your vocation, your commitment, and the path of your specific witness to the presence of God's Kingdom in the world. Your health care ministry, pioneered and developed by Congregations of women Religious and by Congregations of Brothers, is *one of the most vital apostolates* of the ecclesial community and *one of the most significant services* which the Catholic Church offers to society in the name of Jesus Christ.

I have been told that membership in the Catholic Health Association extends to 620 hospitals and 300 long-term care facilities; that Catholic hospital beds number 11 per cent of the total number in the country; that Catholic institutions administer approximately 17 per cent of the health care throughout the nation, and that they cared for nearly 46 million people last year. I am grateful to Sr. Mary Eileen Wilhelm and to your President, Mr. Curley, for illustrating to us this immense network of Christian service.

Jesus' Power Still Active

2. Because of your dedication to caring for the sick and the poor, the aged and the dying, you know from your own daily experience the extent to which illness and suffering are basic problems of human existence. When the sick flocked to Jesus during his earthly life, they recognized in him a friend whose deeply compassionate and loving heart responded to their needs. He restored physical and mental health to many. These cures, however, involved more than just healing sickness. They were also *prophetic signs of his own identity and of the coming of the Kingdom of God*, and they very often caused a new spiritual awakening in the one who had been healed.

The power that went out from Jesus and cured people of his own time (cf. Lk 6:19) has not lost its effect in the two-thousand-year history of the Church. *This power remains, in the life and prayer of the Church, a source of healing and reconciliation*. Ever active, this power confirms the identity of the Church today, authenticates her proclamation of the Kingdom of God, and stands as a sign of triumph over evil.

With all Catholic health care, the immediate aim is to provide for the well-being of the body and mind of the human person, especially in sickness or old age. By his example, Christ teaches the Christian "to do good by his or her suffering and to do good to those who suffer" *(Salvifici Doloris, 30)*. This latter aspect naturally absorbs the greater part of the energy and attention of health care ministry. Today in the United States, Catholic health care extends the mission of the Church in every state of the Union, in major cities, small towns, rural areas, on the campuses of academic institutions, in remote outposts, and in inner-city neighborhoods. By providing health care in all these places, especially to the poor, the neglected, the needy, the newcomer, *your apostolate penetrates and transforms the very fabric of American society*. And sometimes you yourselves, like those you serve, are called to bow in humble and loving resignation to the experience of sickness—or to other forms of pain and suffering.

Special Character of Catholic Health Care

3. *All concern for the sick and suffering is part of the Church's life and mission.* The Church has always understood herself to be charged by Christ with the care of the poor, the weak, the defenseless, the suffering and those who mourn. This means that as you alleviate suffering and seek to heal, you also bear witness to the Christian view of suffering and to the meaning of life and death as taught by your Christian faith.

In the complex world of modern health care in industrialized society, this witness must be given in a variety of ways. First, it requires continual efforts *to ensure that everyone has access to health care.* I know that you have already examined this question in the report of your Task Force on Health Care of the Poor. In seeking to treat patients equally, *regardless of social and economic status,* you proclaim to your fellow citizens and to the world Christ's special love for the neglected and powerless. This particular challenge is a consequence of your Christian dedication and conviction, and it calls for great courage on the part of Catholic bodies and institutions operating in the field of health care. It is a great credit to your zeal and efficiency when, despite formidable costs, you still succeed in preventing the economic factor from being the determinant factor in human and Christian service.

Similarly, the love with which Catholic health care is performed and its professional excellence have the value of a sign testifying to the Christian view of the human person. *The inalienable dignity of every human being is, of course, fundamental to all Catholic health care.* All who come to you for help are worthy of respect and love, for all have been created in the image and likeness of God. All have been redeemed by Christ and, in their sufferings, bear his Cross. It is fitting that our meeting is taking place on the Feast of the Triumph of the Cross. Christ took upon himself the whole of human suffering and radically transformed it through the Paschal Mystery of his Passion, Death and Resurrection. *The Triumph of the Cross gives human suffering a new dimension, a redemptive value* (cf. *Salvifici Doloris,* 24). It is your privilege to bear constant witness to this profound truth in so many ways.

The structural changes which have been taking place within Catholic health care in recent years have increased the challenge of *preserving and even strengthening the Catholic identity of the institutions and the spiritual quality of the services given.* The presence of dedicated women and men Religious in hospitals and nursing homes has ensured in the past, and continues to ensure in the present, that spiritual dimension so characteristic of Catholic health care centers. The reduced number of Religious and new forms of ownership and management should not lead to a loss of a spiritual atmosphere, or to a loss of a sense of vocation in caring for the sick. This is an area in which the Catholic laity, at all levels of health care, have an opportunity to manifest the depth of their faith and to play their own specific part in the Church's mission of evangelization and service.

Moral Dimension—Respect for Life

4. As I have said, Catholic health care must always be carried out within the framework of the Church's saving mission. This mission she has received from her divine Founder, and she has accomplished it down through the ages with the help of the Holy Spirit who guides her into the fullness of truth (cf. Jn 16:13; *Lumen Gentium*, 4). *Your ministry therefore must also reflect the mission of the Church as the teacher of moral truth*, especially in regard to the new frontiers of scientific research and technological achievement. Here too you face great challenges and opportunities.

Many times in recent years the Church has addressed issues related to the advances of biomedical technology. She does so not in order to discourage scientific progress or to judge harshly those who seek to extend the frontiers of human knowledge and skill, but in order to affirm the moral truths which must guide the application of this knowledge and skill. Ultimately, the purpose of the Church's teaching in this field is *to defend the innate dignity and fundamental rights of the human person.* In this regard the Church cannot fail to emphasize the need to safeguard the life and integrity of the human embryo and fetus.

5. The human person is a unique composite—a unity of spirit and matter, soul and body, fashioned in the image of

God and destined to live forever. Every human life is sacred, because every human person is sacred. It is in the light of this fundamental truth that *the Church constantly proclaims and defends the dignity of human life from the moment of conception to the moment of natural death.* It is also in the light of this fundamental truth that we see the great evil of abortion and euthanasia.

Not long ago, in its "Instruction on Respect for Human Life in Its Origin and on the Dignity of Procreation," the Congregation for the Doctrine of the Faith once more dealt with certain vital questions concerning the human person. Once more it defended the sanctity of innocent human life from the moment of conception onward. Once again it affirmed the sacred and inviolable character of the transmission of human life by the procreative act within marriage. It explained that new technologies may afford new means of procreation, but "what is technically possible is not for that very reason morally admissible" (Introduction, 4). To place new human knowledge at the service of the integral well-being of human persons does not inhibit true scientific progress but liberates it. The Church encourages all genuine advances in knowledge, but she also insists on the sacredness of human life at every stage and in every condition. The cause she serves is *the cause of human life and human dignity.*

Forming Society's Moral Vision

6. In the exercise of your professional activities you have a magnificent opportunity, by your constant witness to moral truth, to contribute to *the formation of society's moral vision.* As you give the best of yourselves in fulfilling your Christian responsibilities, you will also be aware of the important contribution you must make to building a society based on truth and justice. Your service to the sick enables you with great credibility *to proclaim to the world the demands and values of the Gospel of Jesus Christ,* and to foster hope and renewal of heart. In this respect, your concern with the Catholic identity of your work and of your institutions is not only timely and commendable, it is essential for the success of your ecclesial mission.

You must always see yourselves and your work as part of the Church's life and mission. You are indeed a very special part of the People of God. You and your institutions have precise responsibilities toward the ecclesial community, just as that community has responsibilities toward you. It is important at every level—national, state and local—that there be *close and harmonious links between you and the Bishops,* who "preside in place of God over the flock whose shepherds they are, as teachers of doctrine, priests of sacred worship and officers of good order" *(Lumen Gentium,* 20). They for their part wish to support you in your witness and service.

Compassion and Service

7. I have come here today *to encourage you in your splendid work* and to confirm you in your vital apostolate. Dear brothers and sisters: for your dedication to meeting the health care needs of all people, especially the poor, I heartily congratulate you. You embody the legacy of those pioneering women and men Religious who selflessly responded to the health care needs of a young and rapidly expanding country by developing an extensive network of clinics, hospitals and nursing homes.

Today you are faced with new challenges, new needs. One of these is the present crisis of immense proportions: that of AIDS and AIDS-Related Complex (ARC). Besides your professional contribution and your human sensitivities toward all affected by this disease, you are called to show the love and compassion of Christ and his Church. As you courageously affirm and implement your moral obligation and social responsibility to help those who suffer, *you are, individually and collectively, living out the parable of the Good Samaritan* (cf. Lk 10:30-32).

The Good Samaritan of the parable showed compassion to the injured man. By taking him to the inn and giving of his own material means, he truly gave of himself. This action, a universal symbol of human concern, has become one of the essential elements of moral culture and civilization. How beautifully the Lord speaks of the Samaritan! He "was neighbor to the man who fell in with the robbers" (Lk

10:36). To be "neighbor" is *to express love, solidarity and service,* and to exclude selfishness, discrimination and neglect. The message of the parable of the Good Samaritan echoes a reality connected with today's Feast of the Triumph of the Cross: "the kindness and love of God our Savior appeared ...that we might be justified by his grace and become heirs, in hope, of eternal life" (Tit 3:4-7). In the changing world of health care, it is up to you *to ensure that this "kindness and love of God our Savior" remains the heart and soul of Catholic health services.*

Through prayer and with God's help, may you persevere in your commitment, providing professional assistance and selfless personal care to those who need your services. I pray that your activities and your whole lives will *inspire and help all the people of America, working together, to make this society a place of full and absolute respect for the dignity of every person,* from the moment of conception to the moment of natural death. And may God, in whom "we live and move and have our being" (Acts 17:28), sustain you by his grace. God bless you and your families and your contribution to America!

We Need More Missionaries

Address to clergy, laity, religious and ecumenical leaders—Sts. Simon and Jude Cathedral, Phoenix, September 14.

Dear Bishop O'Brien,

Dear Brothers and Sisters in Christ,

1. It is a joy for me to come to *the Cathedral of Sts. Simon and Jude*, and to be with you who make up this local Church in Phoenix. This house of prayer and worship, this mother church of the Diocese, is named after two of the Twelve Apostles, two men of courageous faith who personally received from our Risen Savior the mandate to preach the Gospel to the ends of the earth. Jesus said to them and the rest of the Twelve: *"Go,* therefore, and *make disciples of all the nations.* Baptize them in the name of the Father, and of the Son, and of the Holy Spirit. Teach them to carry out everything I have commanded you" (Mt 28:19-20).

Simon and Jude responded wholeheartedly to this summons and spent the rest of their lives seeking "to open up for all people a free and sure path to full participation in the mystery of Christ" *(Ad Gentes, 5).*

The Church, built as she is on the foundation of the Apostles and Prophets (cf. Eph 2:20), has inherited the same mission that Jesus first entrusted to the Twelve. *The Church is by her very nature missionary,* "for it is from the mission of the Son and the mission of the Holy Spirit that she takes her origin, in accordance with the decree of God the Father" *(Ad Gentes,* 2). She has the honor and privilege, and also the obligation, of bringing the Good News of salvation to all nations, to every person. As the Bishops of the United States stated last November in their Pastoral Statement on World Mission: "We are faithful to the nature of the Church to the degree that we love and sincerely promote her missionary activity" *(To the Ends of the Earth,* 2).

Evangelization Is Ongoing

2. *The Church in Phoenix,* like every other local Church in the world, is *the fruit of evangelization.* The Gospel was first brought to Arizona three hundred years ago by the re-

nowned Jesuit missionary, *Father Eusebio Kino,* also known as the "Apostle of Sonora and Arizona." At great personal sacrifice, Father Kino worked tirelessly to establish missions throughout this area so that the Good News concerning our Lord Jesus Christ might take root among the people living here.

And the Gospel did take root, and numerous other missionaries came after Father Kino to continue the evangelizing effort. Perhaps the most zealous among these was the Franciscan, *Francisco Garces.* With particular love for the Indian people, he sought to present the Gospel to them in a way adapted to their culture; at the same time he also encouraged them to live in harmony and peace among themselves. So completely was his life patterned on that of our Lord, that he ended his labors here by shedding his blood for the Gospel.

The missionary efforts continued down through the years, and the Church became firmly established in Arizona. *The rich fruit of this evangelization* is clearly evident today in this quickly growing Diocese of Phoenix and in the expanding dioceses of the surrounding area. The Gospel has truly taken root here and has brought forth fruit in abundance.

3. And yet, the work of evangelization is *not over.* On earth it will never be over. Indeed, so much remains to be done. Let us not forget the words of the Second Vatican Council which said that missionary activity is "a supremely great and sacred task of the Church" (*Ad Gentes,* 29). The duty of carrying forward this work rests on the whole Church and on every member of the Church.

The Church, at the close of the twentieth century, has *need of many more missionaries* with the zeal of Father Kino and Father Garces, persons of heroic faith like *St. Isaac Jogues, St. John Neumann* and *St. Frances Cabrini,* who are willing to leave their own homeland to bring the message of salvation to people in other lands, especially to those who have never heard the word of God.

Who will meet this need? The Gospel message has still not been heard by two-thirds of the world's population. Who will respond to God's missionary call at the end of the twentieth century? Jesus says: "Whoever loves father or mother, son or daughter more than me is not *worthy of me"* (Mt 10:37). We must be *worthy of Christ*.

Not everyone is asked to leave home and loved ones for this task, but *all are called* to bear the burden, to do their part. As the American Bishops have said so well: "Jesus' great commission to the first disciples is now addressed to us.... This mission to the peoples of all nations must involve all of us personally in our parishes and at the diocesan and universal levels of the Church" *(To the Ends of the Earth,* 3).

Missionaries in foreign countries deserve our prayerful support and material help. American Catholics have been especially generous in the past, a generosity and interest that show your genuine missionary spirit. The practice of "twinning" between American parishes and dioceses and those of Africa and Asia has been of great benefit. With gratitude I commend you, and in the name of the universal Church I ask your continued help and prayers. Great assistance has been given to the missions by mission aid societies such as the Society for the Propagation of the Faith and the Association of the Holy Childhood. Nor can we ever forget the generous missionary work that has been carried out for decades by religious Institutes and Missionary Societies of the United States, and also by generous *Fidei Donum* priests and by lay missionaries. The reward of those who have sacrificed everything to spread the Gospel will be great in heaven.

Love Means Sacrifice

4. Dear brothers and sisters: the Letter to the Hebrews tells us that God the Father considered it fitting to make Christ, our leader in the work of salvation, *"perfect through suffering"* (2:10). In a similar way, he led the Apostles Simon and Jude through the suffering of martyrdom to perfection in eternity. In every age of the Church, God makes his chosen ones "perfect through suffering," bringing them to the fullness of life and happiness by giving them on earth a share in the Cross of Christ.

It is easy to understand that God's plan for us passes along the way of the Holy Cross, because it was so for Jesus and his Apostles. Brothers and sisters, never be surprised to find yourselves passing under the shadow of the Cross. *Christian life finds its whole meaning in love, but love does not exist for us without effort, discipline and sacrifice* in every aspect of our life. We are willing to give in proportion as we love, and when love is perfect the sacrifice is complete. God so loved the world that he gave his only Son, and the Son so loved us that he gave his life for our salvation.

On this day when Catholics around the world celebrate the Triumph of the Cross, the Church invites us to look once again at the meaning of our Christian discipleship, to understand the sacrifices it involves, and *place all our hope in our Crucified and Risen Savior.*

O Triumphant Cross of Christ, inspire us to continue the task of evangelization!

O Glorious Cross of Christ, strengthen us to proclaim and live the Gospel of salvation!

O Victorious Cross of Christ, our only hope, lead us to the joy and peace of the Resurrection and eternal life! Amen.

Time for a New Life

Address to 16,000 Native Americans at Veterans' Memorial Coliseum—
September 14.

Dear Brothers and Sisters,

1. I have greatly looked forward to this visit with you, the original peoples of this vast country. *I greet you with love and respect.* I thank you for inviting me to be with you and for sharing with me some aspects of your rich and ancient culture.

I have listened to your concerns and hopes. As your representatives spoke, I traced in my heart the history of your tribes and nations. I was able to see you as *the noble descendants of countless generations of inhabitants of this land,* whose ways were marked by great respect for the natural resources of land and river, of forest and plain and desert. Here your forefathers cherished and sought to pass on to each new generation their customs and traditions, their history and way of life. Here they worshipped the Creator and thanked him for his gifts. In contact with the forces of nature they learned the value of prayer, of silence and fasting, of patience and courage in the face of pain and disappointment.

The Gospel and Indian Rights

2. *The early encounter between your traditional cultures and the European way of life was an event of such significance and change that it profoundly influences your collective life even today.* That encounter was a harsh and painful reality for your peoples. The cultural oppression, the injustices, the disruption of your life and of your traditional societies must be acknowledged.

At the same time, in order to be objective, history must record the deeply positive aspects of your peoples' encounter with the culture that came from Europe. Among these positive aspects I wish to recall the work of *the many missionaries who strenuously defended the rights of the original inhabitants of this land.* They established missions throughout this Southwestern part of the United States. They worked to

155

improve living conditions and set up educational systems, learning your languages in order to do so. Above all, they proclaimed the Good News of salvation in our Lord Jesus Christ, an essential part of which is that all men and women are equally children of God and must be respected and loved as such. *This Gospel of Jesus Christ is today, and will remain forever, the greatest pride and possession of your people.*

3. One priest who deserves special mention among the missionaries is *the beloved Fray Junipero Serra,* who travelled throughout Lower and Upper California. He had frequent clashes with the civil authorities over the treatment of Indians. In 1773 he presented to the Viceroy in Mexico City a *Representación,* which is sometimes termed a "Bill of Rights" for Indians. The Church had long been convinced of the need to protect them from exploitation. Already in 1537, my predecessor *Pope Paul III proclaimed the dignity and rights of the native peoples of the Americas by insisting that they not be deprived of their freedom or the possession of their property (Pastorale Officium,* May 29, 1537: *DS* 1495). In Spain the Dominican priest, Francisco de Vitoria, became the staunch advocate of the rights of the Indians and formulated the basis for international law regarding the rights of peoples.

Unfortunately not all the members of the Church lived up to their Christian responsibilities. But let us not dwell excessively on mistakes and wrongs, even as we commit ourselves to overcoming their present effects. Let us also be grateful to those who came to this land, faithful to the teachings of Jesus, witnesses of his new commandment of love. These men and women, with good hearts and good minds, shared knowledge and skills from their own cultures and shared their most precious heritage, the faith, as well. Now, *we are called to learn from the mistakes of the past and we must work together for reconciliation and healing,* as brothers and sisters in Christ.

The Gospel and Indian Culture

4. It is time to think of the present and of the future. Today, people are realizing more and more clearly that we all belong to the one human family, and are meant to walk and

work together in mutual respect, understanding, trust and love. Within this family *each people preserves and expresses its own identity and enriches others with its gifts of culture,* tradition, customs, stories, song, dance, art and skills.

From the very beginning, the Creator bestowed his gifts on each people. It is clear that stereotyping, prejudice, bigotry and racism demean the human dignity which comes from the hand of the Creator and which is seen in variety and diversity. I encourage you, as native people belonging to the different tribes and nations in the East, South, West and North, *to preserve and keep alive your cultures, your languages, the values and customs* which have served you well in the past and which provide a solid foundation for the future. Your customs that mark the various stages of life, your love for the extended family, your respect for the dignity and worth of every human being, from the unborn to the aged, and your stewardship and care of the earth: these things benefit not only yourselves but the entire human family.

Your gifts can also be expressed even more fully in the Christian way of life. *The Gospel of Jesus Christ is at home in every people. It enriches, uplifts and purifies every culture.* All of us together make up the People of God, the Body of Christ, the Church. We should all be grateful for the growing unity, presence, voice and leadership of Catholic Native Americans in the Church today.

Jesus speaks of the word of God as the seed which falls on good ground and produces abundant fruit (cf. Mt 13:4ff.). The seed has long since been planted in the hearts of many of you. And it has already produced the fruits which show its transforming power—the fruits of holiness. *The best known witness of Christian holiness among the native peoples of North America is Kateri Tekakwitha,* whom I had the privilege, seven years ago, of declaring "Blessed" and of holding up to the whole Church and the world as an outstanding example of Christian life. Even when she dedicated herself fully to Jesus Christ, to the point of taking the prophetic step of making a vow of perpetual virginity, *she always remained what she was, a true daughter of her people,* following her tribe in the hunting seasons and continuing her devotions in the environment most suited to her way of life, before a rough cross carved by herself in the forest. The Gospel of Jesus Christ, which is the great gift of God's love, is never in contrast with what is noble and pure in the life of any tribe or nation, since all good things are his gifts.

5. I would like to repeat what I said at my meeting with native peoples at the Shrine of Saint Anne de Beaupré during my visit to Canada in 1984: "Your encounter with the Gospel has not only enriched you; it has enriched the Church. We are well aware that this has not taken place without its difficulties and, occasionally, its blunders. However, and you are experiencing this today, the Gospel does not destroy what is best in you. On the contrary, it enriches, as it were from within, the spiritual qualities and gifts that are distinctive of your cultures" (n. 3). The American Bishops' Statement on Native Americans rightly attests that our Catholic faith is capable of thriving "within each culture, within each nation, within each race, while remaining the prisoner of none" (Statement of May 4, 1977).

Here too I wish to urge the local Churches to be truly "catholic" in their outreach to native peoples, and *to show respect and honor for their culture and all their worthy traditions.* From your ranks have come a Bishop, a number of priests, many permanent deacons, men and women religious and lay leaders. To all of you who have an active part in the Church's ministry I wish to express my gratitude and support. But the Church has some special needs at this time. And for this reason *I directly appeal to you,* especially to you *young Native Americans, to discover if Jesus is calling you to the priesthood or to the religious life.* Hear him and follow him! He will never let you down! He will lead you, in the Church, to serve your own peoples and others in the best way possible, in love and apostolic generosity.

At the same time I call upon your native Catholic communities *to work together to share their faith and their gifts,* to work together on behalf of all your peoples. There is much to be done in solving common problems of unemployment, inadequate health care, alcoholism and chemical dependency. You have endured much over hundreds of years and your difficulties are not yet at an end. Continue taking steps toward true human progress and toward reconciliation within your families and your communities, and among your tribes and nations.

New Life for Native Americans

6. One day Jesus said: "The thief comes only to steal and slaughter and destroy. I came that they might have life and have it to the full" (Jn 10:10).

Surely, the time has come for the native peoples of America to have a new life in Jesus Christ—the new life of adopted children of God, with all its consequences:

A life in justice and full human dignity!

A life of pride in their own good traditions, and of fraternal solidarity among themselves and with all their brothers and sisters in America!

A deeper life in charity and grace, leading to the fullness of eternal life in heaven!

All consciences must be *challenged*. There are real injustices to be addressed and biased attitudes to be changed. But the greatest challenge is to you yourselves, as Native Americans. You must continue to grow in respect for your own inalienable human dignity, for the gifts of Creation and Redemption as they touch your lives and the lives of your peoples. You must unyieldingly pursue your spiritual and moral goals. You must *trust* in your own future.

As Catholic Native Americans, you are called to become *instruments of the healing power of Christ's love,* instruments of his peace. May the Church in your midst—your own community of faith and fellowship—truly bear witness to the new life that comes from the Cross and Resurrection of our Lord and Savior Jesus Christ!

The Fullest Sign of God's Love

Homily at the Phoenix Eucharist—Arizona State University, September 14.

"The Son of Man must be lifted up."   (Jn 3:14)

Dear Brothers and Sisters,

1. On this day when I have the joy of celebrating the Eucharist with you here in Phoenix, let our first thoughts be directed to *the victorious Cross* of our Savior, to the Son of Man who is lifted up! Let us adore and praise Christ, our Crucified and Risen Lord. To him, and to the Father and the Holy Spirit, be glory and thanksgiving now and forever!

How good it is to join our voices in praise of God on this *feast of the Triumph of the Cross*. And how appropriate to celebrate the feast here in the city of *Phoenix*, which bears the name of an ancient symbol often depicted in Christian art to represent the meaning of the victorious Cross. The phoenix was a legendary bird that, after dying, rose again from its own ashes. Thus, it came to be a symbol of Christ who, after dying on the Cross, rose again in triumph over sin and death.

We can rightly say that, by divine providence, the Church in Phoenix has been called in a particular way to *live the mystery of the victory of the Cross*. Certainly, the Cross of Christ has marked the progress of evangelization in this area since its beginning: from the day, three hundred years ago, when Father *Eusebio Kino* first brought the Gospel to Arizona. The Good News of salvation has brought forth great fruit here in Phoenix, in Tucson and throughout this whole area. The Cross is indeed *the Tree of Life*.

A Summary of the Paschal Mystery

2. *"The Son of Man must be lifted up"* (Jn 3:14).

Today the Church makes special reference to these words of Christ as she celebrates the feast of the Triumph of the Cross. Beyond the particular historical circumstances that contributed to the introduction of this feast in the liturgical calendar, there remain these words that Christ spoke *to*

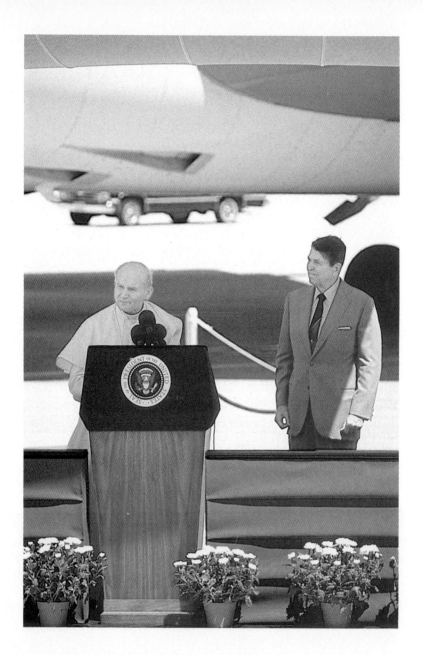

Welcome and beginning of the Holy Father's pastoral visit—International Airport, Miami

Meeting with bishops, priests, religious and laity
of South Carolina—St. Peter's Church, Columbia

Vietnamese dance—Superdome, New Orleans

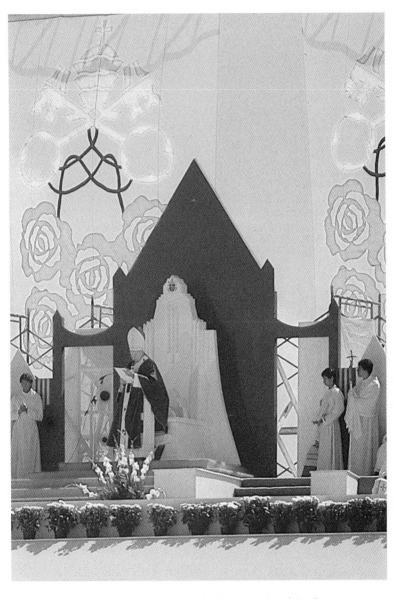

"Today is Sunday: the Lord's Day.... On this day we are called to reflect more deeply on the mystery of creation and therefore of our own lives."
—San Antonio Eucharist

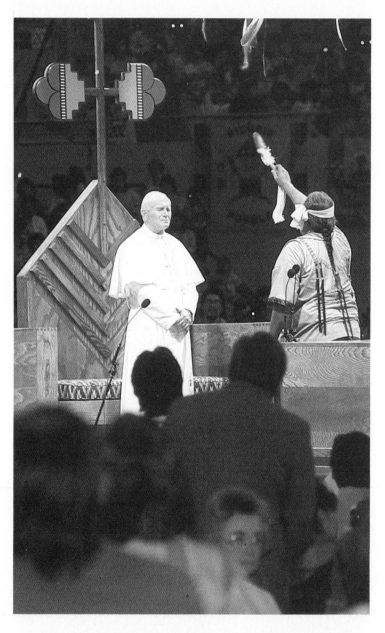

"I have greatly looked forward to this visit with you,
the original peoples of this vast country."
—meeting with Native Americans, Phoenix

"The cross is the tree of life."
—Eucharist, University of Arizona

Warm welcome at the airport from Archbishop Roger Mahony—Los Angeles

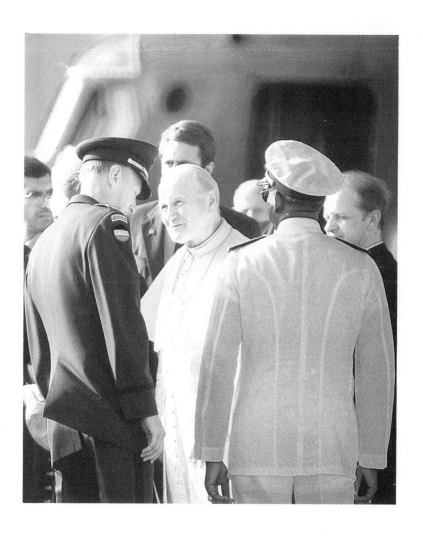

Airport welcome from military personnel in California

Special moment for some young people
—San Francisco Eucharist

Nicodemus during that conversation which took place at night: "The Son of Man must be lifted up."

Nicodemus, as we know, was a man who loved God's word and who studied the word with great attention. Prompted by his hunger for the truth, by his eagerness to understand, Nicodemus came to Jesus at night to find answers to his questions and doubts. It is precisely to him, to Nicodemus, that Jesus speaks these words which still echo in a mysterious way: "The Son of Man must be lifted up, *that all who believe may have eternal life in him*" (Jn 3:14-15).

Nicodemus could not have known at this point that these words contain, in a certain sense, the summary of the whole Paschal Mystery which would crown the messianic mission of Jesus of Nazareth. *When Jesus spoke of being "lifted up," he was thinking of the Cross on Calvary:* being lifted up *on* the Cross, being lifted up *by means of* the Cross. Nicodemus could not have guessed this at the time. And so *Christ referred to an event from the history of the Old Testament* which he knew about, namely, Moses lifting up the serpent in the desert.

3. It was an unusual event that took place *during Israel's journey from Egypt to the Promised Land.* This journey that lasted forty years was full of tests: *the people "tested" God* with their infidelity and lack of trust; in turn this provoked *many tests from the Lord* in order to purify Israel's faith and deepen it. Near Mount Hor a particular test took place, which was that of the *poisonous serpents.* These serpents "bit the people" with the result that many of them died (Nm 21:6). Then *Moses,* ordered by the Lord, *"made a bronze serpent* and mounted it on a pole, and whenever anyone who had been bitten by a serpent looked at the bronze serpent, he recovered" (Nm 21:9).

We might ask: why such a test? *The Lord had chosen Israel to be his own;* he had chosen this people, in order to initiate them gradually into his plan of salvation.

4. Jesus of Nazareth explains the salvific designs of the God of the Covenant. *The bronze serpent* in the desert was *the symbolic figure of the Crucified One.* If someone who had been bitten looked upon the serpent "lifted up" by Moses on a high pole, that person was saved. He remained alive, not

because he had looked upon the serpent, but because *he had believed in the power of God* and his saving love. Thus when the Son of Man is lifted up on the Cross of Calvary, "all who believe will have eternal life in him" (cf. Jn 3:15).

There exists then a profound *analogy between that figure and this reality,* between that sign of salvation and this reality of salvation contained in the Cross of Christ. The analogy becomes even more striking if we keep in mind that the salvation from physical death, caused by the poison of the serpents in the desert, came about through a serpent. *Salvation from spiritual death*—the death that is sin and that was caused by man—*came about through a Man,* through the Son of Man "lifted up" on the Cross.

In this nighttime conversation, Jesus of Nazareth helps Nicodemus to discover the true sense of God's designs. While Jesus is speaking, *the fulfillment of these divine designs belongs to the future,* but at this point the future is not far away. Nicodemus himself will be a witness to this fulfillment. *He will be a witness* to the paschal events in Jerusalem. He will be a witness to the Cross, upon which the One who speaks with him this night—the Son of Man—will be lifted up.

5. Jesus goes on even further. The conversation becomes even deeper: *Why the Cross?* Why must the Son of Man be "lifted up" on the wood of the Cross? Because *"God so loved the world that he gave his only Son* that whoever believes in him may not die but may have eternal life" (Jn 3:16). Yes, eternal life. This is the type of salvation that Jesus is speaking about: *eternal life in God.*

And then Jesus adds: "God did *not* send the Son into the world *to condemn the world,* but that the world might be saved through him" (Jn 3:17). Many thought that the Messiah would be first of all *a severe judge* who would punish, "separating the wheat from the chaff" (cf. Mt 3:12). If at one moment he will have to come as judge—at the end of the world—now "in the fullness of time" (cf. Gal 4:4) *he comes to be judged himself by the sins of the world,* and therefore because of the sins of the world. And thus, Christ lifted up on the Cross becomes the Redeemer of the human race, the Redeemer of the world.

Jesus of Nazareth prepares Nicodemus, the eager student of the Scriptures, so that in time *he will understand the saving mystery contained in the Cross of Christ.* And we know that, in time, Nicodemus did understand, but not during that night.

Jesus Emptied Himself

6. *What, then, does this "being lifted up" mean?*

In the second reading of today's liturgy, taken from St. Paul's Letter to the Philippians, *"being lifted up" means first of all "being brought low."* The Apostle writes about Christ, saying: "Though he was in the form of God, he did not deem equality with God something to be grasped at. Rather, he emptied himself and *took the form of a slave,* being born *in the likeness of men"* (Phil 2:6-7). The God-man! God becoming man. God taking on our humanity: this is the first dimension of "being brought low," and at the same time it is a "lifting up." God is brought low, so that man may be lifted up. Why? *Because "God so loved the world."* Because he is love!

Then the Apostle writes: "[Christ] was known to be of human estate, and it was thus that *he humbled himself, obediently accepting death, death on a Cross"* (Phil 2:7-8). This is *the second and the definitive dimension of being brought low.* It is the dimension of being emptied which confirms in the strongest way the truth of those words: "God so loved the world that he gave his only Son." He *gave. This emptying is itself the gift.* It is the greatest gift of the Father. It surpasses all other gifts. It is the source of every gift. In this absolute lowering, in this emptying, is the beginning and source of every "lifting up," *the source of the lifting up of humanity.*

Jesus Was Exalted

7. The Cross was "lifted up" on Golgotha. And Jesus was nailed to the Cross, and was therefore lifted up with it. *To the human eye,* this was *the culmination of humiliation and disgrace.* But *in the eyes of God* it was different. It was different in the eternal designs of God.

The Apostle continues: "Because of this, God highly exalted him and bestowed on him the name above every other name, so that at Jesus' name every knee must bend in the heavens, on the earth, and under the earth, and every tongue proclaim to the glory of God the Father: *Jesus Christ is Lord''* (Phil 2:9-11).

Christ *is* the Lord! This will be confirmed in the Resurrection, but it is *already* contained in the *Crucifixion.* Precisely in the Crucifixion.

To be crucified, humanly speaking, is to be disgraced and humiliated. But from God's point of view it means being lifted up. Indeed, to be lifted up by means of the Cross. Christ is the Lord, and he becomes Lord of everything and everyone in this elevation by means of the Cross. It is in this way that we look upon the Cross, with the eyes of faith, *instructed by the word of God,* guided by the power of God.

Here then is the mystery of *the Triumph of the Cross.*

The Cross and the Anointing of the Sick

8. This mystery reaches us in a particular way and with a special power when the Church celebrates *the Sacrament of the Anointing of the Sick,* as she does this evening. By means of this Sacrament, and through all her pastoral service, the Church continues *to care for the sick and dying as Jesus did* during his earthly ministry. Through the laying on of hands by the priest, the anointing with oil and the prayers, our brothers and sisters are strengthened with the grace of the Holy Spirit. They are enabled to bear their sufferings with courage and thus to embrace the Cross and follow after Christ with stronger faith and hope.

This holy anointing does not prevent physical death nor does it promise a miraculous healing of the human body. But it does bring *special grace and consolation to those who are dying,* preparing them to meet our loving Savior with lively faith and love, and with firm hope for eternal life. It also brings *comfort and strength to those who are not dying* but who are suffering from serious illness or advanced age. For these the Church seeks healing of both body and soul, praying that the whole person may be renewed by the power of the Holy Spirit.

Every time that the Church celebrates this Sacrament, she is *proclaiming her belief in the victory of the Cross*. It is as if she were repeating the words of St. Paul: "I am certain that *neither death nor life,* neither angels nor principalities, neither the present nor the future, nor powers, neither height nor depth nor any other creature, *will be able to separate us from the love of God* that comes to us in Christ Jesus, our Lord" (Rom 8:38-39).

From the very early days until now, Phoenix has been a city to which people have come for health care, for relief of suffering, for new beginnings and fresh starts. Today as in the past, the Church welcomes such people, offering them love and understanding. She is grateful to the sick and elderly for the special mission which they fulfill in the Kingdom of our Savior. Your hospitality, which I myself have also received, reflects the beautiful saying in Spanish: *"mi casa, su casa."* I pray that you will always remain faithful to this tradition of Christian community and generous service.

By such fidelity to your Christian heritage, through the Sacrament of the Anointing of the Sick, and in the celebration of the Holy Eucharist, you express your deep conviction that suffering and death are not the last words of life. The last word is the Word made flesh, *the Crucified and Risen Christ.*

9. The responsorial psalm of today's liturgy exhorts us:

"Hearken, my people, to my teaching;
Incline your ears to the words of my mouth....
I will utter mysteries from of old" (Ps 77:1-2).

It was exactly in this way that Christ revealed the mystery of salvation to Nicodemus, and to us, and to all people.

The Power
of the Name of Jesus

Address following the official welcome to the Archdiocese of Los Angeles—
St. Vibiana's Cathedral, September 15.

Dear Archbishop Mahony, dear Cardinal Manning,
Dear Brothers and Sisters,

1. I greet you today *in the name of our Lord Jesus Christ.*
Through his love and mercy we are gathered together in the
Church to offer praise and thanksgiving to our heavenly
Father. Grace and peace be to all of you—the clergy, religious
and laity of this city named in honor of Our Lady of the
Angels. May she continue to assist you in praising God both
now and forever with the angels, the patroness of this
Cathedral—St. Vibiana—and all the Saints.

I wish to join my voice to the chorus of praise offered to
God in the name of Jesus in so many languages and by
people of different races and ethnic origins in this great
metropolis. It is his name above all that *unites us in one
household* of faith, hope and love. It is the name of Jesus that
transcends every division and heals every antagonism within
the human family.

As the Successor of Peter, I come to you today in the
name of Jesus. It cannot be otherwise, since every true
minister of the Gospel preaches not himself or any message
of human origin, but he *preaches Jesus Christ* as Lord (cf. 2
Cor 4:5). To the fears, doubts and struggles of individuals
and nations, the Church seeks to apply the healing power of
that name which belongs to him who alone is the Word of
God (cf. Rv 19:13).

The Name of Jesus Saves

2. In a world filled with competing ideologies and so
many false and empty promises, the name of Jesus Christ
brings salvation and life. The Hebrew word *"Jesus" means
"Savior,"* as the Angel said to Joseph in his dream: "You are
to name him Jesus because he will save his people from their
sins" (Mt 1:21). At the very beginning of the Church's mis-

sion, St. Peter proclaims that "there is no salvation in anyone else; for there is no other name in the whole world
given to men by which they are to be saved" (Acts 4:12).
This name is a source of life for those who believe (cf. Jn
20:31); it delivers us from evil and leads us to the truth that
alone can set us free (cf. Jn 8:32).

The name of Jesus is therefore *a cry of deliverance* for all
humanity. It has the power to comfort and heal the sick (cf.
Acts 3:6; Jas 5:14-15), to cast out demons (cf. Mk 16:17; Lk
10:17; Acts 16:18), and to work every kind of miracle (cf. Mt
7:22; Acts 4:30). Most importantly it is in the name of Jesus
and through his power that our sins are forgiven (cf. 1 Jn
2:12).

The *name of Jesus* is at the heart of Christian worship in
this Cathedral and in every church throughout the world:
"Where two or three are gathered in my name, there am I in
their midst" (Mt 18:20). The name of Jesus is at the heart of
all Christian prayer: "All you ask the Father in my name he
will give you" (Jn 15:16). It is a motivation for charity because as Jesus himself explained, "Whoever gives you a cup
of water to drink because you bear the name of Christ, will
by no means lose his reward" (Mk 9:41). It calls forth the gift
of the Holy Spirit, "the Paraclete, whom the Father will send
in my name" (Jn 14:26).

Christians Witness to Christ

3. My dear brothers and sisters: we are called Christians, and therefore the name of Jesus Christ is also our
name. At the baptismal font we received a "Christian name"
which symbolizes our communion with Christ and his
Saints. Our identification with him is reflected in the rule of
life which St. Paul proposes in the Letter to the Colossians:
"Whatever you do, whether in speech or in action, do it in
the name of the Lord Jesus. Give thanks to God the Father
through him" (3:17). We are obliged not only to give thanks,
but also *to speak and act* in the name of Jesus, even at the risk
of being ill-treated, persecuted and hated "for the sake of
the Name" as Jesus foretold (Acts 5:41; cf. also Mk 13:13; Lk
21:12).

As citizens of the United States, you must give thanks to God for the religious liberty which you enjoy under your Constitution, now in its two hundredth year. However, freedom to follow your Catholic faith does not automatically mean that it will be easy to "speak and act" in the name of the Lord Jesus with a conscience formed by the word of God as it is authentically interpreted by the Church's teaching (cf. *Dei Verbum*, 9f.). In a secularized world, to speak and act in the name of Jesus can bring *opposition and even ridicule*. It often means being out of step with majority opinion. Yet if we look at the New Testament, we find encouragement everywhere for perseverance in this testing of our faith. As the First Letter of St. Peter tells us: "If anyone suffers for being a Christian...he ought not to be ashamed. He should rather glorify God in virtue of that name" (1 Pt 4:6). And Jesus himself says, "In the world you will have trouble, but take courage, I have conquered the world" (Jn 16:33).

Is not this message extremely important for young people who are trying *to live a responsible moral life* in the face of a tide of popular culture and peer pressure that is indifferent, if not hostile, to Christian morality? And for their parents, who face daily pressures in the conduct of both their private and public lives? And for the clergy and religious who may sometimes find it difficult to speak the full truth of the Church's teaching because it is a "hard saying" that many will not readily accept?

Life and Salvation

4. Dear brothers and sisters: the name of Jesus, like the Word of God that he is, is a two-edged sword (cf. Heb 4:12). *It is a name that means salvation and life;* it is a name that means a struggle and a cross, just as it did for him. But it is also the name in which we find *strength to proclaim and live the truth* of the Gospel: not with arrogance, but with confident joy; not with self-righteousness, but with humble repentance before God; never with enmity, and always with charity.

Dear people of this great Archdiocese of Los Angeles, with its many problems, its enormous challenges, and its immense possibilities for good: *The name of Jesus is your life and your salvation.* It is your pride and joy, and the pride and joy of your families and your parishes. In this name you find strength for your weaknesses and energy for daily Christian living. In your struggle against evil and the Evil One, and in your striving for holiness, the name of Jesus is the source of your hope, because in the name of Jesus you are invincible!

Continue, then, dear Catholic people of Los Angeles to invoke this holy name of Jesus in your joys and your sorrows; continue to teach this name to your children, so that they in turn can teach it to their children, until the Lord Jesus himself comes in glory to judge the living and the dead!

Hope, Joy and Serving God

Teleconference with young people at Universal Amphitheater, Los Angeles, and in Denver, St. Louis and Portland, Oregon—September 15.

Dear young Friends,

1. I think that you already know, without my saying it, how happy I am to be with you today. Wherever I travel around the world, I always make it a point to meet with young people. A few days ago I was with them in New Orleans and today *I enjoy being with you.* From my early days as a young priest, I have spent many hours talking with students on university campuses or while hiking along lakes or in the mountains and hills. I have spent many evenings singing with young men and women like yourselves. Even now as Pope, during the summer months, various groups of young people come to Castel Gandolfo for an evening and we sing and talk together.

As you probably know, I often say that you who are young bring *hope* to the world. The future of the world shines in your eyes. Even now, you are helping to shape the future of society. Since I have always placed high hopes in young people, I would like to speak to you today precisely *about hope.*

Hope Comes from God

2. *We cannot live without hope.* We have to have some purpose in life, some meaning to our existence. We have to aspire to something. Without hope, we begin to die.

Why does it sometimes happen that a seemingly healthy person, successful in the eyes of the world, takes an overdose of sleeping pills and commits suicide? Why, on the other hand, do we see a seriously disabled person filled with great zest for life? Is it not because of hope? The one has lost all hope; in the other, hope is alive and overflowing. Clearly, then, hope does not stem from talents and gifts, or from physical health and success! It comes from something else. To be more precise, *hope comes from someone else,* someone beyond ourselves.

Hope comes *from God,* from our belief in God. People of hope are those who believe God created them for a purpose and that he will provide for their needs. They believe that God loves them as a faithful Father. Do you remember the advice that Jesus gave his disciples when they seemed to be *fearful of the future?* He said: "Do not be concerned for your life, what you are to eat, or for your body, what you are to wear. *Life is more important* than food and the body more than clothing. Consider the ravens: they do not sow, they do not reap, they have neither cellar nor barn—yet God feeds them. *How much more important you are than the birds!''* (Lk 12:22-24) Yes, God knows all our needs. He is the foundation for our hope.

Faith and Joy

3. But what about people who do not believe in God? This is indeed a serious problem, one of the greatest problems of our time—*atheism,* the fact that many of our contemporaries have no faith in God. When I visited Australia last year, I told a group of children: "The hardest thing about being Pope is to see that many people do not accept the love of Jesus, do not know who he really is and *how much he loves them....* (Jesus) does not force people to accept his love. He offers it to them and leaves them free to say *yes* or *no.* It fills me with joy to see how many people know and love our Lord, how many say *yes* to him. But it saddens me to see that some people say *no''* (November 29, 1986). Without faith in God, there can be no hope, no lasting, authentic hope. To stop believing in God is to start down a path that can lead only to emptiness and despair.

But those who have the gift of faith live with confidence about things to come. They *look to the future with anticipation and joy,* even in the face of suffering and pain; and the future that they are ultimately looking toward is everlasting life with the Lord. This kind of hope was very prominent in the life of St. Paul who once wrote: "We are afflicted in every way possible, but we are not crushed; full of doubts, we never despair. We are persecuted but never abandoned; we are struck down but never destroyed.... *We do not lose heart,* because our inner being is renewed each day" (2 Cor 4:8-9, 16). Only God can renew our inner self each day. Only God can give meaning to life, God who has drawn near to each of us in "Christ Jesus our hope" (1 Tm 1:1).

In the New Testament there are two Letters ascribed to St. Peter. In the first of these, he said: "Venerate the Lord, that is, Christ, in your hearts. Should anyone ask you *the reason for this hope of yours*, be ever ready to reply" (1 Pt 3:15). Dear young friends: I pray that your faith in Christ will always be lively and strong. In this way, you will *always be ready to tell others the reason* for your hope; you will *be messengers of hope for the world*.

The Joy of Serving God

4. I am often asked, especially by young people, *why I became a priest*. Maybe some of you would like to ask the same question. Let me try briefly to reply.

I must begin by saying that it is impossible to explain entirely. For it remains a mystery, even to myself. How does one explain the ways of God? Yet, I know that, at a certain point in my life, I became convinced that Christ was saying to me what he had said to thousands before me: *"Come, follow me!"* There was a clear sense that *what I heard in my heart* was no human voice, nor was it just an idea of my own. Christ was calling me to serve him as a priest.

And you can probably tell, *I am deeply grateful* to God for my vocation to the priesthood. Nothing means more to me or gives me greater joy than *to celebrate Mass each day* and *to serve God's people* in the Church. That has been true ever since the day of my ordination as a priest. Nothing has ever changed it, not even becoming Pope.

Confiding this to you, I would like to invite each of you to listen carefully to God's voice in your heart. *Every human person is called to communion with God*. That is why the Lord made us, to know him and love him and serve him, and—in doing this—to find the secret to lasting joy.

In the past the Church in the United States has been rich in vocations to the priesthood and religious life. And it could be especially true today. At the same time, the Church needs the Gospel witness of holy lay people—in married life and in the single state. Be assured that *the Lord knows each of you by name* and wishes to speak to your heart in a dialogue of love and salvation. *God continues to speak* to young people on the banks of *the Mississippi River* and on the slopes of *the Rocky Mountains*. God continues to speak in the cities on *the West Coast* of America and across *the rolling hills and plains*. God continues to speak to every human person.

Dear young people of America, *listen to his voice*. Do not be afraid. Open up your hearts to Christ. The deepest joy there is in life is the joy that comes from God and is found in Jesus Christ, the Son of God. He is the hope of the world. Jesus Christ is your hope and mine!

An Immense Spiritual Power

Address to 1,600 policy makers in television, radio, motion pictures and the print media—Registry Hotel, Los Angeles, September 15.

Ladies and Gentlemen of the Communications Industry,
Dear Friends,

1. I am very pleased to be here with you. I would like to be able to greet each one of you personally and to express my regard for you individually. Although this is not possible, I wish to express my sincere respect for *all the categories of the media* that you represent—the film industry, the music and recording industry, radio, electronic news, television and all those who inform the world through the written word—and for *the diverse functions* that you perform as workers, writers, editors, managers and executives. I greet you in the full range of your activities, from the very visible to the relatively hidden.

My visit to Los Angeles, and indeed to the United States, would seem incomplete without this meeting, since you represent *one of the most important American influences on the world today.* You do this in every area of social communications and contribute thereby to the development of a mass popular culture. Humanity is profoundly influenced by what you do. *Your activities affect communication itself:* supplying information, influencing public opinion, offering entertainment. The consequences of these activities are numerous and diverse. You help your fellow citizens to enjoy leisure, to appreciate art and to profit from culture. You often provide the stories they tell and the songs they sing. You give them news of current events, a vision of humanity and motives for hope. Yours is indeed a profound influence on society. Hundreds of millions of people see your films and television programs, listen to your voices, sing your songs and reflect your opinions. It is a fact that your smallest decisions can have global impact.

Communication Implies Responsibility

2. Your work can be *a force for great good or great evil.* You yourselves know the dangers, as well as the splendid opportunities open to you. Communication products can be works

of great beauty, revealing what is *noble and uplifting* in humanity and promoting what is just and fair and true. On the other hand communications can appeal to and promote what is *debased* in people: dehumanized sex through pornography or through a casual attitude toward sex and human life; greed through materialism and consumerism or irresponsible individualism; anger and vengefulness through violence or self-righteousness. All the media of popular culture which you represent can build or destroy, uplift or cast down. You have untold possibilities for good, ominous possibilities for destruction. It is the difference between death and life—the death or life of the spirit. And it is a matter of choice. The challenge of Moses to the people of Israel is applicable to all of us today: "I set before you life and death.... Choose life" (Dt 30:19).

3. There is something of great interest for all of us in the Constitution of the United States. The same Amendment that guarantees freedom of speech and freedom of the press also guarantees freedom of religious practice. *The link between the art of human expression and the exercise of religion is profound. Social communications,* in fact, provide an important first step in uniting human beings in mutual love, and this first step is also a step to God, "for God is love" (1 Jn 4:8). *Religious practice* for its part fosters communication with God. But it also fosters human communication, since *human communication is part of that relationship of love for neighbor* that is mandated in both the Old and New Testaments.

It is easy to see why the Church has recognized and taught that people have a right to communicate. Linked to this right is *the right to information,* about which the Second Vatican Council speaks in these words: "Because of the progress of modern society and the increasing interdependence of its members, it is clear that information has become very useful and generally necessary.... There exists therefore in human society a right to information on the subjects that are of concern to people" (*Inter Mirifica,* 5).

In this way, then, the Church recognizes the need for freedom of speech and freedom of the press, just as does your Constitution. But she goes further. *Rights imply corresponding duties.* The proper exercise of the right to information demands that the content of what is communicated be true and—within the limits set by justice and charity—complete (cf. *ibid.*). Your very profession invites you to reflect on this *obligation to truth and its completeness*. Included here is the obligation *to avoid any manipulation of truth for any reason*. This manipulation in fact takes place when certain issues are deliberately passed over in silence, in order that others may be unduly emphasized. It also occurs when information is altered or withheld so that society will be less able to resist the imposition of a given ideology.

The obligation to truth and its completeness applies not only to the coverage of news, but to all your work. Truth and completeness should characterize the content of artistic expression and entertainment. You find a real meaning in your work when you exercise your role as collaborators of truth—*collaborators of truth in the service of justice, fairness and love.*

4. Your industry not only speaks to people and for people; it makes communication possible among them. In this we see how your activities transcend the categories of both rights and duties and confer upon you *inestimable privileges*. Just before joining you this afternoon, I met with young people in several cities by using satellite links. For me this is just one example of how your industry can help foster communication and unite people in fraternal love. It is within your power to use technology to promote what is deeply human and to direct it to the work of peace. You have *marvelous tools* which others lack. They must be employed *in the service of people's right to communicate.*

In today's modern world there is always the danger of communication becoming exclusively one-way, depriving audiences of the opportunity *to participate in the communication process*. Should that happen with you, you would no longer be communicators in the full, human sense. The people themselves, the general public whom you serve, should not be excluded from having the opportunity for public dialogue.

In order to foster such a dialogue, you yourselves, as communicators, must listen as well as speak. You must seek to communicate with people, and not just speak to them. This involves learning about people's needs, being aware of their struggles and *presenting all forms of communications with the sensitivity that human dignity requires*—your human dignity and theirs. This applies especially to all audio-visual programs.

Respect for Human Dignity

5. *At the basis of all human rights is the dignity of the human person* created in the image and likeness of God (Gn 1:27). A recognition of this human dignity is also part of your civil tradition in the United States, and is expressed in the declaration of your nation's independence: all people are created equal in their human dignity and are endowed by their Creator with inalienable rights to life, liberty, and the pursuit of happiness. All other rights too are rooted in human dignity, including the right to maintain one's privacy and not to be exploited in the intimacy of one's family.

The fundamental dignity of the human person is still more strongly *proclaimed by the Church*. She raises her voice on behalf of people everywhere, declaring the dignity of every human being, every man, woman and child. None is excluded because all bear the image of God. Physical and mental handicaps, spiritual weaknesses and human aberrations cannot obliterate the dignity of man. You will understand why the Church attaches such importance to this principle found on the first page of the Bible; it will later become the basis of the teaching of Jesus Christ as he says: "Always treat others as you would like them to treat you" (Mt 7:12).

In particular, *social communications must support human dignity* because the world is constantly tempted to forget it. Whether in news or in drama, whether in song or in story, you are challenged to respect what is human and to recognize what is good. Human beings must never be despised because of limitations, flaws, disorders, or even sins.

Twenty years ago, my predecessor Pope Paul VI, speaking to a gathering much like this one, told that creative community in Rome: "It is a fact that when, as writers and artists, you are able to reveal in the human condition, however lowly or sad it may be, a spark of goodness, at that very instant a glow of beauty pervades your whole work. We are not asking that you should play the part of moralists, but we are expressing confidence in your mysterious power of opening up the glorious regions of light that lie behind the mystery of human life" (Allocution of May 6, 1967).

As you do precisely this—open up the glorious regions of light that lie behind the mystery of human life—you must ask yourselves *if what you communicate is consistent with the full measure of human dignity*. How do the weakest and the most defenseless in society appear in your words and images: the most severely handicapped, the very old, foreigners and the undocumented, the unattractive and the lonely, the sick and the infirm? Whom do you depict as having—or not having—human worth?

6. Certainly your profession subjects you to *a great measure of accountability*—accountability to God, to the community and before the witness of history. And yet at times it seems that everything is left in your hands. Precisely because your responsibility is so great and your accountability to the community is not easily rendered juridically, society relies so much on your good will. In a sense the world is at your mercy. Errors in judgment, mistakes in evaluating the propriety and justice of what is transmitted, and wrong criteria in art can offend and wound consciences and human dignity. They can encroach on sacred fundamental rights. The *confidence* that the community has in you *honors you deeply and challenges you mightily*.

7. I would encourage you in yet another way: *to respect also your own dignity*. All that I have said about the dignity of human beings applies to you.

Daily cares oppress you in ways different from those arising in other kinds of work. Your industry reflects the fast pace of the news and changing tastes. It deals with vast amounts of money that bring with them their own problems. It places you under extreme pressure to be successful, without telling you what "success" really is. Working constantly with images, you face the temptation of seeing them as reality. Seeking to satisfy the dreams of millions, you can become lost in a world of fantasy.

At this point, you must cultivate *the integrity consonant with your own human dignity*. You are more important than success, more valuable than any budget. Do not let your work drive you blindly; for if work enslaves you, you will soon enslave your art. Who you *are* and what you *do* are too important for that to happen. Do not let money be your sole concern, for it too is capable of enslaving art as well as souls. In your life there must also be room for your families and for leisure. You need time to rest and be re-created, for only in quiet can you absorb the peace of God.

You yourselves are called to what is noble and lofty in human living, and you must study the highest expressions of the human spirit. You have *a great part in shaping the culture* of this nation and other nations. To you is entrusted an important portion of the vast heritage of the human race. In fulfilling your mission you must always be aware of *how your activities affect the world community*, how they serve the cause of universal solidarity.

A Vision of Unity

8. *The Church* wishes you to know that she *is on your side*. For a long time she has been a patron and defender of the arts; she has promoted the media and been in the forefront of the use of new technology. The first book for the printing press of Johannes Gutenberg, the inventor of movable type, was the inspired word of God, the Bible. Vatican Radio was established under the direction of the inventor of radio, Guglielmo Marconi.

Today, too, the Church stands ready to help you by her encouragement and *to support you in all your worthy aims*. She offers you her challenge and her praise. I pray that you will welcome that help and never be afraid to accept it.

Ladies and gentlemen of the communications industry: I have set before you the broad outlines of *a choice for good within the framework of your profession*. I ask you to choose the common good. It means honoring the dignity of every human being.

I am convinced that to a great extent we can share a common hope, rooted in *a vision of the human race harmoni-*

ously united through communication. I am sure, too, that all of you, whether Christian or not, will permit me to allude to the great fascination that surrounds the mystery of the communicating word. For Christians, the communicating word is the explanation of all reality as expressed by St. John: "In the beginning was the Word; the Word was in God's presence, and the Word was God" (Jn 1:1). And for all those who hold the Judeo-Christian tradition, the nobility of communication is linked to the wisdom of God and expressed in his loving revelation. Thus the Book of Deuteronomy records God's communication to Israel: "You shall love the Lord your God with all your heart, and with all your soul, and with all your strength. Take to heart these words which I enjoin on you today" (Dt 6:6).

Ladies and gentlemen: *as communicators of the human word, you are the stewards and administrators of an immense spiritual power* that belongs to the patrimony of mankind and is meant to enrich the whole of the human community. The challenge that opens up before you truly requires generosity, service and love. I am sure that you will strive to meet it. And, as you do, I pray that you will experience in your own lives a deep satisfaction and joy. And may the peace of God dwell in your hearts.

Mary, Mother of Compassion

Homily at the Los Angeles Eucharist—Los Angeles Coliseum, September 15.

"And you yourself shall be pierced with a sword."
(Lk 2:35)

Dear Brothers and Sisters of the Archdiocese of Los Angeles, and of the Dioceses of Orange, San Diego, San Bernardino and Fresno,

1. The Church's meditation today focuses on the sufferings of Mary, the Mother standing at the foot of her Son's Cross. This *brings to completion* yesterday's feast of the Triumph of the Cross. Jesus had said, "Once I am lifted up, I will draw all men to myself" (Jn 12:32). These words were fulfilled when he was "lifted up" *on the Cross*.

The Church, which constantly lives this mystery, feels very deeply the suffering of the Mother on Golgotha. The agony of the Son who in his terrible pain entrusts the whole world to his Father—that agony is united with the agony in the heart of the Mother there on Calvary. Today's Gospel reminds us that, when Jesus was only forty days old, *Simeon* had foretold this agony in the heart of the Mother when he said: "And you yourself shall be pierced with a sword" (Lk 2:35).

The entire *mystery of obedience to the Father* is encompassed by the Son's agony: "he humbled himself, obediently accepting even death, death on a cross" (Phil 2:8), as yesterday's liturgy proclaimed. And today we read in the Letter to the Hebrews: "In the days when he was in the flesh, [Christ] offered prayers and supplications with loud cries and tears to God, who was able to save him from death" (Heb 5:7). These words have special application to the agony in the Garden of Gethsemane when he prayed: "My Father, if it is possible, let this cup pass me by" (Mt 26:39-42). The author of the Letter to the Hebrews immediately adds that Christ "was heard because of his reverence" (5:7). Yes, he was heard. He had said, "not as I will but as you will" (Mt 26:39). And so it came to pass.

The agony of Christ was, and still is, the mystery of his obedience to the Father. *At Gethsemane. On Calvary.* "Son though he was," the text continues, "he learned obedience from what he suffered" (Heb 5:8). This includes Christ's obedience even unto death—the perfect sacrifice of Redemption. "And when perfected, he became the source of eternal salvation for all who obey him" (v. 9).

Mary's Pilgrimage of Faith

2. As we celebrate Our Lady of Sorrows during this Marian Year, let us call to mind the teaching of the Second Vatican Council concerning the presence of Mary, the Mother of God, in the mystery of Christ and of the Church. Let us recall in particular the following words: "The Blessed Virgin advanced in her *pilgrimage of faith*, and loyally persevered in her union with her Son unto the Cross, where she stood, in keeping with the divine plan" *(Lumen Gentium, 58)*.

Mary's pilgrimage of faith! It is precisely at the foot of the Cross that this pilgrimage of faith, which began at the Annunciation, *reaches its high point*, its culmination. There it is united with the agony of Mary's maternal heart. "Suffering grievously with her only-begotten Son...she lovingly consented to the immolation of this Victim which she herself had brought forth" *(Lumen Gentium, 58)*. At the same time, the agony of her maternal heart also represents a fulfillment of the words of Simeon: "And you yourself shall be pierced with a sword" (Lk 2:35). Surely these prophetic words express *the "divine plan"* by which Mary is destined to stand at the foot of the Cross.

Compassion and Exultant Faith

3. Today's liturgy makes use of the ancient poetic text of the sequence which begins with the Latin words *Stabat Mater:*

By the Cross of our salvation
Mary stood in desolation
While the Savior hung above.
All her human powers failing,
Sorrow's sword, at last prevailing,
Stabs and breaks her heart of love....

Virgin Mary, full of sorrow,
From your love I ask to borrow
Love enough to share your pain.
Make my heart to burn with fire,
Make Christ's love my one desire,
Who for love of me was slain.

The author of this sequence sought, in the most eloquent way humanly possible, to present *the "compassion" of the Mother* at the foot of the Cross. He was inspired by those words of Sacred Scripture about the sufferings of Mary which, though few and concise, are deeply moving.

It is appropriate that *Mary's song of praise, the Magnificat,* should also find a place in our celebration: "My being proclaims the greatness of the Lord.... For he has looked upon his servant in her lowliness.... God who is mighty has done great things for me.... His mercy is from age to age.... Even as he promised our fathers, Abraham and his descendants forever" (Lk 1:46-55).

Can we not suppose that these words, which reflect the fervor and exultation of the young mother's heart, still ring true at the foot of the Cross? That they still reveal her heart now that she finds herself in agony with her Son? Humanly speaking, it does not seem possible to us. However, within the fullness of divine truth, the words of the Magnificat actually *find their ultimate meaning* in the light of Christ's Paschal Mystery, from the Cross through the Resurrection.

It is precisely in this Paschal Mystery that the "great things," which God who is mighty, has done for Mary find their *perfect fulfillment,* not only for her, but for all of us and for all of humanity. It is precisely at the foot of the Cross that the promise is fulfilled which God once made to Abraham and to his descendants, the People of the Old Covenant. It is also at the foot of the Cross that there is an overflow of *the mercy* shown to humanity from generation to generation by him whose name is holy.

Yes, at the foot of the Cross, the "humility of the Lord's servant"—the one upon whom "God has looked" (cf. Lk 1:48)—reaches its full measure together with the absolute humiliation of the Son of God. But from that same spot *the "blessing" of Mary by "all ages to come"* also begins. There, at the foot of the Cross—to use the description of the prophet Isaiah in the first reading—the Virgin of Nazareth is fully "clothed with a robe of salvation" (cf. Is 61:10): she whom already at the Annunciation the Archangel hailed as "full of grace" (Lk 1:28); she who was redeemed in the most perfect manner; she who was conceived without stain in view of the merits of her Son. At the price of the Cross. In virtue of Christ's Paschal Mystery.

The Mystery of Human Suffering

4. Dear brothers and sisters of Los Angeles and Southern California: it is a joy for me to celebrate this liturgy today with you. California has been a symbol of hope and promise for millions of people who continue to come here to make a home for themselves and their families. Today the people of California play a *major role in shaping the culture of the United States,* which has such a profound influence on the rest of the world. Your state also leads in research and technology designed to improve the quality of human life and to transcend the limitations which impede human freedom and progress.

Yet amid the many blessings that you enjoy within this beautiful and prosperous state, I know that the mention of Mary as a Mother of sorrows and suffering still strikes a responsive chord in your hearts. This is because all of us, in some way, experience *sorrow and suffering in our lives.* No amount of economic, scientific or social progress can eradicate our vulnerability to sin and to death. On the contrary, progress creates new possibilities for evil as well as for good. Technology, for example, increases what we can do, but it cannot teach us the right thing to do. It increases our choices, but it is we who must choose between evil and good. Besides moral suffering, physical and emotional sufferings are part of every human life. The Gospel message is certainly no enemy of human progress or of the promotion of our temporal welfare, but neither does the Paschal Mystery allow us to run away from human sorrow and suffering.

5. The message of the crucified Son and of his Mother at the foot of the Cross is that the mysteries of suffering, love, and Redemption are inseparably joined together. In bitterness and alienation from God and our fellow human beings we will never find the answer to the question—the "why?" of suffering. Calvary teaches us that we will find an answer only *through the "obedience"* mentioned in the Letter to the Hebrews. It is not obedience to a cruel or unjust god of our own making, but obedience to the God who "so loved the world that he gave his only Son" (Jn 3:16). Jesus prayed: "Not as I will, but as you will.... Your will be done" (Mt 26:39, 42). And Mary began her pilgrimage of faith with the words, "I am the servant of the Lord. Let it be done to me as you say" (Lk 1:38).

Looking upon the suffering Son and Mother in the light of Scripture, we cannot equate their obedience with fatalism or passivity. Indeed, the Gospel is the *negation of passivity* in the face of suffering *(Salvifici Doloris, 30)*. What we find is a loving act of self-giving on the part of Christ for the salvation of the world, and on the part of Mary as an active participant from the beginning in the saving mission of her Son. When we have striven to alleviate or overcome suffering, when like Christ we have prayed that "the cup pass us by" (cf. Mt 26:39), and yet suffering remains, then we must walk "the royal road" of the Cross. As I mentioned before, Christ's answer to our question "why?" is above all *a call, a vocation.* Christ does not give us an abstract answer, but rather he says, "Follow me!" He offers us the opportunity through suffering to take part in his own work of saving the world. And when we do take up our cross, then gradually the salvific meaning of suffering is revealed to us. It is then that in our sufferings we find inner peace and even spiritual joy (cf. *Salvifici Doloris,* 26).

The Letter to the Hebrews also speaks of being made perfect through suffering (cf. Heb 5:8-10). This is because the purifying flames of trial and sorrow have the power *to transform us from within* by unleashing our love, teaching us compassion for others, and thus drawing us closer to Christ. Next to her Son, Mary is the most perfect example of this. It is precisely in being the Mother of Sorrows that she is a mother to each one of us and to all of us. The spiritual sword that pierces her heart opens up a river of compassion for all who suffer.

Compassion for Others

6. My dear brothers and sisters: as we celebrate this Marian Year in preparation for the Third Millennium of Christianity, let us join the Mother of God in her pilgrimage of faith. Let us learn the *virtue of compassion* from her whose heart was pierced with a sword at the foot of the Cross. It is the virtue that prompted the Good Samaritan to stop beside the victim on the road, rather than to continue on or to cross over to the other side. Whether it be the case of the person next to us or of distant peoples and nations, we must be Good Samaritans to all those who suffer. We must be the compassionate "neighbor" of those in need, not only when it is emotionally rewarding or convenient, but also when it is demanding and inconvenient (cf. *Salvifici Doloris*, 28-30). Compassion is a virtue we cannot neglect in a world in which the human suffering of so many of our brothers and sisters is needlessly increased by oppression, deprivation and underdevelopment—by poverty, hunger and disease. Compassion is also called for in the face of the spiritual emptiness and aimlessness that people can often experience amid material prosperity and comfort in developed countries such as your own. Compassion is a virtue that brings healing to those who bestow it, not only in this present life but in eternity: "Blessed are they who show mercy, mercy shall be theirs" (Mt 5:7).

Humility and a Clear Conscience

7. Through the faith of Mary, then, let us fix our gaze on *the mystery of Christ*. The mystery of the Son of Man, written in the earthly history of humanity, is at the same time the definitive manifestation of God in that history.

Simeon says: "This child is destined to be the downfall and the rise of many in Israel, a sign that will be opposed" (Lk 2:34). How profound these words are! How far down these words reach into the history of man! Into the history of us all: Christ is destined for the ruin and the resurrection of many! Christ is a sign of contradiction! Is this not also true in our own time? In our age? *In our generation?*

And standing next to Christ is Mary. To her Simeon says: "...so that the thoughts of many hearts may be laid bare. And you yourself shall be pierced with a sword" (Lk 2:35).

Today we ask for *humility of heart* and for a clear conscience:

before God
through Christ.

Yes, we ask that the thoughts of our hearts may be laid bare. We ask that our *consciences may be pure:*

before God
through the Cross of Christ
in the heart of Mary. Amen.

A Living Sign of Christ

Homily given to the U.S. Bishops at morning prayer—San Fernando Mission, September 16.

"God's flock is in your midst; give it a shepherd's care. *Watch over it willingly as God would have you do*" (1 Pt 5:2).

Dear Brothers in our Lord Jesus Christ,

1. A very full day lies before us, *a day that the Lord has made.* It is good that we begin it by joining our voices in praise of the living God.

On this feast of Sts. Cornelius and Cyprian, we have listened to the words of Peter as he appeals to his "fellow elders" to *be generous* in caring for the People of God, and to *"be examples* to the flock" (1 Pt 4:3), the Church. These words of Peter are most appropriate for us as we begin this day together.

Peter describes himself as *"a witness* of Christ's sufferings and *a sharer* in the glory that is to be revealed" (1 Pt 4:1). There is no doubt in Peter's mind about the witness he is called to bear. He is a witness of *the suffering Christ.* Perhaps he was mindful, however, of an earlier time in his life, precisely during the Passion itself, when out of fear for his own safety he had denied that he ever knew his Master. How far Peter has come from that day of sorrow and despair. For *love is more powerful than fear,* and the Lord is merciful and forgiving. The same Peter who denied his Master is now, in word and in deed, bearing witness with courage to the Crucified and Risen Christ.

2. Our task as Bishops in the Church today is still centered on the person of Jesus Christ. We are witnesses to his Cross and Resurrection. Each of us has been consecrated by the Holy Spirit to be for our people a *living sign of Jesus Christ:*

— a living sign of *the praying Christ,* who himself took time during his public ministry to be alone with his Father in prayer;

— a living sign of *the compassionate Redeemer,* who healed the sick, forgave sinners and comforted the sorrowful;

— a living sign of *the love of our Savior,* a love which is stronger than sin and death;

— a living sign of *the fidelity of the Lord,* and therefore like Christ *a sign of contradiction.*

In the midst of our priests and among ourselves as Bishops, each of us is meant to be *a sign of Jesus' fraternal love.* And for our people we are called to be *a sign of the Good Shepherd, who came to serve* and not to be served.

"Be examples to the flock," Peter tells us. And we shall be precisely that to the extent that our lives are centered on the person of Jesus Christ.

"To him whose power now at work in us can do immeasurably more than we ask or imagine—*to him be glory in the Church* and in Christ Jesus through all generations, world without end. Amen!" (Eph 3:20-21)

Particular Pastoral Issues

Address to the U.S. Catholic Bishops at Queen of the Angels Minor Seminary—Los Angeles, September 16.

I

Dear Brothers in our Lord Jesus Christ,

1. Before beginning to respond in the context of our fraternal exchanges, I wish to express to you *my deep gratitude:* gratitude for your many invitations to make this pastoral visit, gratitude for your presence here today, and gratitude for the immense amount of preparation which this visit required. Over and above all this, I thank you for your daily toil, and *your partnership with me in the Gospel.* In a word, I thank you for "your work of faith and labor of love and steadfastness of hope in our Lord Jesus Christ" (1 Thes 1:3).

Ecclesiastical Communion

Cardinal Bernardin has given us an introduction to *the extremely important reality of "communio,"* which is the best framework for our conversation. As Bishops, we can never tire of prayerfully reflecting on this subject. Since, as the Extraordinary Session of the Synod of Bishops in 1985 indicated, "the ecclesiology of communion is the central and fundamental idea of the Council's documents" *(Relatio Finalis,* C, 1), it follows that we must return time and again to those same documents in order to be imbued with *the profound theological vision of the Church* which the Holy Spirit has placed before us, and which constitutes *the basis of all pastoral ministry* in the Church's pilgrimage through human history.

The program of our collegial ministry cannot be other than to release into the lifestream of ecclesial life all the richness of the Church's self-understanding, which was given by the Holy Spirit to the community of faith in the celebration of the Second Vatican Council. *The renewal of Catholic life* which the Council called for *is to be measured* not primarily in terms of external structures, but *in deeper understanding and more effective implementation of the core vision of her true nature and mission* which the Council offered to the Church at the close of the second millennium of the Christian era. That renewal depends on the way the Council's fundamental insights are authentically received in each particular Church and in the universal Church.

At the heart of the Church's self-understanding is the notion of *communio:* primarily, *a sharing through grace in the life of the Father given us through Christ and in the Holy Spirit.* "God chose us in him"—in Christ—"before the world began, to be holy and blameless in his sight, to be full of love" (Eph 1:4). This communion has its origin in a divine call, the eternal decree which predestined us to share the image of the Son (cf. Rom 8:28-30). It is realized through sacramental union with Christ and through organic participation in all that constitutes the divine and human reality of the Church, the Body of Christ, which spans the centuries and is sent into the world to embrace all people without distinction.

2. It is clear that in the decades since the Council this *"vertical dimension"* of ecclesial communion has been less deeply experienced by many who, on the other hand, have a vivid sense of its *"horizontal dimension."* Unless, however, the entire Christian community has a keen awareness of the marvelous and utterly gratuitous outpouring of "the kindness and love of God our savior" which saved us "not because of any righteous deeds we had done, but because of his mercy" (Tit 3:4-5), the whole ordering of the Church's life and the exercise of her mission of service to the human family will be radically weakened and never reach the level intended by the Council.

The ecclesial body is healthy in the measure in which Christ's grace, poured out through the Holy Spirit, is *accepted* by the members. Our pastoral efforts are fruitful, in the last analysis, when the People of God—we Bishops with the clergy, religious and laity—are led to Christ, grow in faith, hope and charity, and become authentic witnesses of God's love in a world in need of transfiguration.

Cardinal Bernardin has stated very well that just as there is but one faith, one Lord, one baptism, so there can be but *one loyalty—to the word of God perennially proclaimed in the Church,* entrusted to the Episcopal College with the Roman

Pontiff as its visible head and perpetual source of unity. The word of God, which is the power of God leading all who believe to salvation (cf. Rom 1:16; *Dei Verbum*, 17), is fully revealed in the Paschal Mystery of the Death and Resurrection of Jesus Christ. This Paschal Mystery brings about a salvation that is transcendent and eternal: "He died for us, that all of us...together might live with him" (1 Thes 5:10). It is the Church's task therefore, while she seeks in every way possible to increase her service to the human family in all its needs, *to preach Christ's call to conversion and to proclaim Redemption in his blood.*

3. The "vertical dimension" of ecclesial communion is of profound significance in understanding *the relationship of the particular Churches to the universal Church*. It is important to avoid a merely sociological view of this relationship. "In and from such individual Churches there comes into being the one and only Catholic Church" *(Lumen Gentium,* 23), but this universal Church cannot be conceived as the sum of the particular Churches, or as a federation of particular Churches.

In the celebration of the Eucharist these principles come fully to the fore. For, as the Council document on the Liturgy specifies: "the principal manifestation of the Church consists in the full, active participation of all God's holy people in the same liturgical celebrations, especially in the same Eucharist, in one prayer, at one altar, at which the Bishop presides, surrounded by his presbyterate and by his ministers" *(Sacrosanctum Concilium,* 41). Wherever a community gathers around the altar under the ministry of a Bishop, there Christ is present and there, because of Christ, the one, holy, Catholic and apostolic Church gathers together (cf. *Lumen Gentium,* 26).

The Catholic Church herself subsists in each particular Church, which can be truly complete only through effective communion in faith, in the Sacraments, and in unity with the whole Body of Christ. Last November, in my letter to you during your meeting in Washington, I dealt at some length with this aspect of communion. At that time I wrote: "The very *mystery of the Church* impels us to recognize that the one, holy, Catholic and apostolic Church is present in each particular Church throughout the world. And since the Successor of Peter has been constituted for the whole Church as Pastor and as Vicar of Christ (cf. *Lumen Gentium*, 22), all the particular Churches—precisely because they are Catholic, precisely because they embody in themselves the mystery of the universal Church—are called to live in communion with him.

"*Our own relationship of ecclesial communion—collegialitas effectiva et affectiva*—is discovered in the same mystery of the Church. It is precisely because you are Pastors of particular Churches in which there subsists the fullness of the universal Church that you are, and must always be, in full communion with the Successor of Peter. To recognize your ministry as 'vicars and delegates of Christ' for your particular Churches (cf. *Lumen Gentium*, 27) is to understand all the more clearly the ministry of the Chair of Peter, which 'presides over the whole assembly of charity, protects legitimate variety, and at the same time sees to it that differences do not hinder unity but rather contribute to it' *(Lumen Gentium*, 13)" (Letter of November 4, 1986).

Collegiality

4. In this perspective too, we must see *the ministry of the Successor of Peter*, not only as a "global" service, reaching each particular Church from "outside" as it were, but *as belonging already to the essence of each particular Church from "within."* Precisely because this relationship of ecclesial communion—our *collegialitas effectiva et affectiva*—is such an intimate part of the structure of the Church's life, its exercise calls for each and every one of us to be completely one in mind and heart with the will of Christ regarding our different roles in the College of Bishops. The Council took pains not only to formulate these roles but also to place the exercise of authority in the Church in its proper perspective, which is precisely the perspective of *communio*. In this respect also the Council was—in the words of the Extraordinary Synod—"a legitimate and valid expression and interpretation of the deposit of faith as it is found in Sacred Scripture and in the living tradition of the Church" *(Relatio Finalis*, I, 2).

As I also wrote to you last year, I have endeavored to fulfill my role as Successor of Peter in a spirit of fraternal solidarity with you. I wish only to be of service to all the Bishops of the world, and—in obedience to my specific responsibility at the service of the Church's unity and universality—to confirm them in their own collegial ministry. I have always been greatly encouraged in this task by your fraternal support and your partnership in the Gospel, for which I express to you again my profound gratitude. It is of great importance to the Church *that in the full power of the Church's communion we continue to proclaim together Jesus Christ and his Gospel.* In this way we ourselves live fully, as Successors of the Apostles, the mystery of ecclesial communion. At the same time through our ministry we enable the faithful to enter ever more deeply into the Church's life of communion with the Most Holy Trinity.

II

5. Archbishop Quinn has spoken of the Church as a community that wishes to remain faithful to *the moral teaching of our Lord Jesus Christ.* To proclaim a body of moral teaching is in fact an inseparable part of the Church's mission in the world. From the beginning, the Church under the guidance of the Holy Spirit has striven to apply God's revelation in Christ to all the many aspects of our living in this world, knowing that we are called to "lead a life worthy of the Lord and pleasing to him in every way" (Col 1:10).

The Gospel Challenges

It is sometimes reported that a large number of Catholics today do not adhere to the teaching of the Church on a number of questions, notably sexual and conjugal morality, divorce and remarriage. Some are reported as not accepting the Church's clear position on abortion. It has also been noted that there is a tendency on the part of some Catholics to be selective in their adherence to the Church's moral teachings. It is sometimes claimed that dissent from the Magisterium is totally compatible with being a "good Catholic" and poses no obstacle to the reception of the Sacraments. This is a grave error that challenges the teaching office of the Bishops of the United States and elsewhere. I wish to encourage you in the love of Christ to address this situation courageously in your pastoral ministry, *relying on the power of God's truth* to attract assent *and on the grace of the Holy Spirit* which is given both to those who proclaim the message and to those to whom it is addressed.

We must also constantly recall that the teaching of Christ's Church—like Christ himself—is a "sign of contradiction." It has never been easy to accept the Gospel teaching in its entirety, and it never will be. The Church is committed, both in faith and morals, to make her teaching as clear and understandable as possible, presenting it in all the attractiveness of divine truth. And yet *the challenge of the Gospel remains inherent in the Christian message* transmitted to each generation. Archbishop Quinn has made reference to a principle with extremely important consequences for every area of the Church's life: "...the revelation of God *par excellence* is found in the Cross of Christ which makes God's folly wiser than human wisdom. Often human wisdom in a given age appears to have the last word. But the Cross brings a perspective that changes judgments radically." Yes, dear Brothers, *the Cross—in the very act of revealing mercy, compassion and love—changes judgments radically.*

Theology and Pastoral Practice

6. A number of other general points may be made. First, the Church is a community of faith. To accept faith is to give assent to the word of God as transmitted by the Church's authentic *Magisterium.* Such assent constitutes the basic attitude of the believer, and is an act of the will as well as of the mind. It would be altogether out of place to try to model this act of religion on attitudes drawn from secular culture.

Within the ecclesial community, *theological discussion takes place within the framework of faith.* Dissent from Church doctrine remains what it is, dissent; as such it may not be proposed or received on an equal footing with the Church's authentic teaching.

Moreover, as Bishops we must be especially responsive to our role as authentic teachers of the faith when opinions at variance with the Church's teaching are proposed *as a basis for pastoral practice.*

I wish to support you as you continue to engage in fruitful dialogue with theologians regarding *the legitimate freedom of inquiry* which is their right. You rightly give them sincere encouragement in their difficult task, and assure them how much the Church needs and deeply appreciates their dedicated and constructive work. They, on their part, will recognize that the title of *Catholic* theologian expresses a vocation and a responsibility at the service of the community of faith, and subject to the authority of the Pastors of the Church. In particular your dialogue will seek to show the inacceptability of dissent and confrontation as a policy and method in the area of Church teaching.

Conversion and Catholic Identity

7. Speaking on your behalf, Archbishop Quinn has shown full awareness of the seriousness of the challenge facing your teaching ministry. He has spoken of the dual task of *the conversion of the mind* and *the conversion of the heart.* The way to the heart very often passes through the mind, and throughout the length and breadth of the Church there is need today for *a new effort of evangelization and catechesis directed to the mind.* Elsewhere I have mentioned the relationship between the Gospel and culture. Here I wish to underline the importance of the formation of the mind at every level of Catholic life.

Catholic children and young people need to be given *an effective opportunity to learn the truths of the faith,* in such a way that they become capable of formulating their Catholic identity in terms of doctrine and thought. *Here the Catholic press can make a magnificent contribution* to raising the general level of Catholic thought and culture. Seminaries, especially, have the responsibility of ensuring that future priests should acquire a high level of intellectual preparation and competence. Continuing education programs for priests, religious and laity play an important part in stimulating a necessary and serious intellectual approach to the multitude of questions confronting faith in our contemporary world.

A crucial aspect of this "apostolate of the mind" concerns the *duty and right of Bishops to be present in an effective way in Catholic* colleges and universities and institutes of higher studies in order *to safeguard and promote their Catholic character,* especially in what affects the transmission of Catholic doctrine. It is a task which requires personal attention on the part of Bishops, since it is a specific responsibility stemming from their teaching office. It implies frequent contacts with teaching and administrative personnel, and calls for providing serious programs of pastoral care for students and others within the academic community. Much is already being done, and I take the opportunity to encourage you to seek ways of intensifying these apostolates.

One of the greatest services we Bishops can render to the Church is to consolidate present and future generations of Catholics in a sound and complete understanding of their faith. The ecclesial community will thus be wonderfully strengthened for all aspects of Christian moral living and for generous service. The intellectual approach that is needed, however, is one intimately linked to faith and prayer. *Our people must be aware of their dependence on Christ's grace* and on the great need to open themselves ever more to its action. Jesus himself wants us all to be convinced of his words: *"Apart from me you can do nothing"* (Jn 15:5).

III

8. The Synod to be held this coming month in Rome will undoubtedly deal in further detail with the many important points raised by Archbishop Weakland in his presentation on *the role of the laity.* These remarks, like my own, particularly concern the Catholic laity in the United States.

The Laity and Society

It has been stated that "the Church in the United States of America can boast of having the largest number of educated faithful in the world." This statement has many implications. The situation which it describes is *cause for humble rejoicing and gratitude* because it represents a major achievement: the sustained educational effort by the Church in this country for many, many decades. At the same time the education of the faithful offers great promise and potential in the years ahead. For "it can be assumed they will continue to take a prominent role in U.S. society and culture in the future."

Primarily through her laity, the Church is in a position to exercise great influence upon *American culture*. This culture is *a human creation*. It is created through shared insight and communication. It is built by an exchange among the people of a particular society. And culture, while having a certain dynamic endurance, is always changing and developing as a way of life. Thus the American culture of today stands in continuity with your culture of fifty years ago. Yet it has changed; it has been greatly influenced by attitudes and currents of thought.

But *how is the American culture evolving today?* Is this evolution being influenced by the Gospel? Does it clearly reflect Christian inspiration? Your music, your poetry and art, your drama, your painting and sculpture, the literature that you are producing—are all those things which reflect the soul of a nation being influenced by the spirit of Christ for the perfection of humanity?

I realize these are difficult questions to answer, given the complexity and diversity of your culture. But they are relevant to any consideration of the role of the Catholic laity, "the largest number of educated faithful in the world." And it is above all *the laity*, once they have themselves been inspired by the Gospel, who *bring the Gospel's uplifting and purifying influence to the world of culture,* to the whole realm of thought, and artistic creativity, to the various professions and places of work, to family life and to society in general. As Bishops, with the task of leading the laity and of encouraging them to fulfill their ecclesial mission in the world, we must continue to support them as they endeavor to make their specific contribution to the evolution and development of culture and to its impact on society.

The Bishops and the Laity

9. With reference to this question, and in such areas as politics, economics, mass media and international life, *the service we bring is primarily a priestly service:* the service of preaching and teaching the word of God with fidelity to the truth, and of drawing the laity ever more into the dialogue of salvation. We are charged to lead our people to holiness, especially through the grace of the Eucharist and the whole sacramental life. The service of our pastoral leadership, purified in personal prayer and penance, far from bearing an authoritarian style in any way, must listen and encourage, challenge and at times correct. Certainly, there is no question of condemning the technological world but rather of urging the laity to transform it from within so that it may receive the imprint of the Gospel.

10. We serve our laity best when we make every effort to provide for them, and in collaboration with them, *a comprehensive and solid program of catechesis* with the aim of "maturing the initial faith and of educating the true disciple of Christ by means of a deeper and more systematic knowledge of the person and the message of our Lord Jesus Christ" *(Catechesi Tradendae,* 19). Such a program will also assist them in developing that habit of discernment which can distinguish the spirit of the world from the Spirit of God, and which can distinguish authentic culture from elements that degrade human dignity. It can provide them with a solid basis for growing in their knowledge and love of Jesus Christ through continual conversion and personal commitment to the demands of the Gospel.

Family Values

11. In speaking of the laity, I feel a particular desire to support you in all you are doing on behalf of *family life.* Archbishop Weakland has mentioned "the large number of divorces and the breakup of so many families" as a special pastoral problem. I know that all of us feel great sadness and deep pastoral concern for all those whose lives are affected in this way.

As you will recall, on the occasion of your *ad limina* visits, four years ago, I spoke at some length on the topic of *marriage*. Without repeating all that I said on that occasion, I wish to encourage you to continue in your many zealous and generous efforts to provide *pastoral care to families*. I also urge you in the face of all the trends which threaten the stability of marriage, the dignity of human love, and the dignity of human life, as well as its transmission, never to lose confidence and courage. Through the grace given us as pastors we must endeavor to present as effectively as possible the whole teaching of the Church, including the prophetic message contained in *Humanae Vitae* and in *Familiaris Consortio*.

The faithful teaching of the intrinsic relationship between the unitive and procreative dimensions of the marriage act is of course only a part of our pastoral responsibility. With pastoral solicitude for couples, *Familiaris Consortio* pointed out that "the ecclesial community at the present time must take on the task of instilling conviction and offering practical help to those who wish to live out their parenthood in a truly responsible way.... This implies a broader, more decisive and more systematic effort to make the natural methods of regulating fertility known, respected and applied" (n. 35).

On the occasion of the last *ad limina* visits I stated: "Those couples who choose the natural methods perceive the profound difference—both anthropological and moral—between contraception and natural family planning. Yet they may experience difficulties; indeed they often go through a certain conversion in becoming committed to the use of the natural methods, and they stand in need of competent instruction, encouragement and pastoral counseling and support. We must be sensitive to their struggles and have a feeling for the needs that they experience. We must encourage them to continue their efforts with generosity, confidence and hope. As Bishops we have the charism and the pastoral responsibility to make our people aware of *the unique influence that the grace of the sacrament of marriage has on every aspect of married life, including sexuality* (cf. *Familiaris Consortio*, 33). The teaching of Christ's Church is not only light and strength for God's people, but it uplifts their hearts in gladness and hope.

"Your Episcopal Conference has established a special program to expand and coordinate efforts in the various dioceses. But the success of such an effort requires the abiding pastoral interest and support of each Bishop in his own diocese, and I am deeply grateful to you for what you do in this most important apostolate" (Address of September 24, 1983).

Life Issues

12. My profound gratitude to you extends to the many other areas in which, with generous dedication, you have worked *for and with the laity.* These include your persevering efforts at *promoting peace, fostering justice* and *supporting the missions.* In the area of *the defense of human life,* you have worked with exceptional commitment and constancy. Already during the *ad limina* visits of 1978, Paul VI drew attention to this activity of yours, assuring you of the appreciation of the Holy See. Because of their exceptional importance, I wish to quote at some length his words of strong support for you and make them my own:

"In the name of Jesus Christ, we thank you for your ministry at the service of life. We know that you have labored precisely in order that the words of the Good Shepherd would be fulfilled: 'that they may have life and have it to the full.' Under your leadership, so many of the Catholic people—priests, deacons, religious and laity—have joined in numerous initiatives aimed at defending, healing and promoting human life.

"With the enlightenment of faith, the incentive of love and an awareness of your pastoral accountability, you have worked to oppose whatever wounds, weakens or dishonors human life. Your pastoral charity has found a consistent expression in so many ways—all related to the question of life, all aimed at protecting life in its multiple facets. You have endeavored to proclaim in practice that all aspects of human life are sacred.

202 John Paul II in America

"In this regard, *your efforts have been directed to the eradication of hunger, the elimination of subhuman living conditions, and the promotion of programs on behalf of the poor, the elderly and minorities. You have worked for the improvement of the social order itself.* At the same time, we know that you have held up to your people the goal to which God calls them: the life above, in Christ Jesus (cf. Phil 3:14).

"Among your many activities at the service of life there is one which, especially at this juncture of history, deserves our strongest commendation and our firmest support: it is the continuing struggle against what the Second Vatican Council calls the 'abominable crime' of abortion (*Gaudium et Spes*, 51). Disregard for the sacred character of life in the womb weakens the very fabric of civilization; it prepares a mentality, and even a public attitude, that can lead to the acceptance of other practices that are against the fundamental rights of the individual. This mentality can, for example, completely undermine concern for those in want, manifesting itself in insensitivity to social needs; it can produce contempt for the elderly, to the point of advocating euthanasia; it can prepare the way for those forms of genetic engineering that go against life, the dangers of which are not yet fully known to the general public.

"It is therefore very encouraging to see the great service you render to humanity by constantly holding up to your people the value of human life. We are confident that, relying on the words of the Good Shepherd, who inspires your activity, you will continue to exercise leadership in this regard, sustaining the entire ecclesial community in their own vocation at the service of life.

"It is also a source of worldwide honor that, in your country, so many upright men and women of differing religious convictions are united in a profound respect for the laws of the Creator and Lord of life, and that, by every just means at their disposal, they are endeavoring, before the witness of history, to take a definitive stand for human life" (Address of May 26, 1978).

Nine years have passed since these words were spoken and yet they are *still relevant today*—relevant in their prophetic vision, relevant in the needs they express, relevant in the defense of life.

The Advancement of Women

13. In his Encyclical *Pacem in Terris*, Pope John XXIII placed the question of *the advancement of women* in the context of the characteristics of the present day, "the signs of the times." He made it clear that the cause in question was one of *human dignity.* This is indeed the aim of all the Church's efforts on behalf of women: to promote their human dignity. The Church proclaims *the personal dignity of women as women*—a dignity equal to that of men's dignity. This dignity must be affirmed in its ontological character, even before consideration is given to any of the special and exalted roles fulfilled by women as wives, mothers or consecrated women.

There are many other aspects involved in the question of women's equal dignity and responsibility, which will undoubtedly be properly dealt with in the forthcoming Synod of Bishops. At the basis of all considerations are two firm principles: *the equal human dignity of women and their true feminine humanity.* On the basis of these two principles *Familiaris Consortio* has already enunciated much of the Church's attitude toward women, which reflects the "sensitive respect of Jesus toward the women that he called to his following and his friendship" (n. 22). As I have stated and as Archbishop Weakland has pointed out, women are not called to the priesthood. Although the teaching of the Church on this point is quite clear, it in no way alters the fact that women *are indeed an essential part of the Gospel plan to spread the Good News of the Kingdom.* And the Church is irrevocably committed to this truth.

IV

14. My interest in the question of *vocations* is well known to all of you. It is a recurring theme in my conversations with Bishops around the world. It is one of the subjects I frequently speak about in my meetings with young people.

It is a crucial factor for the future of the Church as we draw
near to the beginning of the third millennium. Therefore, I
am very pleased that you have chosen this topic as one of
those to be emphasized today.

Priestly and Religious Vocations

Archbishop Pilarczyk has presented an "overview of the
ministerial realities of the Church in this country," mention-
ing aspects that offer *much consolation* to you as Bishops and
aspects which are cause for pastoral *concern*. He mentioned
that it was important "to speak of some of the very positive
implications of lay, religious and clerical vocations in America." In doing this, he rightly drew attention to the way that
the Holy Spirit is at work in your midst, something that we
must indeed be ever attentive to and grateful for. As *Lumen
Gentium* reminds us, "The Spirit guides the Church into the
fullness of truth (cf. Jn 16:13) and gives her unity of fellowship and service.... By the power of the Gospel the Spirit
makes the Church grow, perpetually renews her, and leads
her to perfect union with her Spouse" (n. 4).

It is indeed encouraging to note how *lay people,* in ever-
increasing numbers, have become involved in the life of the
Church, and how this has led to "a depth and variety of
ministry far greater than ever before." Certainly, *the more
active participation of the laity in the mission of the Church is an
eloquent sign of the fruitfulness of the Second Vatican Council,* one
for which we all give thanks. And I am confident that the
forthcoming Synod of Bishops will give fresh impetus to this
participation and solid direction for its continued growth
and consolidation.

It is important for our people to see clearly that *the
ministry of the ordained priest and the involvement of the laity in
the Church's mission* are not at all opposed to one another. On
the contrary, the *one complements the other.* Just as the priestly
ministry is not an end in and of itself, but serves to awaken
and unify the various charisms within the Church, so too
the involvement of the laity does not replace the priesthood,
but supports it, promotes it and offers it space for its own
specific service.

At this time, I would like to make a few remarks about *vocations to the priesthood and to the religious life.*

The *insufficient number of seminarians and candidates for religious life is indeed a cause of pastoral concern* for all of us, for we know that their public witness to the Gospel and their specific roles in the Church are irreplaceable. In many parts of the world the Church is experiencing, as Archbishop Pilarczyk observed, that "society is becoming increasingly secular and therefore increasingly inhospitable to Christian belief." It is especially difficult today for young people to make the generous sacrifices entailed in accepting God's call. Yet it is possible for them to do so through grace and with the support of the community. And it is precisely in this situation that we are called to bear witness to the hope of the Church.

In our pastoral mission we must often evaluate a situation and decide on a course of action. We must do this with prudence and pastoral realism. At the same time we know that today, as always, there are "prophets of doom." We must resist them in their pessimism, and *continue in our efforts to promote vocations to the priesthood and the religious life.*

Prayer for vocations remains the primary way to success, since Jesus himself left us the commandment: *"Beg the harvest master* to send out laborers to gather his harvest" (Mt 9:38). I ask you therefore to encourage prayer for vocations among all the people, particularly among priests and religious themselves, but also in families, where the first seeds of vocations are usually planted, and in schools and religious education programs. The prayers of the elderly and the sick have an efficacy that must not be forgotten.

In addition to prayer, young people *must be invited.* It was Andrew who brought his brother Peter to the Lord. It was Philip who brought Nathanael. And how many of us and of our priests and religious came to hear the Lord's call through the invitation of someone else? Your own presence among the youth is a blessing and an opportune time to extend this invitation to them and to ask young people themselves to pray for vocations.

Just last Thursday, speaking in Miami about vocations to the priesthood, I emphasized the basis of our hope: "There

is still one more factor to be considered in evaluating the
future of vocations, and it is *the power of Christ's Paschal
Mystery*. As the Church of Christ, we are all called to profess
his power before the world; to proclaim that he is able, in
virtue of his Death and Resurrection, to draw young people
to himself, in this generation as in the past; to declare that
he is strong enough to attract young men even today to a life
of self-sacrifice, pure love and total dedication to the priesthood. As we profess this truth, as we proclaim with faith the
power of the Lord of the harvest, we have a right to expect
that he will grant the prayers that he himself has commanded to be offered. *The present hour calls for great trust* in
him who has overcome the world."

Priestly Formation

15. I would like to thank you for all you are doing to
ensure *a solid formation for the priesthood* in the United States.
The apostolic visitation to the seminaries has been carried
out with generous collaboration. And I am grateful for the
letters many of you have sent me expressing your appreciation for this initiative and telling me of the many positive
effects which have resulted from it.

At the same time, your pastoral interest and personal
involvement in seminary training is something that can
never end. It is too central a task and too important a
priority in the life of the Church. The Church of tomorrow
passes through the seminaries of today. With the passing of
time, the pastoral responsibility will no longer be ours. But
at present the responsibility *is* ours and it is heavy. Its
zealous fulfillment is a great act of love for the flock.

In particular, I ask you to be vigilant that *the dogmatic and
moral teaching of the Church* is faithfully and clearly presented
to the seminarians, and fully accepted and understood by
them. On the opening day of the Second Vatican Council,
October 11, 1962, John XXIII told his brother Bishops: "The
greatest concern of the Ecumenical Council is this: *that the
sacred deposit of Christian doctrine should be more effectively
guarded and taught.*" What Pope John expected of the Council
is also a primary concern for priestly formation. We must

ensure that our future priests have a solid grasp of the entirety of the Catholic faith; and then we must prepare them to present it in turn to others in ways that are intelligible and pastorally sound.

16. I cannot let this opportunity pass without expressing once again my gratitude for the great interest you have taken in the *religious life*. I am pleased to note, as Archbishop Pilarczyk has said, that there is "an increased understanding of and appreciation for religious life on the part of bishops and priests, thanks, in large part, to the pontifical commission" established in 1983.

In asking the commission to study *the problem of vocations*, I did so "with a view to encouraging a new growth and fresh move forward in this most important sector of the Church's life." The response which you have all made to this request has been most gratifying. And I know you will continue with this important effort. *The religious life is a precious gift from the Lord,* and we must continue to assure religious of the love and esteem of the Church.

+   +   +

17. There are many other issues, dear brother Bishops, which come to mind as we reflect together in this extraordinary hour of ecclesial communion. All of them touch us in our role as Pastors and challenge our apostolic love and zeal.

Confession

Because of its importance in the life of the Church, I spoke to the priests in Miami about *Confession* and our own need to receive the Sacrament regularly. I also expressed my gratitude for their generous ministry in making Confession available to the faithful. In this regard I would ask you as Bishops to make every effort to ensure that the important norms of the universal Church with regard to *the use of general absolution* are understood and observed in a spirit of faith. In this regard I would ask that the Post-Synodal Apostolic Exhortation *Reconciliatio et Paenitentia* continue to be the object of prayerful reflection.

Homosexual Persons

18. I wish to encourage you also in the pastoral care that you give to *homosexual persons*. This includes a clear explanation of the Church's teaching, which by its nature is unpopular. Nevertheless your own pastoral experience confirms the fact that the truth, howsoever difficult to accept, brings grace and often leads to a deep inner conversion. No matter what problem individual Christians have, and no matter what degree of response to grace they make, they are always worthy of the Church's love and Christ's truth. All homosexuals and other persons striving to fulfill the Gospel precept of chastity are worthy of special encouragement and esteem.

Sex Education

19. From time to time the question of *sex education*, especially as regards programs being used in schools, becomes a matter of concern to Catholic parents. The principles governing this area have been succinctly but clearly enunciated in *Familiaris Consortio*. First among these principles is the need to recognize that sex education is *a basic right and duty of parents themselves*. They have to be helped to become increasingly more effective in fulfilling this task. Other educational agencies have an important role, but always in a subsidiary manner, with due subordination to the rights of parents.

Many parents will undoubtedly be heartened by the reference in the Pastoral Letter of the Bishops of California, *A Call to Compassion*, to an absolutely essential aspect of this whole question: "The recovery of the virtue of chastity"—they wrote—"may be one of the most urgent needs of contemporary society." We cannot doubt that the Catholic Church in the United States, as elsewhere, is called to make great efforts to assist parents in teaching their children the sublime value of self-giving love; young people need great support in living this fundamental aspect of their human and Christian vocation.

The Military Ordinariate

20. Among your many pastoral obligations is *the need to provide for the spiritual care of the military and their dependents.* This you do through the Military Ordinariate. The functioning of this extended Archdiocese requires the fraternal and sensitive collaboration of all the Bishops in permitting and encouraging priests to commit themselves to this worthy ministry. The Church is grateful to all the chaplains who generously serve God's people in this particular situation, with its special needs.

The Service and Identity of Bishops

21. I wish at this time to offer you my encouragement as you seek to guide the Church of God in so many areas: as you seek to lead your people *in fulfilling their mission within the United States and well beyond her boundaries.* Everything you do to help your people to look outside themselves to *Christ in need* is a great ecclesial and apostolic service.

My final word is about *our pastoral identity as Bishops of Jesus Christ and his Church.* Because of this identity we are called to *holiness* and to daily conversion. In speaking to you eight years ago in Chicago I stated: *"The holiness of personal conversion is indeed the condition* for our fruitful ministry as Bishops of the Church. It is our union with Jesus Christ that determines the credibility of our witness to the Gospel and the supernatural effectiveness of our activity" (Discourse of October 5, 1979). May God give us all this great gift of *union with Jesus* and allow us to live it *together* in strength and joy, *in the communion of the Church of God.*

You Are Learning How to Live

Address to pupils at Immaculate Conception School—Los Angeles, September 16.

Dear Students of Immaculate Conception School,

It is a real pleasure for me to visit your school today, together with your Archbishop and with Mrs. Reagan, the wife of the President of the United States. When I speak about visiting your school I mean visiting *you!*

What Catholic Students Learn

1. I consider *your school*—and all the other parochial schools in America—*to be very important* for your future and for the future of the Church and of your country.

In this school, you learn not only reading, writing and arithmetic, but also—and most important—*religion*. You learn about God, about God's Son, Jesus Christ, and about God's love. You learn that God made you to know him, to love him and to serve him in this life and to be happy with him forever in the next. You learn how much *God loves you* and how much he wants you to share that love with others, as Jesus taught us.

You learn to love God, and to see his image and *to love him* in your parents, your teachers, your fellow students, and *in all God's children*. You learn to love your country and all the people in it, no matter who they are. And you learn to love the people outside the United States, those in other countries—both near and far away.

You learn how important it is, in order to be truly happy, *to follow God's commandments*. You learn how important it is therefore to be truthful, honest, kind and considerate, and to avoid cheating and fighting and lying. You learn to know the difference between good and bad influences, and how important it is to avoid those things—such as the use of drugs—which hurt yourselves and others and which give offense to God. Sometimes they can even destroy your lives and the lives of others. You have seen this happen around you.

2. In short, in this school you learn how to live in a way

that is *pleasing to God* and that will bring *happiness and peace to you,* your families and your community. You learn *skills* which help you to become a more complete person and a more conscientious citizen, and which prepare you for your future. You learn how to be morally good and how to build a better society.

One of the most important things you can ever learn here is *to pray:* to speak to God, to express what is in your heart, to show your dependence on him, to thank him for the gift of life, for your families, and for everything you have received. Here you also learn how to pray as a community, at Mass, together with Christ and with each other.

Heritage of Catholic Schools

3. For many, many years, Catholic schools—such as Immaculate Conception—have been *an important part of education in the United States of America.* They have truly helped to form this nation. Catholic schools have educated the first Americans, the Native Americans; they have educated black Americans and white Americans and the children of immigrants *from every race and from every nation*—and indeed from many *different religious denominations.* Catholic schools continue to provide not only a vision of life's purpose but a gateway to life's opportunities.

Students of Immaculate Conception School: you can be proud of your school. Make sure that your school can always be proud of you. *Your parents, your parish and your Archdiocese* have made great efforts to give you this Catholic education. Do not let them down.

The Golden Rule

4. Finally, dear boys and girls, I ask you to do me a favor: *to think frequently about these words of Jesus:* "Treat others the way you would have them treat you" (Mt 7:12). The words that are important in life are not "me," but

"others"; not "to get," but "to give" and "to serve"—*to give* and *to serve* the way Jesus did, with love and sacrifice *for others*.

May God bless you, and your teachers, your families and all *those who work and sacrifice* to make this school and every Catholic school a place that prepares students to lead a good Christian life and to be happy with God forever in heaven.

Cooperation for Peace

Address to leaders of non-Christian religions (Buddhist, Moslem, Hindu and Jewish representatives)—Japanese Cultural Center, Los Angeles, September 16.

Dear Brothers and Sisters,
Representatives of World Religions and Religious Leaders,
Dear Friends,

1. It is a great joy for me to meet with you, the local representatives of great religions of the world, during the course of my pastoral visit. I wish to thank in particular the Japanese community of Los Angeles for their kind hospitality at this Center, which is a symbol of cultural diversity within the United States as well as a symbol of dialogue and interaction at the service of the common good. I understand that the Japanese community has been present in this area of Los Angeles for a century. May God continue to bless you with every good gift now and in the future. I also wish to extend *cordial greetings to all* religious leaders and to all people of goodwill who honor us with their presence today.

It is my conviction that we must make use of every *opportunity to show love and respect* for one another in the spirit of *Nostra Aetate* which, as the theme of our meeting affirms, is indeed alive twenty-two years after its promulgation among the documents of the Second Vatican Council. This Declaration, on the Relation of the Catholic Church to Non-Christian Religions, speaks of "that which people have in common and of those things which tend to promote fellowship among them" *(Nostra Aetate, 1)*. This continues to be the basis of our efforts to develop a fruitful relationship among all the great religions of the world.

Dialogue among Religions

2. As I stated earlier this year, the Catholic Church remains firmly committed to the proclamation of the Gospel and to dialogue with people of other religions: *proclamation of the Gospel*, because as *Nostra Aetate* points out, the Church "must ever proclaim Christ, 'the way, the truth, and the life' (Jn 14:6) in whom people find the fullness of religious life,

213

and in whom God has reconciled all things to himself (cf. 2 Cor 5:18-19)" *(Nostra Aetate,* 2); *dialogue and collaboration with the followers of other religions,* because of the spiritual and moral goods that we share (cf. *ibid.).* That dialogue "is a complex of human activities, all founded upon respect and esteem for people of different religions. It includes the daily living together in peace and mutual help, with each bearing witness to the values learned through the experience of faith. It means a readiness to cooperate with others for the betterment of humanity, and a commitment to search to-gether for true peace. It means the encounter of theologians and other religious specialists to explore, with their counter-parts from other religions, areas of convergence and diver-gence. Where circumstances permit, it means a sharing of spiritual experiences and insights. This sharing can take the form of coming together as brothers and sisters to pray to God in ways which safeguard the uniqueness of each reli-gious tradition" (Address to the Members and Staff of the Secretariat for Non-Christians, April 28, 1987).

Throughout my pontificate it has been my constant con-cern to fulfill this twofold task of proclamation and dialogue. On my pastoral visits around the world I have sought to encourage and strengthen the faith of the Catholic people and other Christians as well. At the same time I have been pleased to meet with leaders of all religions in the hope of promoting greater interreligious *understanding and cooperation* for the good of the human family. I was very gratified at the openness and goodwill with which the *World Day of Prayer for Peace in Assisi* last October was received, not only by the various Christian Churches and Ecclesial Communities, but by the other religions of the world as well. I was also pleased that another World Day of Prayer subsequently took place in Japan at Mount Hiei.

Serving the Good of Humanity

3. What I said in Assisi also applies to our meeting today: "The fact that we have come here does not imply any intention of seeking a religious consensus among ourselves or of negotiating our faith convictions. Neither does it mean

that religions can be reconciled at the level of a common commitment in an earthly project which would surpass them all. Nor is it a concession to relativism in religious beliefs, because every human being must sincerely follow his or her upright conscience with the intention of seeking and obeying the truth. Our meeting attests only—and this is its real significance for the people of our time—that in the great battle for peace, humanity, in its very diversity, must draw from its deepest and most vivifying sources where its conscience is formed and upon which is founded the moral action of all people" (Message to the Participants at the World Day of Prayer for Peace, Assisi, October 27, 1986).

It is in that spirit that I wish, through you, to greet each of your communities before saying something further about the concern for peace that we all share.

To the Buddhist Community, which reflects numerous Asian traditions as well as American: I wish respectfully to acknowledge your way of life, based upon compassion and loving kindness and upon a yearning for peace, prosperity and harmony for all beings. May all of us give witness to compassion and loving kindness in promoting the true good of humanity.

To the Islamic Community: I share your belief that mankind owes its existence to the One, Compassionate God who created heaven and earth. In a world in which God is denied or disobeyed, in a world that experiences so much suffering and is so much in need of God's mercy, let us then strive together to be courageous bearers of hope.

To the Hindu Community: I hold in esteem your concern for inner peace and for the peace of the world, based not on purely mechanistic or materialistic political considerations, but on self-purification, unselfishness, love and sympathy for all. May the minds of all people be imbued with such love and understanding.

To the Jewish Community: I repeat the Second Vatican Council's conviction that the Church "cannot forget that she received the revelation of the Old Testament through the people with whom God in his mercy established the Ancient Covenant. Nor can she forget that she draws sustenance from the root of that good olive tree onto which has been grafted the wild olive branches of the Gentiles (cf. Rom 11:17-24)" *(Nostra Aetate,* 4). With you, I oppose every form of anti-Semitism. May we work for the day when all peoples and nations may enjoy security, harmony and peace.

The Quest for Peace

4. Dear brothers and sisters of these religions and of every religion: so many people today experience inner emptiness even amid material prosperity because they overlook the *great questions of life:* "What is man? What is the meaning and purpose of life? What is goodness and what is sin? What gives rise to suffering and what purpose does it serve? What is the path to true happiness? What is death, judgment and retribution after death? What, finally, is that ultimate, ineffable mystery which embraces our existence, from which we take our origin and toward which we move?" *(Nostra Aetate,* 1)

These profoundly spiritual questions, which are shared to some degree by all religions, also draw us together in a *common concern* for man's earthly welfare, especially world peace. As I said at Assisi: "[World Religions] share a common respect of and obedience to conscience, which teaches all of us to seek the truth, to love and serve all individuals and peoples, and therefore to make peace among individuals and among nations" (Message at the Conclusion of the World Day of Prayer for Peace, Assisi, October 27, 1986).

In the spirit of the kind words with which you addressed me earlier as an advocate of peace, let us continue *to seek peace for the human family:* through prayer, since peace transcends our human efforts; through penance, since we have not always been "peacemakers"; through prophetic witness, since old divisions and social evils need to be challenged; and through constant initiatives on behalf of the rights of individuals and nations, and on behalf of justice everywhere. The fragile gift of peace will survive only if there is a concerted effort on the part of all, to be concerned with the "glaring inequalities not merely in the enjoyment of possessions but even more in the exercise of power" *(Populorum Progressio,* 9). In this regard world leaders and international bodies have their special role to play. But universal sensitivity is also called for, particularly among the young.

I believe that the *Prayer of St. Francis* of Assisi, universally recognized as a man of peace, touches the conscience of us all. It is that prayer that best expresses my sentiments in meeting with all of you today:

Lord, make me an instrument of your peace;
where there is hatred, let me sow love;
where there is injury, pardon;
where there is doubt, faith;
where there is despair, hope;
where there is darkness, light;
and where there is sadness, joy.

O Divine Master, grant that I may not so much seek to be consoled as to console; to be understood as to understand; to be loved as to love; for it is in giving that we receive, it is in pardoning that we are pardoned, and it is in dying that we are born to eternal life.

Unity in Diversity

Homily at the Los Angeles Eucharist—Dodger Stadium, September 16.

"The Lord has made his salvation known in the sight of the nations." (Ps 97[98]:2)

Dear brother Bishops,
Dear Brothers and Sisters in Christ,
People of this City of our Lady of the Angels, once known as
El Pueblo de Nuestra Señora de los Angeles,
Citizens of this State of California,

1. Today, from this City of Los Angeles on the Pacific Coast, in which are gathered all the Bishops of the United States, we return together to *the Upper Room* in Jerusalem. We hear words from the prayer which Christ pronounced there. Surrounded by his Apostles, *Jesus prays for the Church of every time and place.* He says to the Father: "I do not pray for them alone. I pray also for those who will believe in me through their word" (Jn 17:20). Christ, the one Eternal Priest of the new and everlasting covenant, *prays for us,* for all of us gathered here, for everyone who lives here in Los Angeles on the West Coast of the United States of America, for everyone in the world. Yes, *every one of us is included in this priestly prayer of the Redeemer.*

The Church in Los Angeles

2. Jesus says to the Father: "I pray also for *those who will believe in me through their word''* (Jn 17:20). This is *the Church* of all ages that he is praying for. How many generations of disciples have already heard these words of Christ! How many Bishops, priests, men and women religious, and how many parents and teachers in the course of the centuries *have passed on this word of salvation!* In how many places of the world, among how many peoples and nations, has this mystery of the Redemption continued to unfold and bear fruit! It is the word of salvation from which *the Church* has grown and *continues to grow.* This is true for the universal Church and for each local Church. It is true for the Church in Los Angeles which is visited today by the Bishop of Rome, the Successor of Peter.

218

In 1769, Father Junipero Serra and his Franciscan companions brought the word of God to California. Leaving behind all that was familiar and dear to them, they freely chose to come to this area to preach the Good News of our Lord Jesus Christ. This initial effort of evangelization very quickly showed impressive results as thousands of Native Americans accepted the Gospel and were baptized. Soon, a whole series of missions was established all along *El Camino Real,* each of them bearing the name of a Saint or a mystery of the Christian faith: San Diego, San Bernardino, San Gabriel, San Buenaventura, Santa Barbara, San Fernando and all the rest.

Within years of this first missionary effort, *immigrants began to settle in California.* Coming mostly from Mexico and Spain, these early settlers had *already* been *evangelized* and thus they brought as part of their heritage the Catholic and apostolic faith. Little did they know at the time that, in God's providence, they were initiating a pattern which would characterize California for years to come.

Subsequently California has become *a haven for immigrants,* a new home for refugees and migrants, a place where people from every continent have come together to fashion a society of the most varied ethnic diversity. Many of these, like their earliest predecessors, have brought not only their specific cultural traditions but also the Christian faith. As a result, the Church in California, and particularly the Church in Los Angeles, is *truly catholic in the fullest sense,* embracing peoples and cultures of the widest and richest variety.

Today, in the Church in Los Angeles, Christ is Anglo and Hispanic, Christ is Chinese and Black, Christ is Vietnamese and Irish, Christ is Korean and Italian, Christ is Japanese and Filipino, Christ is Native American, Croatian, Samoan, and many other ethnic groups. In this local Church, the *one Risen Christ,* the one Lord and Savior, is living in each person who has accepted the word of God and been washed clean in the saving waters of Baptism. And *the Church, with all her different members, remains the one Body of Christ,* professing the same faith, united in hope and in love.

Unity—Modelled on the Trinity

3. *What does Jesus pray for in the Upper Room* the night before his Passion and Death? *"That all may be one* as you, Father, are in me, and I in you; I pray that they may be one in us, that the world may believe that you sent me" (Jn 17:21). "One in us"—the mystery of the inscrutable divine Being, the mystery of the intimate life of God: the divine Unity and at the same time *the Trinity.* It is the divine "We" of the Father, and the Son, and the Holy Spirit. And even though it is not attainable in its absolute fullness, this most perfect Unity is the real *model for the Church.* According to the teaching of the Second Vatican Council, "the Church shines forth as a people made one by the unity of the Father, the Son, and the Holy Spirit" (*Lumen Gentium*, 4).

It is for this type of unity for the Church of all times that Christ prays in the Upper Room: "That they may be one, as *we* are one—*I living in them, you living in me*—that their unity may be complete. So shall the world know that you sent me, and that you loved them as you loved me" (Jn 17:22-23). This is the unity of the Church's communion which is *born from the communion of Three Persons in the Most Holy Trinity.*

All Are Called to Unity

4. People of all times and places are called to this communion. This truth of revelation is first presented to us in today's liturgy, *through the image of the holy city of Jerusalem* found in the reading from the Prophet Isaiah, who writes: "Nations shall walk by your light, and kings by your shining radiance. Raise your eyes and look about; they all gather and come to you: your sons *come from afar,* and your daughters in the arms of their nurses" (Is 60:3-5). Isaiah spoke these words in Jerusalem as he foresaw *a great light* which would descend upon the city. *This light is Christ.* The awesome movement toward Christ of people from all over the world begins as a result of the Gospel. Animated by the Holy Spirit, in the power of the Cross and Resurrection of Christ, *this movement of people culminates in a new unity* of humanity. Thus, the words of Jesus come to pass: "And I—once I am

lifted up from the earth—will draw all men to myself" (Jn 12:32).

The Second Vatican Council gave prominence to this dimension of the unity of the Church, above all *in the teaching on the People of God.* "This People, while remaining one and unique, is to be spread throughout the whole world and must exist in all ages, so that the purpose of God's will may be fulfilled" *(Lumen Gentium,* 13).

The Body of Christ

5. However, that *People is at the same time the Body of Christ.* The Body is yet another image, and in a certain sense another dimension, of the same truth of the unity that we all constitute in Christ under the action of the Holy Spirit. Accordingly, St. Paul exhorts us: "Make every effort to preserve *the unity which has the Spirit as its origin* and peace as its binding force. There is but *one body* and *one Spirit,* just as there is but one hope given all of you by your call. There is *one Lord, one faith, one baptism;* one God and Father of all, who is over all, and works through all, and is in all" (Eph 4:3-6). The unity for which Christ prayed in the Upper Room is realized in this way. It does not come from us, but *from God: from the Father, through the Son, in the Holy Spirit.*

Diversity and Communion

6. *This unity does not at all erase diversity.* On the contrary, *it develops it.* There is constantly "unity in diversity." Through the work of the one Lord, by means of the one faith and the one baptism, this diversity—a diversity of human persons, of individuals—tends toward unity, a unity which is *communion* in the likeness of God the Trinity.

The unity of the Body of Christ gives life; at the same time, it *serves diversity* and develops it. This is the diversity of "everyone" and at the same time of "each one." It is the truth that we find in the Letter to the Ephesians where Paul writes: *''Each of us has received God's favor* in the measure in which Christ bestows it.... It is he who gave apostles, prophets, evangelists, pastors and teachers in roles of service for the faithful to build up the body of Christ" (Eph 4:7, 11-12). As such then, it is *the Holy Spirit* who is the source of both the unity and the diversity in the Church: *the unity* because it finds its origin solely in the Spirit; the diversity since the Spirit bestows *the variety of gifts*, the variety of vocations and ministries found in the Church, which is the Body of Christ and at the same time the People of God.

7. The Saints whom we honor in today's liturgy, *Cornelius and Cyprian*, remind us of one concrete example of unity in diversity: *the unity of the universal Church* which is served by the Successor of St. Peter, and the diversity of the particular Churches which help to build up the whole Body through the leadership of the local Bishops.

Pope St. Cornelius was called to shepherd the universal Church in the middle of the third century, a time of religious persecution from without and a time of painful dissension within. His efforts to strengthen the Church's communion were greatly aided by the persuasive talents of the Bishop of Carthage, St. Cyprian, who while caring for his own flock also promoted unity throughout North Africa. These two men of different backgrounds and temperaments were united *by a mutual love for the Church* and by their *zeal for the unity of the faith*. How appropriate that we should observe their feast on the day when the present Successor of Peter is meeting with the Bishops of the United States.

The feast focuses our attention on a basic truth, namely that *the unity of the members of the Church* is deeply affected by *the unity of the Bishops* among themselves and by their communion with the Successor of Peter. The Second Vatican Council put it this way: "The Roman Pontiff, as the Successor of Peter, is the perpetual and visible source and foundation of the unity of the Bishops and of the multitude of the faithful. The individual Bishop, however, is the visible principle and foundation of unity in his particular Church, fashioned after the model of the universal Church. In and from such individual Churches there comes into being the one and only Catholic Church" *(Lumen Gentium, 23)*.

8. The Church's concrete *methods of evangelization* and her efforts to promote peace and justice are shaped to a large extent by the fact that the Church is one and yet diverse.

The Good News of Jesus must be proclaimed in *the language that particular people understand,* in *artistic symbols* that give meaning to their experience, in ways that correspond as far as possible to their own aspirations and needs, their manner of looking at life and the way in which they speak to God. At the same time, there must be *no betrayal of the essential truth* while the Gospel is being translated and the Church's teaching is being passed down.

The *ethnic universality of the Church* demands a keen sensitivity to authentic cultures and a real sense of what is required by the process of inculturation. In this regard, Pope Paul VI stated very accurately the task to be done: "The question is undoubtedly a delicate one. Evangelization loses much of its force and effectiveness if it does not take into consideration the actual people to whom it is addressed, if it does not use their language, their signs and symbols, if it does not answer the questions they ask, and if it does not have an impact on their concrete life. But on the other hand evangelization risks losing its power and disappearing altogether if one empties or adulterates its content under the pretext of translating it; if, in other words, one sacrifices this reality and destroys the unity without which there is no universality" *(Evangelii Nuntiandi, 63).*

Closely aligned with the Church's evangelization is her *action on behalf of peace and justice,* and this too is deeply influenced by her pastoral concern for particular peoples, especially for refugees, immigrants and the poor. For over two hundred years, *the Church has welcomed* the waves of *new immigrants* to the shores of your country. It was the love and compassion of the Church that so many new arrivals first felt when they stepped onto the soil of this young nation. While that continuous pastoral care of the immigrant was focused primarily on the East Coast in the early decades, that *pastoral outreach* now extends to virtually every major city in the country. Los Angeles—where this evening we celebrate the diversity of peoples who make up your country—has now become the new major point of entry for the latest waves of immigrants.

I commend you, my brother Bishops and all of those working closely with you, for your active collaboration in helping several million undocumented immigrants to become legal residents. This pastoral care of the immigrant in our own day reflects the love of Christ in the Gospels and the legitimate work of the Church in carrying on the challenge of the Lord, *"I was a stranger and you welcomed me"* (Mt 25:35).

Sacrament of Salvation

9. The Church faces a particularly difficult task in her efforts to preach the word of God in all *cultures* in which the faithful are constantly challenged by *consumerism and a pleasure-seeking mentality,* where utility, productivity and hedonism are exalted while God and his law are forgotten. In these situations, where ideas and behavior directly contradict the truth about God and about humanity itself, the Church's witness must be *unpopular.* She must take a *clear* stand on the word of God and proclaim the whole Gospel message with great confidence in the Holy Spirit. In this effort, just as in all others, the Church shows herself to be *the Sacrament of salvation* for the whole human race, the people God has chosen to be his channel of peace and reconciliation in a world torn by division and sin.

While the Church's unity is not her own achievement but a precious gift from the Lord, it is nonetheless her serious responsibility to be an instrument for *guarding and restoring unity* in the human family. She does this by being faithful to the truth and by directly opposing the devil, who is "the Father of lies." She does this by efforts to break down prejudice and ignorance as she fosters new understanding and trust. She also promotes unity by being a faithful channel of Christ's mercy and love.

The Wondrous Deeds of God

10. Today, with *the very prayer for unity said by Christ* in the Upper Room, we celebrate the liturgy of the Eucharist here, on the rim of the Pacific, in the city that takes its *name from the Angels.* And with the Psalmist, we say: "Sing to the Lord a new song, for he has done wondrous deeds" (Ps 97[98]:1).

Yes, God has done so many wondrous deeds that confirm his salvific action in our world—the "God and Father of all, who is over all, and works through all, and is in all" (Eph 4:6). "The Lord has made his salvation known.... He has revealed his justice." He constantly remembers "his kindness and his faithfulness" (Ps 97[98]:2-3). *This is the way God is, the God of our faith,* the Father of our Lord Jesus Christ.

The angels in heaven see "the face of God" in the beatific vision of glory. All of us, people of this planet, *walk in faith* toward that same vision. And we walk *in hope.* We draw the strength of this hope from the same prayer of Christ in the Upper Room. Did not Christ say in the words addressed to the Father: "I have given them the glory you gave me that they may be one, as we are one—I living in them, you living in me" (Jn 17:22-23)?

"The glory...I gave to them." We are called in Christ *to share in the glory* that is part of the beatific vision of God.

Truly, "all the ends of the earth have seen the salvation by our God." For this reason: "Sing to the Lord a new song!" (Ps 97[98]:3, 1) Amen.

Prayer to Mary
for the Church in the U.S.

Act of Entrusting the whole Church in the United States to the Blessed Virgin Mary—Los Angeles, September 16.

1. I wish at this time to turn my thoughts once more to *the Woman of faith and of all salvation history:* Mary the Mother of Jesus and Mother of his Church; Mary, the Patroness of the United States under the title of her Immaculate Conception.

I entrust to you, Virgin Mother of God, *all the faithful* of this land. I entrust them to you, not only as individual men and women in the nobility of their personhood, but as the Christian community, living corporately the life of your divine Son.

I entrust to you *my brother Bishops* in their great mission as servant pastors of God's people, in communion with the Successor of Peter. I entrust to you all *the priests* who minister generously in the name of the Good Shepherd; all *the deacons* bearing witness to Christ's servanthood; all *women and men religious* proclaiming by their lives the holiness of God; all *the laity* working in virtue of their Baptism and Confirmation to order all temporal affairs according to the plan of God.

I entrust to you *all the holy People of God*—the pilgrim People of God—called to be mindful of their Christian dignity, called to conversion, called to eternal life.

In particular I entrust to you *the families* of America, in their quest for holiness, in their struggle against sin, in their vocation to be vital cells in the Body of Christ. I ask you to bless all *husbands and wives,* all *fathers and mothers,* and to confirm them in their high vocation of human love and openness to life. I entrust to you *the children* of this generation, asking·you to preserve them in innocence, to protect them from all harm and abuse, and to let them grow up in a world of peace and justice and fraternal love.

I entrust to you *all the women of the Church* and the cause of their true human advancement in the world and their ever fuller participation in the life of the Church, according to the authentic plan of God. May they discover in you, O Mary, and in the freedom that was yours—from that moment of supreme liberation in your Immaculate Conception—the secret of living their femininity totally in fulfillment, progress and love.

I commend to your protection *the young people* that make up the future of the United States. I pray that in your Son Jesus Christ they may grasp the meaning of life, and come to understand deeply their call to serve their fellow human beings; that they may discover the profound fulfillment of chaste love, and the joy and strength that come from Christian hope.

I offer to your loving care *the elderly people* with all their sufferings and joys, and with their yet unfinished mission of service in your Church. I ask you to console and assist *the dying,* and to renew within the whole community a sense of the importance of human life at every stage, even when it is weak and defenseless.

I ask you to assist *the single people* with their special needs and special mission. Give them strength to live according to the Beatitudes and to serve with generosity and gladness.

2. I entrust to you all *those engaged in the great Christian struggle of life:* all those who, despite human weaknesses and repeated falls, are striving to live according to the word of God; all those who are confused about the truth and are tempted to call evil good and darkness light; all those who are yearning for truth and grasping for hope.

I ask you to show yourself once again as a Mother with that deep human concern which was yours at Cana of Galilee. Help *all those weighed down by the problems of life.* Console the suffering. Comfort the sad and dejected, those tormented in spirit, those without families, loved ones or friends.

Assist *the poor and those in need,* and those subjected to discrimination or other forms of injustice. Come to the help of the unemployed. Heal the sick. Aid the handicapped and disabled, so that they may live in a manner befitting their dignity as children of God. *Stir up the consciences of us all* to respond to the needs of others with justice, mercy and love.

3. Through your intercession I ask *that sinners may be reconciled,* and that the whole Church in America may become ever more attentive to Christ's call to conversion and to holiness of life.

I pray that all those baptized in Christ your Son will be strengthened in the great cause of Christian unity, according to his will.

I ask your prayers so *that citizens may work together to conquer evil with good,* oppose violence, reject war and its weapons, satisfy hunger, overcome hatred, and remedy all forms of personal, social, national, and international injustice.

I ask you *to strengthen the Catholic people* in truth and love, in their obedience to the commandments of God, and in their fidelity to the Sacraments.

Virgin Mother of God, Our Lady of the Angels: I entrust to you *the whole Church in America.* Help her to excel in sacrifice and service. Purify her love, renew her life, and convert her constantly to the Gospel of your Son. Lead her children with *all their Christian and non-Christian brethren* to eternal life, for the glory of your Son Jesus Christ, who lives and reigns with the Father in the unity of the Holy Spirit, for ever and ever. Amen.

Persons Before Economics

Homily at Monterey Eucharist—Laguna Seca Recreation Area, September 17.

"Be careful not to forget the Lord, your God" (Dt 8:11).

Dear Brothers and Sisters of the Monterey Peninsula,
Brothers and Sisters of California and other areas of the
United States,

1. Originally these words were addressed by Moses to the Israelite people as they were on the point of entering the promised land—a land with streams of water, with springs and fountains welling up in the hills and valleys, a land producing an abundance of every fruit and food, a land where the people would lack nothing (cf. Dt 8:7-9). Today, these words are addressed to the People of God here in Monterey, in the state of California, against the background of an extraordinary beauty of land and sea, of snowcapped mountains and deep lakes, oak groves and forests of fir and pine and mighty redwoods, a land among the richest and most fruitful of the earth. Yes, today, these words are addressed to all of us gathered here: *"Be careful not to forget the Lord, your God."*

Temptations to Forget God

2. These words, pronounced thousands of years ago, have still today a special meaning and relevance. Moses, the great teacher of his people, was concerned that in their future prosperity the people might abandon God—the God who brought them out of the land of slavery and guided them through the desert with its parched ground, feeding them with manna along the way (cf. Dt 8:15-16). Moses knew the tendency of the human heart to cry out to the Lord in time of need, but easily "to neglect his commandments and decrees and statutes" (cf. Dt 8:11) in the time of well-being and prosperity. He knew that *God is easily forgotten.*

In our own day are we not perhaps witnesses of the fact that often in rich societies, where there is an abundance of material well-being, permissiveness and moral relativism find easy acceptance? And where the moral order is undermined, God is forgotten and questions of ultimate responsibility are set aside. *In such situations a practical atheism pervades private and public living.*

From the moment of *original sin,* man has been inclined to see himself in the place of God. He often thinks, just as Moses warned he might: "It is my own power and the strength of my own hand that has obtained for me this wealth" (Dt 8:17). He acts as if the One who is the source of all life and goodness were just not there. He ignores a fundamental truth about himself: *the fact that he is a creature;* that he has been created and owes everything to his Creator, who is also his Redeemer.

In these closing years of the twentieth century, on the eve of the Third Millennium of the Christian era, a part of the human family—the most economically and technically developed part—is being specially tempted, perhaps as never before, to imitate the ancient model of all sin—the original rebellion that expressed itself saying: "I will not serve." *The temptation today is to try to build a world for oneself,* forgetting the Creator and his design and loving providence. But sooner or later we must come to grips with this: that *to forget God, to feign the death of God, is to promote the death of man* and of all civilization. It is to threaten the existence of individuals, communities and all societies.

We Are to Reflect God's Goodness

3. Today's readings from the New Testament are in contrast to such a position. They speak of *God's presence which permeates the human heart and the whole of created reality.* Jesus teaches that the Reign of God is like the growth of the seed that a man scatters on the ground (cf. Mk 4:26-29). Certainly, human activity is essential. Man "goes to bed and gets up every day...." He plants. And "when the crop is ready he wields the sickle." Even the rich valleys of California would produce nothing without human ingenuity and toil. But the word of God says that *"the soil produces of itself* first the blade, then the ear, finally the ripe wheat in the ear" (v. 28), as if to say: the growth of the wheat and its maturing, which greatly depends on the fertility of the soil, comes from the

nature and vitality of creation itself. Consequently there is *another source of growth:* the One who is *above nature and above the man who cultivates the earth.*

In a sense, the Creator *"hides himself"* in this life-giving process of nature. It is the human person, with the help of intellect and faith, who is called to "discover" and "unveil" the presence of God and his action in all of creation: *"So may your way be known upon earth; among all nations, your salvation"* (Ps 67:3).

If the parable of the seed indicates the growth of the Kingdom of God *in the world,* the words of St. Paul in the second reading speak of how God's generous giving aims at drawing "good works" *from the human heart:* "God can multiply his favors among you...for good works." The whole of human activity must be finalized in works of justice, peace and love. All human work—including, in a very direct way, the noble work of agriculture in which many of you are engaged—is to be carried out at the service of man and for the glory of God.

Work Is a Vocation

4. *The land is God's gift.* From the beginning, God has entrusted it to the whole human race as a means of sustaining the life of all those whom he creates in his own image and likeness. We must use the land to sustain every human being in life and dignity. Against the background of the immense beauty of this region and the fertility of its soil, let us proclaim together our gratitude for this gift, with the words of the responsorial psalm: *"The earth has yielded its fruit, the Lord our God has blessed us"* (Ps 67:7).

As we read in Genesis, human beings earn their bread by the sweat of their brows (cf. Gn 3:17). We toil long hours and grow weary at our tasks. Yet *work is good for us.* "Through work man not only transforms nature, adapting it to his own needs, but he also achieves fulfillment as a human being and indeed in a sense becomes 'more a human being'" (*Laborem Exercens,* 9).

The value of work does not end with *the individual.* The full meaning of work can only be understood in relation to *the family* and *society* as well. Work supports and gives stability to the family. Within the family, moreover, children first learn the human and positive meaning of work and responsibility. In each community and in the nation as a whole, work has a fundamental social meaning. It can, moreover, either join people in the solidarity of a shared commitment, or set them at odds through exaggerated competition, exploitation and social conflict. *Work is a key to the whole social question,* when that "question" is understood as being concerned with *making life more human* (cf. *Laborem Exercens,* 3).

5. Agricultural work exemplifies all these principles—the potential of work for the fulfillment of the human person, the "family" dimension of work, and social solidarity. *Agricultural work is*—as Pope John XXIII described it—*a vocation, a God-given mission, a noble task and a contribution to civilization* (cf. *Mater et Magistra,* 149). God has blessed the United States with some of the richest *farm land* in the world. The productivity of American agriculture is a major success story. Clearly, it is a history of hard and wearying work, of courage and enterprise, and it involves the interaction of many people: growers, workers, processors, distributors, and finally consumers.

I know too that recently thousands of *American farmers* have been introduced to poverty and indebtedness. Many have lost their homes and their way of life. Your Bishops and the whole Church in your country are deeply concerned; and they are listening to the voices of so many farmers and farmworkers as they express their anxieties over the costs and the risks of farming, the difficult working conditions, the need for a just wage and decent housing, and the question of a fair price for products. On an even wider scale is heard *the voice of the poor,* who are bewildered in a land of plenty, and still experience the pangs of hunger.

Solidarity and Stewardship

6. All agree that the situation of the farming community in the United States and in other parts of the world is highly complex, and that simple remedies are not at hand. The Church, on her part, while she can offer no specific technical

solutions, does present a social teaching based on the primacy of the human person in every economic and social activity. At every level of the agricultural process, *the dignity, rights and well-being of people must be the central issue.* No one person in this process—grower, worker, packer, shipper, retailer or consumer—is greater than the other in the eyes of God.

Giving voice therefore to the sufferings of many, I appeal to all involved to work together to find appropriate solutions to all farm questions. This can only be done in a community marked by a sincere and effective *solidarity*—and, where still necessary, *reconciliation*—among all parties to the agricultural productive process.

And what of our responsibility to future generations? The earth will not continue to offer its harvest, except with *faithful stewardship.* We cannot say we love the land and then take steps to destroy it for use by future generations. I urge you to be sensitive to the many issues affecting the land and the whole environment, and to unite with each other to seek the best solutions to these pressing problems.

Concern for Those in Most Need

7. *Each one of us is called to fulfill his or her respective duties before God and before society.* Since the Church is constrained by her very nature to focus her attention most strongly on those least able to defend their own legitimate interests, I appeal to landowners, growers and others in positions of power to respect the just claims of their brothers and sisters who work the land. These claims include the right to share in decisions concerning their services and the right to free association with a view to social, cultural and economic advancement (cf. *Laborem Exercens,* 21). I also appeal to all workers to be mindful of their own obligations of justice and to make every effort to fulfill a worthy service to mankind.

New legislation in your country has made it possible for many people, especially migrant farmworkers, *to become citizens* rather than remain strangers among you. Many of these people have worked here with the same dream that your ancestors had when they first came. I ask you to welcome these new citizens into your society and to respect the human dignity of every man, woman and child.

Two hundred years after the Constitution confirmed the United States as a land of opportunity and freedom, it is right to hope that there may be a general and renewed *commitment to those policies needed to ensure that within these borders equity and justice will be preserved and fostered.* This is an ever present requirement of America's historical destiny.

It is also important for America at this time *to look beyond herself* and all her own needs *to see the even greater needs of the poorer nations of the world.* Even as local communities mobilize to work ever more effectively for the integral human advancement of their own members, they must not forget their brothers and sisters elsewhere. We must be careful not to forget the Lord, but we must be careful also not to forget those whom he loves.

Tourism

8. The hidden attributes of the Creator are reflected in the beauty of his creation. The beauty of the Monterey Peninsula attracts a great number of visitors; as a result, many of you are involved in *the tourist industry.* I greet you and encourage you to see your specific work as a form of service and of solidarity with your fellow human beings.

Work—as we have seen—is an essential aspect of our human existence, but so also is the necessary rest and recreation which permits us to recover our energies and strengthen our spirit for the tasks of life. Many worthwhile values are involved in tourism: relaxation, the widening of one's culture and the possibility of using leisure time for spiritual pursuits. These include prayer and contemplation, and pilgrimages, which have always been a part of our Catholic heritage; they also include fostering human relationships within the family and among friends. Like other human activities, tourism can be a source of good or evil, a place of grace or sin. I invite all of you who are involved in tourism *to uphold the dignity of your work* and to be always willing *to bear joyful witness to your Christian faith.*

Work's Transformation in the Eucharist

9. Dear brothers and sisters: it is *in the Eucharist* that the fruits of our work—and all that is noble in human affairs—become an offering of the greatest value in union with the Sacrifice of Jesus Christ, our Lord and Savior. In fostering what is authentically human through our work and through deeds of justice and love, we set upon the altar of the Lord those elements which will be transformed into Christ: "Blessed are you, Lord, God of all creation. Through your goodness we have this bread to offer, which earth has given and human hands have made. *It will become for us the bread of life.*"

I ask you to join with me *in praising the Most Holy Trinity* for the abundance of life and goodness with which you have been gifted: "The earth has yielded its fruit. God, our God, has blessed us" (Ps 67:7). But may your abundance never lead you to forget the Lord or cease to acknowledge him as the source of your peace and well-being. Your prayer for yourselves and for all your brothers and sisters must always be an echo of the psalm:

"May God have pity on us and bless us;
     may he let his face shine on us" (Ps 67:2).

For years to come may the Lord's face shine on this land, on the Church in Monterey, and on all America: "From sea to shining sea." Amen.

Single-Minded Devotion and Witness

Address given at Carmel Mission Basilica—Monterey, September 17.

Dear Bishop Shubsda,
Dear Brothers and Sisters,

1. I come today as a pilgrim to this Mission of San Carlos, which so powerfully evokes the heroic spirit and heroic deeds of Fray Junipero Serra and which enshrines his mortal remains. This serene and beautiful place is truly *the historical and spiritual heart of California.* All the missions of *El Camino Real* bear witness to the challenges and heroism of an earlier time, but not a time forgotten or without significance for the California of today and the Church of today.

These buildings and the men who gave them life, especially their spiritual father, Junipero Serra, are reminders of an age of discovery and exploration. The missions are the result of a conscious moral decision made by people of faith in a situation that presented many human possibilities, both good and bad, with respect to the future of this land and its Native Peoples. It was a decision rooted in a love of God and neighbor. It was *a decision to proclaim the Gospel* of Jesus Christ at the dawn of a new age, which was extremely important for both the European settlers and the Native Americans.

Junipero Serra

2. Very often, at crucial moments in human affairs, God raises up men and women whom he thrusts into roles of decisive importance for the future development of both society and the Church. Although their story unfolds within the ordinary circumstances of daily life, they become larger than life within the perspective of history. We rejoice all the more when their achievement is coupled with a holiness of life that can truly be called heroic. So it is with Junipero Serra, who in the providence of God was destined to be *the Apostle of California,* and to have a permanent influence over the spiritual patrimony of this land and its people, whatever

their religion might be. This apostolic awareness is captured in the words ascribed to him: "In California is my life and there, God willing, I hope to die." Through Christ's Paschal Mystery, that death has become a seed in the soil of this state that continues to bear fruit "thirty- or sixty- or a hundredfold" (Mt 13:9).

Father Serra was a man *convinced of the Church's mission,* conferred upon her by Christ himself, to evangelize the world, to "make disciples of all the nations, baptizing them in the name of the Father and of the Son and of the Holy Spirit" (Mt 28:19). The way in which he fulfilled that mission corresponds faithfully to the Church's vision today of what evangelization means: "...The Church evangelizes when she seeks to convert, solely through the divine power of the message she proclaims, both the personal and collective consciences of people, the activities in which they engage, and the lives and concrete milieux which are theirs" *(Evangelii Nuntiandi,* 18).

He not only brought the Gospel to the Native Americans, but as one who lived the Gospel he also became their *defender and champion.* At the age of sixty he journeyed from Carmel to Mexico City to intervene with the Viceroy on their behalf—a journey which twice brought him close to death—and presented his now famous *Representación* with its "bill of rights," which had as its aim the betterment of every phase of missionary activity in California, particularly the spiritual and physical well-being of its Native Americans.

3. Father Serra and his fellow missionaries shared the conviction found everywhere in the New Testament that the Gospel is a matter of life and salvation. They believed that in offering Jesus Christ to people, they were doing *something of immense value,* importance and dignity. What other explanation can there be for the hardships that they freely and gladly endured, like St. Paul and all the other great missionaries before them: difficult and dangerous travel, illness and isolation, an ascetical life-style, arduous labor, and also, like St. Paul, that "concern for all the churches" (2 Cor 11:28) which Junipero Serra, in particular, experienced as "Presidente" of the California Missions in the face of every vicissitude, disappointment and opposition.

Call to Evangelize

Dear brothers and sisters: like Father Serra and his Franciscan brethren, we too are *called to be evangelizers*, to share actively in the Church's mission of making disciples of all people. The way in which we fulfill that mission will be different from theirs. But their lives speak to us still because of their sure faith that the Gospel is true, and because of their passionate belief in the value of bringing that saving truth to others at great personal cost. Much to be envied are those who can give their lives for something greater than themselves in loving service to others. This, more than words or deeds alone, is what draws people to Christ.

This *single-mindedness* is not reserved for great missionaries in exotic places. It must be at the heart of each priest's ministry and the evangelical witness of every religious. It is the strength that one senses in this place of prayer so filled with his presence. It is the key to their personal sense of well-being, happiness and fulfillment in what they are and what they do. This single-mindedness is also essential to the Christian witness of the Catholic laity. The covenant of love between two people in marriage and the successful sharing of faith with children require the effort of a lifetime. If couples cease believing in their marriage as a sacrament before God, or treat religion as anything less than a matter of salvation, then the Christian witness they might have given to the world is lost. Those who are unmarried must also be steadfast in fulfilling their duties in life if they are to bring Christ to the world in which they live.

"In him who is the source of my strength I have strength for everything" (Phil 4:13). These words of the great missionary, St. Paul, remind us that *our strength is not our own*. Even in the martyrs and saints, as the liturgy reminds us, it is "(God's) power shining through our human weakness" *(Preface of Martyrs)*. It is the strength that inspired Father Serra's motto: "Always forward, never back." It is the strength that one senses in this place of prayer so filled with his presence. It is the strength that can make each one of us, dear brothers and sisters, missionaries of Jesus Christ, witnesses of his message, doers of his word.

God Loves Everyone

Address to retired priests, AIDS patients, parishioners and others—Mission Dolores Basilica, San Francisco, September 17.

Dear Archbishop Quinn,
Dear Brothers and Sisters in Christ,

1. Thank you for your very kind welcome to *San Francisco*. It is a joy to be here with all of you. As I begin my pastoral visit to your historic city, I extend fraternal greetings to all the citizens of this metropolitan area. In the love of Christ I greet my brothers and sisters of the Catholic community. And in a special way I welcome this opportunity to be with you who are present in this *Basilica dedicated to Our Lady of Sorrows*. May the grace and peace of God our Father and our Lord Jesus Christ be with you all.

San Francisco! Both in name and by history you are linked to *the spirit of St. Francis of Assisi*. And thus, as I come to your city on this pastoral visit, I think of all that St. Francis means, not only to yourselves but to people all around the world. There is something about this man, who was born over eight hundred years ago in a little Italian town, that continues in our day to inspire people of vastly different cultures and religions.

St. Francis was a man of peace and gentleness, a poet and lover of beauty. He was a man of poverty and simplicity, a man in tune with the birds and animals, enchanted by all of God's creation. Above all, Francis was a man of prayer whose whole life was shaped by *the love of Jesus Christ*. And he wished to live in a way that spoke in the clearest terms of the everlasting love of God.

As I come today, then, to the city of San Francisco, I come in the spirit of this saint whose *whole life proclaims the goodness and mercy of God*.

God's Love Is Freely Given

2. Accordingly, I wish to speak to you about the all-embracing love of God. St. John says: *"Love, then, consists in this:* not that we have loved God but *that he has loved us* and *has sent his Son as an offering for our sins"* (1 Jn 4:10). God's

love for us is freely given and unearned, surpassing all we could ever hope for or imagine. He does not love us because we have merited it or are worthy of it. God loves us, rather, because he is true to his own nature. As St. John puts it, *"God is love,* and he who abides in love abides in God, and God in him" (1 Jn 4:16).

The greatest proof of God's love is shown in the fact that he loves us in our human condition, with our weaknesses and our needs. Nothing else can explain the mystery of the Cross. The Apostle Paul once wrote: "You can depend on this as worthy of full acceptance: that *Christ Jesus came into the world to save sinners.* Of these, I myself am the worst. But on that very account I was dealt with mercifully, so that in me, as an extreme case, Jesus Christ might display *all his patience,* and that I might become an example to those who would later have faith in him and gain everlasting life" (1 Tm 1:15-16).

The love of Christ is more powerful than sin and death. St. Paul explains that Christ came to forgive sin, and that his love is greater than any sin, stronger than all my personal sins or those of anyone else. This is the faith of the Church. This is the Good News of God's love which the Church proclaims throughout history, and which I proclaim to you today: God loves you with an everlasting love. He loves you in Christ Jesus, his Son.

God Is Our Father

3. God's love has many aspects. In particular, *God loves us as our Father.* The parable of the prodigal son expresses this truth most vividly. You recall that moment in the parable when the son came to his senses, decided to return home and set off for his father's house. *"While he was still a long way off,* his father caught sight of him and was deeply moved. *He ran out to meet him,* threw his arms around his neck, and kissed him" (Lk 15:20). This is the fatherly love of God, a love always ready to forgive, eager to welcome us back.

God's love for us as our Father is a strong and faithful love, a love which is full of mercy, a love which *enables us to hope for the grace of conversion* when we have sinned. As I said in my Encyclical on the Mercy of God: "The parable of the prodigal son expresses in a simple but profound way *the reality of conversion.* Conversion is the most concrete expression of the working of love and of the presence of mercy in the human world.... Mercy is manifested in its true and proper aspect when it restores to value, promotes and *draws good from all the forms of evil* existing in the world" *(Dives in Misericordia,* 6).

It is the reality of God's love for us as our Father that explains why Jesus told us *when we pray* to address God as *"Abba, Father"* (cf. Lk 11:2; Mt 6:9).

His Love Is Tender

4. It is also true to say that *God loves us as a Mother.* In this regard, God asks us, through the Prophet Isaiah: "Can a mother forget her infant, be without *tenderness for the child of her womb?* Even should she forget, *I will never forget you"* (Is 49:15). God's love is tender and merciful, patient and full of understanding. In the Scriptures, and also in the living memory of the Church, the love of God is indeed depicted and has been experienced as *the compassionate love of a mother.*

Jesus himself expressed a compassionate love when he wept over Jerusalem, and when he said: "O Jerusalem, Jerusalem.... How often would I have gathered your children together *as a hen gathers* her brood under her wings" (Lk 13:34).

His Love Is Unconditional

Dear friends in Christ: the love of God is so great that it goes *beyond the limits of human language,* beyond the grasp of artistic expression, beyond human understanding. And yet, it is *concretely embodied in God's Son, Jesus Christ,* and in his Body, the Church. Once again this evening, here in Mission Dolores Basilica, I repeat to all of you the ageless proclamation of the Gospel: God loves you!

God loves you all, without distinction, without limit. He loves those of you who are elderly, who feel the burden of the years. He loves those of you who are sick, those who are suffering from AIDS and from AIDS-Related Complex. He loves the relatives and friends of the sick and those who care for them. He loves us all with an unconditional and everlasting love.

In the spirit of St. Francis, then, I urge you all to open your hearts to God's love, to respond by your prayers and by the deeds of your lives. Let go of your doubts and fears, and let the mercy of God draw you to his heart. *Open the doors of your hearts* to our God who is rich in mercy.

"See what love the Father has bestowed on us in letting us be called children of God! Yet that is what we are" (1 Jn 3:1). Yes, that is what we are today and forever: children of a loving God!

Prophetic Signs of Truth

Address to representatives of U.S. Religious Congregations—St. Mary's Cathedral, San Francisco, September 17.

Dear Sisters and Brothers in Christ,
Dear Religious of the United States of America,

1. In their deepest spiritual significance, the Vespers that we are praying together are *the voice of the Bride* addressing the Bridegroom (cf. *Sacrosanctum Concilium,* 84). They are also *the voice of the Bridegroom,* "the very prayer which Christ himself, together with his body, addresses to the Father" *(ibid.).* With one and the same voice the Bride and the Bridegroom praise the Father in the unity of the Holy Spirit.

In this liturgical song of praise we give expression to "the real nature of the true Church"—"both human and divine, visible and yet invisibly endowed, eager to act and yet devoted to contemplation, present in the world and yet not at home in it" *(ibid.,* 2). It is precisely *the presence of God* in human life and human affairs that you proclaim through your religious consecration and the practice of the evangelical counsels. It is to the reality of *God's love in the world* that you bear witness by means of the many forms of your loving service to God's people

Importance of This Meeting

2. Dear religious sisters, and religious priests and brothers: for me, this is one of the most important moments of my visit. Here, with all of you, men and women religious of the United States, and in the spiritual presence of all the members of your Congregations spread throughout this land or serving in other countries, *I give heartfelt thanks to God for each and every one of you.* He who is mighty has done great things for you, holy is his name! (cf. Lk 1:49)

I greet each one of you with love and gratitude. I thank you for the warm welcome you have given me and I thank Sister Helen Garvey and Father Stephen Tutas, who have presented a picture of your dedicated lives. I rejoice because of your deep love of the Church and your generous service to God's people. Every place I have visited in this vast country bears the marks of the diligent labor and immense spiritual energies of religious of both contemplative and active Congregations in the Church. The extensive Catholic educational and health care systems, the highly developed network of social services in the Church—none of this would exist today, were it not for your highly motivated dedication and the dedication of those who have gone before you. The spiritual vigor of so many Catholic people testifies to the efforts of generations of religious in this land. The history of the Church in this country is in large measure *your history at the service of God's people.*

As we remember your glorious past, let us be filled with hope that *your future* will be no less beneficial for the Church in the United States, and no less a prophetic witness of God's Kingdom to each new generation of Americans.

The Period of Renewal

3. The single most extraordinary event that has affected the Church in every aspect of her life and mission during the second half of the twentieth century has been the Second Vatican Council. The Council called the whole Church to conversion, to "newness of life," to renewal—to a *renewal that consists essentially in an ever increasing fidelity to Jesus Christ her divine Founder.* As "men and women who more closely follow and more clearly demonstrate the Savior's self-giving" (*Lumen Gentium*, 42), it is only natural that religious should have experienced the call to renewal in a radical way. Thousands of religious in the United States have generously responded to this call, and continue to live it with profound commitment. The results, the good fruits of this response are evident in the Church: we see a Gospel-inspired spirituality, which has led to a deepening of personal and liturgical prayer; a clearer sense of the Church as a communion of faith and love in which the grace and responsibility entrusted to each member are to be respected and encouraged; a new appreciation of the legacy of your founders and foundresses, so that the specific charism of each Congregation stands out more clearly; a heightened awareness of the urgent needs of the modern world where reli-

gious, in close union with the Bishops and in close collaboration with the whole Church, seek to carry on the work of the Good Shepherd, the Good Samaritan and the Good Teacher.

It would be unrealistic to think that such a deep and overall process of renewal could take place without risks and errors, without undue impatience on the part of some and undue fears on the part of others. Whatever the tension and polarization occasioned by change, whatever the mistakes made in the past, I am sure that all of you are convinced that the time has come *to reach out once again to one another in a spirit of love and reconciliation,* both within and beyond your Congregations.

During the past two decades there have also been profound insights into the meaning and value of religious life. Many of these insights, conceived in the experience of prayer and penance and authenticated by the teaching charism of the Church, have contributed greatly to ecclesial life. These insights have borne witness to *the enduring identity of religious consecration and mission* in the life of the Church. At the same time they have testified to the need for religious to adapt their activity to the needs of the people of our times.

Religious and the Church

4. Fundamental to the Council's teaching on religious life is an emphasis on *the ecclesial nature of the vocation to observe the evangelical counsels.* Religious consecration "belongs inseparably to the life and holiness of the Church" *(Lumen Gentium,* 44). "The counsels are a divine gift, which the Church has received from her Lord and which she ever preserves with the help of his grace" *(ibid.,* 43). It was precisely within this ecclesial context that in 1983 I asked the Bishops of the United States to render a pastoral service by offering to those of you whose Institutes are engaged in apostolic works special encouragement and support in living your ecclesial vocation to the full. I now wish to thank the Bishops and all of you for your very generous collaboration in this important endeavor. In particular I thank the Pontifical Commission headed by Archbishop John Quinn. By

God's grace there now exists a fresh cooperative spirit between your religious Institutes and the local Churches.

Your continuing participation in the mission of the Church at the diocesan and parish levels is of inestimable value to the well-being of the local Churches. Your communion with the local Bishops and collaboration with the pastoral ministry of the diocesan clergy contributes to a strong and effective spiritual growth among the faithful. Your creative initiatives in favor of the poor and all marginalized persons and groups, whose needs might otherwise be neglected, are deeply appreciated. Your evangelizing and missionary work both at home and in other parts of the world is one of the great strengths of the Church in the United States. Alongside your traditional apostolates—which are as important now as ever before and which I encourage you to appreciate in their full significance—you are engaged in almost every area of defending human rights and of building a more just and equitable society. This is *a record of unselfish response to the Gospel of Jesus Christ.* Yes, the entire Church in the United States benefits from the dedication of American Religious to their ecclesial mission..

Challenges

5. At the same time you are concerned about certain weaknesses affecting the structure of your Institutes. The decline in vocations and the aging of your membership are serious challenges for each one of your Institutes and for the corporate reality of religious life, and yet these are not new phenomena in the long experience of the Church. History teaches us that in ways generally unpredictable *the radical "newness" of the Gospel message is`always able to inspire successive generations* to do what you have done, to renounce all for the sake of the Kingdom of God, in order to possess the pearl of great price (cf. Mt 13:44-45).

You are called at this hour to fresh courage and trust. Your *joyful witness to consecrated love*—in chastity, poverty and obedience—will be the greatest human attraction for young people to religious life in the future. When they sense the authenticity of renewal in you and your communities, they too will be disposed to come and see! The invitation is directly from Christ, but they will want to hear it from you too. Your own essential contribution to vocations will come *through fidelity, penance and prayer,* and through confidence in *the power of Christ's Paschal Mystery to make all things new.*

In the best traditions of Christian love, you will know how to show your special appreciation for the aged and infirm members of your communities, whose contribution of prayer and penance, suffering and faithful love is of immense value to your apostolates. May they always be comforted in knowing that they are respected and loved within their own religious families.

6. Your vocation is, of its very nature, a radical response to the call which Jesus extends to all believers in their baptismal consecration: *"Seek first his kingship over you, his way of holiness"* (Mt 6:33). Your response is expressed by your vowed commitment to embrace and live in community the evangelical counsels. Through chastity, poverty and obedience you live in expectation of an eschatological kingdom where "they neither marry nor are given in marriage" (Mt 22:30). And so, even now, "where your treasure is there your heart is also" (Mt 6:21).

Through your religious profession, the consecration which the Holy Spirit worked in you at Baptism is *powerfully directed anew to the perfection of charity.* By practicing the vows, you constantly die with Christ in order to rise to new life with him (cf. Rom 6:8). In fidelity to your vow of *chastity* you are empowered to love with the love of Christ and to know that deep encounter with his love which inspires and sustains your apostolic love for your neighbor. Treading the path of *poverty* you find yourselves truly open to God and aligned with the poor and suffering in whom you see the image of the poor and suffering Christ (cf. Mt 25:31ff.). And through *obedience* you are intimately united with Jesus in seeking always to fulfill the Father's will. Through such obedience there is unlocked in you *the full measure of Christian freedom* which enables you to serve God's people with selfless and unfailing devotion. The Catholic people, and indeed the vast majority of your fellow-citizens, have the highest respect for your religious consecration, and they

look to you for the "proof" of the transcendent Christian
hope that is in you (cf. 1 Pt 3:15).

7. The disciple, though, is not above the Master. It is
only right for you to expect, as has always been the Church's
understanding, that if you follow the laws of Christ's
Kingdom—in essence, the new commandment of love and
the new values proclaimed in the Beatitudes—you will be in
conflict with the "wisdom of this age" (cf. 1 Cor 2:6). In a
particularly personal and courageous way, religious have
always been in the front line of this never ending struggle.

Today, the encounter between the saving message of the
Gospel and the forces that shape our human culture calls for
a profound and prayerful discernment of Christ's will for his
Church at this moment of her life. In this regard the Second
Vatican Council remains the necessary point of reference and
the guiding light. This discernment is the work of the whole
Church. No person or group of people can claim to possess
sufficient insights so as to monopolize it. All members of the
Church, according to the ministry received for the good of
the whole Body, must be humbly attuned to the Holy Spirit
who guides the Church into the fullness of truth (cf. Jn
16:13; *Lumen Gentium*, 4), and produces in her the fruits of
his action, which St. Paul lists as "love, joy, peace, patient
endurance, kindness, generosity, faith, mildness and chastity" (Gal 5:22-23). And since the Holy Spirit has placed in
the Church the special pastoral charism of the Magisterium,
we know that *adherence to the Magisterium is an indispensable
condition for a correct reading of "the signs of the times"* and
hence a condition for the supernatural fruitfulness of all
ministries in the Church.

You indeed have an important role in the Church's dialogue with the complex and varied cultural environment of
the United States. The first law of this dialogue is *fidelity to
Christ and to his Church*. And in this fundamental act of faith
and trust you already show the world the basis of your
special position within the community of God's people. Also
required for this dialogue is *a true understanding of the values
involved in America's historical experience*. At the same time the
Christian concepts of the common good, of virtue and conscience, of liberty and justice, must be distinguished from

what is sometimes inadequately presented as the expression of these realities. As religious, you are especially sensitive to the implications of this dialogue with the world in which you are called to live and work. As men and women consecrated to God, you are aware of having a special responsibility to be a sign—an authentic prophetic sign—that will speak to the Church and to the world, not in terms of easy condemnation, but humbly *showing forth the power of God's word to heal and uplift, to unite and bind with love.*

At this important moment of the history of the human family it is essential for the Church to proclaim the full truth about God—Father, Son and Holy Spirit—and the full truth about our human condition and destiny as revealed in Christ and authentically transmitted through the teaching of the Church. The faithful have the right to receive the true teaching of the Church in its purity and integrity, with all its demands and power. When people are looking for a sure point of reference for their own values and their ethical choices, they turn to the special witnesses of the Church's holiness and justice—to you religious. They expect and want to be convinced by the example of your acceptance of God's word.

Union with Christ

8. Dear sisters and brothers: *the life we now live is not our own; Christ is living in us.* We still live our human life, but it is a life of faith in the Son of God, who loved us and gave himself for us (cf. Gal 2:20). In these words St. Paul sums up the core of our Christian experience, and even more so *the heart of religious life.* The validity and fruitfulness of religious life depends upon *union with Jesus Christ.*

Union with Christ demands *a true interior life of prayer,* a life of closeness to him. At the same time it enables you to be effective witnesses before the world of the healing and liberating power of the Paschal Mystery. It means that above all in your own lives and in your own communities the Paschal Mystery is first being celebrated and experienced through *the Eucharist and the Sacrament of Penance.* In this way your works of charity and justice, of mercy and compassion will be true signs of Christ's presence in the world.

"Examples to the Flock"

9. The challenges which you faced yesterday you will face again tomorrow. The thousand tasks that now draw upon your courage and your energies will hardly disappear next week, next month, next year. What then is the meaning of our meeting? What "word of the Lord" is addressed to us here? As the one who for the time being has been given the place of the Fisherman from Galilee, as the one who occupies the Chair of Peter for this fleeting hour in the Church's life, allow me to make my own the sentiments of the Reading from our Evening Prayer: *"Be examples to the flock"* (1 Pt 5:3)—examples of faith and charity, of hope and joy, of obedience, sacrifice and humble service. And "when the Chief Shepherd appears, you will win for yourselves the unfading crown of glory" (v. 4).

To the *contemplative religious* of the United States, whose lives are hidden with Christ in God, I wish to say a word of profound thanks for reminding us that "here we have no lasting city" (Heb 13:14), and that all life must be lived in the heart of the living God. May the whole Church in this land recognize the primacy and efficacy of the spiritual values which you represent. The Second Vatican Council deliberately chose to call you "the glory of the Church" *(Perfectae Caritatis, 7).*

Brothers and Sisters, men and women religious of the United States: your country needs the witness of your deep spirituality and your commitment to the life-giving power of the Gospel. America needs to see all the power of love in your hearts expressed in evangelizing zeal. The whole world needs to discover in you "the kindness and love of God our Savior" (Tit 3:4). Go forward, therefore, in the mystery of the dying and rising of Jesus. *Go forward in faith, hope and charity, expending yourselves in the Church's mission of evangelization and service.* Always be examples to the flock. And know that "when the Chief Shepherd appears, you will win for yourselves the unfading crown of glory" (1 Pt 5:4).

In this Marian Year of grace may you find joy and

strength in an ever greater devotion to Mary, the Virgin Mother of the Redeemer. As "the model and protectress of all consecrated life" (Can. 663, §4, may she lead each one of you to perfect union with her Son, our Lord Jesus Christ, and to ever closer collaboration in his redemptive mission. And may the example of *Mary's discipleship* confirm you all in generosity and love.

Incarnating Gospel Values

Address to over 3,000 representatives of the laity—St. Mary's Cathedral, San Francisco, September 18.

"To him whose power now at work in us can do immeasurably more than we ask or imagine—to him be glory in the Church and in Christ Jesus through all generations...."

(Eph 3:20-21)

Dear Brothers and Sisters,
Dear Catholic Lay People of America,

1. I am grateful to you for your kind welcome and pleased *to be with you* this morning in glorifying the Father, "in the Church and in Christ Jesus," through the working of the Holy Spirit. I also wish to thank you for the informative presentations which have been made in the name of the Catholic laity of the United States.

The reading from the Letter of St. Paul to the Ephesians which we heard a few moments ago has a deep meaning for the life of each one of us. The text movingly describes *our relationship with God* as he reveals himself to us in the mystery of the Most Holy Trinity. St. Paul reminds us of two fundamental truths: first, that our ultimate vocation is to glorify the God who created and redeemed us; and secondly, that our eternal and highest good is to "attain to the fullness of God himself"—to participate in the loving communion of the Father and the Son and the Holy Spirit for all eternity. God's glory and our good are perfectly attained in the Kingdom of heaven.

The Apostle Paul also reminds us that *salvation*, which comes as a free gift of divine love in Christ, is not offered to us on a purely individual basis. It comes to us *through and in the Church*. Through our communion with Christ and with one another on earth, we are given a foretaste of that perfect communion reserved for heaven. Our communion is also meant to be *a sign or sacrament* which draws other people to Christ, so that all might be saved.

This gift of the Redemption, which originates with the Father and is accomplished by the Son, is brought to fruition in our individual lives and in the life of the world by *the Holy Spirit*. Thus we speak of the gifts of the Spirit at work within the Church—gifts which include the hierarchical office of shepherding the flock, and gifts given to the laity so that they may live the Gospel and make their specific contribution to the Church's mission.

The Council tells us that "everyone in the Church does not proceed by the same path, nevertheless all are called to sanctity and have received an equal privilege of faith through the justice of God (cf. 2 Pt 1:1). And if by the will of Christ some are made teachers, dispensers of mysteries, and shepherds on behalf of others, yet all share a true equality with regard to the dignity and activity common to all the faithful for the building up of the Body of Christ" (*Lumen Gentium,* 32). *Through a great diversity* of graces and works, the children of God bear witness to that *wonderful unity* which is the work of one and the same Spirit.

Leaven in the Secular World

2. Dear brothers and sisters: it is in the context of these mysteries of faith that I wish to reflect with you on your role as laity in the Church today. What is most fundamental in your lives is that *by your Baptism and Confirmation you have been commissioned by our Lord Jesus Christ himself to share in the saving mission of his Church* (cf. *Lumen Gentium,* 33). To speak of the laity is to speak of hundreds of millions of people, like yourselves, of every race, nation and walk of life, who each day seek, with the help of God, to live a good Christian life. To speak of the laity is to speak of the many of you who draw from your *parish* the strength and inspiration to live your vocation in the world. It is to speak also of those of you who have become part of national and international *ecclesial associations and movements* that support you in your vocation and mission.

Your struggles and temptations may differ according to your various situations, but all of you cherish the same basic hope to be faithful to Christ and to put his message into practice. You all cherish the same basic hope for a decent life for yourselves and an even better life for your children. All of you must toil and work and bear the sufferings and disappointments common to humanity, but as believers you are endowed with faith, hope and charity. And often your charity reaches heroic dimensions within your families or among your neighbors and co-workers. To the extent that your resources and duties in life permit, you are called to support and actively to participate in Church activities.

It is within the everyday world that you the laity must bear *witness to God's Kingdom;* through you the Church's mission is fulfilled by the power of the Holy Spirit. The Council taught that *the specific task of the laity* is precisely this: to "seek the Kingdom of God by engaging in temporal affairs and by ordering them according to the plan of God" *(Lumen Gentium,* 31). You are called to live in the world, *to engage in secular professions and occupations,* to live in those ordinary circumstances of family life and life in society from which is woven the very web of your existence. You are called by God himself *to exercise your proper functions according to the spirit of the Gospel* and to work for the sanctification of the world from within, in the manner of leaven. In this way you can make Christ known to others, especially by the witness of your lives. It is for you as lay people *to direct all temporal affairs to the praise of the Creator and Redeemer* (cf. *ibid.).*

The temporal order of which the Council speaks is vast. It encompasses the social, cultural, intellectual, political and economic life in which all of you rightly participate. As lay men and women actively engaged in this temporal order, you are being called by Christ to sanctify the world and to transform it. This is true of *all work, however exalted or humble,* but it is especially urgent for those whom circumstances and special talent have placed in positions of leadership or influence: men and women in public service, education, business, science, social communications, and the arts. As Catholic lay people you have an important moral and cultural *contribution of service to make to the life of your country.* "Much will be required of the person entrusted with much" (Lk 12:48). These words of Christ apply not only to the sharing of material wealth or personal talents, but also to the sharing of one's faith.

The Family—Love and Life

3. Of supreme importance in the mission of the Church is *the role that the laity fulfill in the Christian family.* This role is above all a *service of love* and a *service of life.*

The love of husband and wife, which is blessed and sealed in the Sacrament of Marriage, constitutes the first way that couples exercise their mission. They serve by being true to themselves, to their *vocation of married love.* This love, which embraces all the members of the family, is aimed at forming *a community of persons* united in heart and soul, an indissoluble communion where the love of spouses for each other is a sign of Christ's love for the Church.

The service of life rests on the fact that husband and wife cooperate with God in transmitting the gift of human life, in the procreation of children. In this most sacred responsibility, the service of life is intimately united to the service of love in the one conjugal act, which must always be open to bringing forth new life. In his Encyclical *Humanae Vitae,* Pope Paul VI explained that in the task of transmitting life, husband and wife are called to "conform their activity to the creative intention of God, expressed in the very nature of marriage and of its acts, and manifested by the constant teaching of the Church" (n. 10).

While "love and life constitute the nucleus of the saving mission of the Christian family in the Church and for the Church *(Familiaris Consortio,* 50), the family also performs *a service of education,* particularly within the home, where the parents have the original and primary role of educating their children. The family is likewise *an evangelizing community,* where the Gospel is received and put into practice, where prayer is learned and shared, where all the members, by word and deed and by the love they have for one another, bear witness to the Good News of salvation.

At the same time we must recognize the *difficult situation* of so many people with regard to family living. There are many with special burdens of one kind or another. There are the single-parent families and those who have no natural family; there are the elderly and the widowed. And there are those separated and divorced Catholics who, despite their loneliness and pain, are striving to preserve their fidelity and to face their responsibilities with loving generosity. All of these people share deeply in the Church's mission by faith, hope and charity, and by all their many efforts to be faithful to God's will. The Church assures them not only of her prayers and spiritual nourishment, but also of *her love, pastoral concern and practical help.*

Although, in fidelity to Christ and to his teaching on Christian marriage, the Church reaffirms her practice of not admitting to Eucharistic Communion those divorced persons who have remarried outside the Church, nevertheless, she assures these Catholics too of her deep love. She prays for them and encourages them to persevere in prayer, to listen to the word of God and to attend the Eucharistic Sacrifice, hoping that they will "undertake a way of life that is no longer in contradiction to the indissolubility of marriage" *(Familiaris Consortio,* 84). At the same time *the Church remains their mother, and they are part of her life.*

The Dignity of Women

4. I wish to express the deep gratitude of the Church for *all the contributions made by women* over the centuries to the life of the Church and of society. In speaking of the role of women special mention must of course be made of their contribution, in partnership with their husbands, in begetting life and in educating their children. "The true advancement of women requires that clear recognition be given to the value of their maternal and family role, by comparison with all other public roles and all other professions" *(Familiaris Consortio,* 23). The Church is convinced, however, that all the special gifts of women are needed in an ever-increasing measure in her life, and for this reason hopes for their fuller participation in her activities. Precisely because of their equal dignity and responsibility, the access of women to public functions must be ensured. Regardless of the role they perform, the Church proclaims *the dignity of women as women*—a dignity equal to men's dignity, and revealed as such in the account of creation contained in the word of God.

Lay Participation in the Church's Life

5. The renewal of the Church since the Council has also been an occasion for *increasing lay participation* in all areas of ecclesial life. More and more, people are joining with their pastors in collaboration and consultation for the good of their diocese and parish. An increasing number of lay men and women are devoting their professional skills on a full-time basis to the Church's efforts in education, social services, and other areas, or to the exercise of administrative responsibilities. Still others build up the Body of Christ by direct collaboration with the Church's pastoral ministry, especially in bringing Christ's love to those in the parish or community who have special needs. I rejoice with you at this great flowering of gifts in the service of the Church's mission.

At the same time we must ensure both in theory and in practice that these positive developments are always rooted in *the sound Catholic ecclesiology taught by the Council.* Otherwise we run the risk of "clericalizing" the laity or "laicizing" the clergy, and thus robbing both the clerical and lay states of their specific meaning and their complementarity. Both are indispensable to the "perfection of love," which is the common goal of all the faithful. We must therefore recognize and respect in these states of life a diversity that builds up the Body of Christ in unity.

Worship and Service

6. As lay men and women you can fulfill this great mission authentically and effectively only to the extent that you *hold fast to your faith,* in communion with the Body of Christ. You must therefore live in the conviction that there can be no separation between your faith and your life, and that apart from Christ you can do nothing (cf. Jn 15:5). Since union with God in Christ is the goal of all Christian living, *the laity are called to prayer:* personal prayer, family prayer, liturgical prayer. Generations of devout lay people have found great strength and joy in invoking the Blessed Virgin Mary, especially through her rosary, and in invoking the saints.

In particular, the laity must realize that they are *a people of worship called to service*. In the past I had occasion to emphasize this aspect of the life of the laity in the United States: "All the striving of the laity *to consecrate the secular field of activity to God* finds inspiration and magnificent confirmation in the Eucharistic Sacrifice. Participating in the Eucharist is only a small portion of the laity's week, but the total effectiveness of their lives and all Christian renewal depends on it: the primary and indispensable source of the true Christian spirit!" (*ad Limina* Discourse, July 9, 1983).

Challenges to the Laity

7. Every age poses *new challenges and new temptations* for the People of God on their pilgrimage, and our own is no exception. We face a growing *secularism* that tries to exclude God and religious truth from human affairs. We face an insidious *relativism* that undermines the absolute truth of Christ and the truths of faith, and tempts believers to think of them as merely one set of beliefs or opinions among others. We face a materialistic *consumerism* that offers superficially attractive but empty promises conferring material comfort at the price of inner emptiness. We face an alluring *hedonism* that offers a whole series of pleasures that will never satisfy the human heart. All these attitudes can influence our sense of good and evil at the very moment when social and scientific progress requires strong ethical guidance. Once alienated from Christian faith and practice by these and other deceptions, people often commit themselves to passing fads, or to bizarre beliefs that are either shallow or fanatical.

We have all seen how these attitudes have a profound influence on the way people think and act. It is precisely in this society that lay men and women like yourselves, all the Catholic laity, are called *to live the Beatitudes*, to become leaven, salt and light for the world, and sometimes a "sign of contradiction" that challenges and transforms that world according to the mind of Christ. No one is called to impose religious beliefs on others, but to give the strong example of a life of justice and service, resplendent with *the virtues of faith, hope and charity*.

On moral issues of fundamental importance, however, it is at times necessary to challenge publicly *the conscience of society*. Through her moral teaching the Church seeks to defend—for the benefit of all people—those basic human values that uphold the good which humanity seeks for itself and that protect the most fundamental human rights and spiritual aspirations of every person.

The greatest challenge to the conscience of society comes from your fidelity to your own Christian vocation. It is up to you the Catholic laity to *incarnate without ceasing the Gospel in society*—in American society. You are in the forefront of the struggle to protect authentic Christian values from the on-slaught of secularization. Your great contribution to the evangelization of your own society is made through your lives. Christ's message must live in you and in the way you live and in the way you refuse to live. At the same time, because your nation plays a role in the world far beyond its borders, you must be conscious of the impact of your Chris-tian lives on others. *Your lives must spread the fragrance of Christ's Gospel throughout the world.*

St. Paul launched a great challenge to the Christians of his time and today I repeat it to all the laity of America: "Conduct yourselves, then, in a way worthy of the gospel of Christ, so that, whether I come and see you or am absent, I may hear news of you, that you are standing firm in one spirit, with one mind, struggling together for the faith of the gospel, not intimidated in any way..." (Phil 1:27-28).

Mary—Model and Intercessor

8. Dear brothers and sisters, representatives of the mil-lions of faithful and dedicated Catholic laity of the United States: in bringing my reflections to a conclusion I cannot fail to mention the Blessed Virgin Mary who reveals the Church's mission in an unparalleled manner. She, more than any other creature, shows us that *the perfection of love* is the only goal that matters, that it alone is the measure of holi-ness and the way to perfect communion with the Father, the Son and the Holy Spirit. Her state in life was that of *a*

laywoman, and she is at the same time the Mother of God, the Mother of the Church and our Mother in the order of grace.

The Council concluded the Dogmatic Constitution on the Church with *an exhortation* on the Blessed Virgin. In doing so, the Council expressed the Church's ancient sentiments of love and devotion for Mary. Let us, especially during this Marian Year, make our own these sentiments, imploring her to intercede for us with her Son, for the glory of the Most Holy and Undivided Trinity (cf. *Lumen Gentium*, 69).

Christians Must
Witness to Christ

Homily at San Francisco Eucharist—Candlestick Park, September 18.

"Go...and make disciples of all nations."   (Mt 28:19)

"It was in Antioch that the disciples were called Christians for the first time."   (Acts 11:26)

Dear fellow Christians,
Dear Brothers and Sisters,

1. Today, here on the west coast of America, *in San Francisco*, we hear once again the words with which *Jesus sends the Apostles* into the world after his Resurrection. He hands on to them a mission. He sends them forth as he himself had been sent by the Father.

The Apostles' Mission

These words of Christ come at the end of his earthly *messianic mission*. In his Cross and Resurrection are found the basis for his "authority both in heaven and on earth" (Mt 28:18). This is *the authority of the Redeemer,* who through the blood of his Cross has ransomed the nations. In them he has established the beginning of a new creation, a new life in the Holy Spirit; in them he has planted *the seed of the Kingdom of God.* In the power of his authority, as he is leaving the earth and going to the Father, Christ says to his Apostles: *"Go...and make disciples of all nations.* Baptize them in the name of the Father, and of the Son, and of the Holy Spirit. Teach them to carry out everything I have commanded you. And know that I am with you always, until the end of time" (Mt 28:19-20).

2. The Acts of the Apostles describes *the beginning of this mission.* The point of departure was the Upper Room in Jerusalem. *From Jerusalem* the travels of the Apostles and of their first collaborators led them first to the neighboring countries and to the people who lived there. In today's

second reading, we hear that the witnesses of the Crucified and Risen Christ reached *Phoenicia, Cyprus and Antioch* (cf. Acts 11:19).

This occurred also as a result of the dispersion which began with the death of the deacon Stephen and *with the persecution of the disciples of Jesus*. We know that, at the stoning of Stephen, Saul of Tarsus was present as a persecutor. But the Acts of the Apostles later present him as Paul, after his conversion on the road to Damascus. Together with Barnabas, Paul worked for a whole year in Antioch, and there "they instructed many people." And it was precisely "in Antioch that the disciples were *called Christians* for the first time" (Acts 11:26).

Christian Identity

3. *What does it mean to be a Christian?*

It means accepting the testimony of the Apostles concerning the Crucified and Risen Christ. Indeed, it means *accepting Christ himself who works in the power of the Holy Spirit*. This acceptance is expressed in *Baptism*, the Sacrament in which we are born again of water and the Holy Spirit (cf. Jn 3:5). In this Sacrament, *Christ comes to meet us spiritually*. As St. Paul teaches, we are baptized into Christ's death. Together with him we die to sin, in order to rise with him, *to pass from the death of sin to life in God*, to the life of sanctifying grace. To new life!

Christians then are those who have been baptized. We are *those to whom Christ has come with the salvific power of his Paschal Mystery*. Those whose lives have been totally shaped by this salvific power. Indeed, Baptism gives us *an indelible sign*—called a character—with which we are marked throughout all our earthly life and beyond. This sign is with us when we die and when we find ourselves before the judgment of God. Even if in practice our lives are not Christian, this indelible sacramental sign of Baptism *remains with us for all eternity*.

Spiritual Progress

4. The readings of today's liturgy permit us *to respond still more fully* to the question: What does it mean to be a Christian?

In the book of the Prophet Isaiah we read about "the mountain of the Lord's house" (Is 2:2), raised above all things. The Prophet says: "All nations shall stream toward it; many peoples shall come and say: 'Come, *let us climb the Lord's mountain,* to the house of the God of Jacob, that he may instruct us in his ways, and we may walk in his paths.' For from Zion shall go forth instruction, and the word of the Lord from Jerusalem" (Is 2:2-3). Yes, *the word of the Lord did go forth from Jerusalem.* This word is the word of the Gospel. The word of the Cross and Resurrection. Christ charged his Apostles to go forth with this word to all the nations—to proclaim it and to baptize.

Through Baptism Christ comes to every person with the power of his Paschal Mystery. To accept Christ through Baptism, to receive new life in the Holy Spirit—this is what it means to become a Christian. In this way, through the centuries, individuals and entire nations have become Christian.

To be a Christian means to go up to the mountain to which Christ leads us. To enter into the temple of the living God that is formed in us and in our midst by the Holy Spirit. To be Christian means to continue to become Christian, learning from Christ *the ways of the Lord* so as to be able "to walk in his paths" (cf. Is 2:3). To be a Christian *means to become one every day,* ascending spiritually toward Christ and *following him.* In fact, as we recall, when Christ first called those who were to become his disciples, he said to them: "Follow me."

San Francisco's Heritage

5. "It was in Antioch that the disciples were called Christians for the first time." And it was more than two hundred years ago that *people in the San Francisco area* were called Christians for the first time. Since the arrival of the first settlers and the missionary efforts of Father Palou and

his companions, there have always been Christians in San Francisco—people of the most varied cultural backgrounds who have believed God's word, been baptized, and followed in the footsteps of the Lord.

Here is *a City built on hopes:* the hopes of Father Serra's Franciscan missionaries who came to preach the Good News, the hopes of pioneers who came to make their fortunes, the hopes of people who came here to seek peace, the hopes of those who still come to find refuge from violence, persecution or dire poverty. It is the city in which, some forty years ago, statesmen met to establish the United Nations Organization, an expression of our common hopes for a world without war, a world committed to justice and governed by fair laws.

But this city was built also with hard work and effort. Here the Church advanced from the little Mission Dolores to the establishment of the Archdiocese of San Francisco in 1853. It took effort and determination for the City and the Church to recover from the devastating effects of the severe earthquake and terrible fire in the spring of 1906. Yes, it takes great effort to move from initial enthusiasm to *something that will really last.* "There are in the end," St. Paul tells us, *"three things that last: faith, hope and love,* and the greatest of these is love" (1 Cor 13:13). It is precisely these virtues— faith and hope and love—that have directed and sustained all the efforts of the Church in San Francisco in the past, and that will sustain her well into the future.

"Devotion to Instruction"

6. "It was in Antioch that the disciples were *called Christians* for the first time." Here in San Francisco, and in every city and place, it is necessary for the followers of Jesus *to deepen their communion* with him so that they are not just Christians in name. The primary means the Church has always employed for this task is *a systematic catechesis.*

When Jesus sent his disciples forth on mission, he told them *to baptize and to teach.* Baptism alone is not sufficient. The initial faith and the new life in the Holy Spirit, which are received in Baptism, need *to advance to fullness.* After having begun to experience the mystery of Christ, his followers must develop their understanding of it. They must come to know better Jesus himself and the Kingdom which he proclaimed; they must discover God's promises in the Scriptures, and learn the requirements and demands of the Gospel.

In the Acts of the Apostles we are told that the members of the first Christian community in Jerusalem "devoted themselves to *the Apostles' instruction* and the *communal life,* to *the breaking of bread* and *the prayers''* (Acts 2:42). Here we have a model of the Church that can serve as a goal of all catechesis. For the Church needs continually to feed on God's word which comes to us from the Apostles, and she needs to celebrate the Eucharist, to be faithful to regular prayer and to bear witness to Christ in the ordinary life of the community.

The experience of history has proved the importance of a carefully programmed study of the whole of the Christian mystery. *''Teach them to carry out everything* I have commanded you,'' Jesus tells the Apostles (cf. Mt 28:20). There is no substitute for a *systematic presentation of all the essentials* of our Catholic faith, a presentation which can provide the basis for sound judgments about the problems of life and society, and which can prepare people to stand up for what they believe, with both humility and courage. As I stated in my Apostolic Exhortation on Catechesis: "Firm and well-thought-out convictions lead to courageous and upright action.... Authentic catechesis is always an orderly and systematic initiation into the revelation that God has given of himself to humanity in Christ Jesus, a revelation stored in the depths of the Church's memory and in Sacred Scripture, and constantly communicated from one generation to the next by a living, active *traditio'' (Catechesi Tradendae,* 22).

Identification with Christ

7. What is the purpose of catechesis? What does it mean, not only to be called Christians, but truly to be Christians? It means *being identified with Christ,* not only at Mass on Sunday—which is extremely important—but also in

all the other activities of life. In speaking about our relationship to him, Jesus himself said: "Remember what I told you: no slave is greater than his master. If they persecuted me, they will also persecute you. If they kept my word, they will also keep yours" (Jn 15:20).

To be identified with Christ means that we must live according to God's word. As the Lord told his first disciples: "You will live in my love *if you keep my commandments*, even as I have kept my Father's commandments and live in his love" (Jn 15:10). For this reason the Church never ceases to proclaim the whole of the Gospel message, whether it is popular or unpopular, convenient or inconvenient. And the Church is ever mindful of her great task to call people to conversion of mind and heart, just as Jesus did. The first words spoken by Jesus in the Gospel are these: "This is the time of fulfillment. The reign of God is at hand! *Reform your lives and believe in the Gospel*" (Mk 1:15).

Signs of Contradiction

8. Those who accept the grace of conversion and who live according to God's word find that, with God's grace, they begin to put on the mind and heart of Christ. They become increasingly identified with *Christ*, who is a *sign of contradiction*. It was Simeon who first foretold that the newborn Son of Mary would be for his own people a sign of contradiction. He tells the Virgin Mother: "This child is destined to be the downfall and the rise of many in Israel, *a sign that will be opposed*" (Lk 2:34). And so it happened. Jesus met with opposition in the message that he preached, and in the all-embracing love that he offered to everyone. Almost from the beginning of his public ministry, he was in fact "a sign that people opposed."

Simeon's words hold *true for every generation*. Christ remains today a sign of contradiction—a sign of contradiction in his Body, the Church. Therefore, it should not surprise us if, in our efforts to be faithful to Christ's teachings, we meet with criticism, ridicule or rejection. *"If you find that the world hates you,"* the Lord told the Twelve, *"know that it has hated me before you. If you belonged to the world, it would love you* as its own; the reason it hates you is that you do not belong to the world. But *I chose you out of the world"* (Jn 15:18-19).

These words of our loving Savior are true for us not only as individuals but *also as a community.* In fact, the witness to Christ of the entire Christian community has a greater impact than that of a single individual. How important, then, is the Gospel witness of every Christian community, but especially that most fundamental of them all, *the Christian family.* In the face of many common evils, the Christian family that truly lives the truth of the Gospel in love is most certainly a sign of contradiction; and at the same time it is a source of great hope for those who are eager to do good. Parishes, too, and dioceses, and all other Christian communities which "do not belong to the world," find themselves meeting opposition *precisely because they are faithful to Christ.* The mystery of the Cross of Christ is renewed in every generation of Christians.

Never Cease Proclaiming and Working

9. When Jesus Christ sent his Apostles throughout all the world, he ordered them to *"teach all the nations"* (cf. Mt 28:19-20).

The Gospel, and together with it the salvific power of Christ's Redemption, is addressed to every person in every nation. It is also addressed to *entire nations and peoples.* In his vision, the Prophet *Isaiah sees the peoples* who go up to the mountain of the house of the Lord, asking to be instructed in his ways and to walk in *his paths* (cf. Is 2:2-3). We too ask to walk in the paths of the living God, the Creator and Redeemer, the one God who lives in inscrutable unity as Father, Son and Holy Spirit.

Continuing to describe his vision, Isaiah says:

"He shall judge between the nations,
and impose terms on many peoples.
They shall beat their swords into plowshares
and their spears into pruning hooks;
One nation shall not raise the sword against another,
nor shall they train for *war* again" (Is 2:4).

How greatly we desire to see the future of humanity in the light of these Prophetic words! *How greatly we desire a world* in which *justice and peace* prevail! Can the Church, which has come forth from such a prophecy—the Church of the Gospel—ever cease to proclaim *the message of peace* on earth? Can she ever cease to work for the true progress of peoples? Can she ever cease to work for the true dignity of every human person?

To be Christian also means to proclaim *this message* untiringly in every generation, in our generation, at the end of the second millennium and at the threshold of the third!

"O house of Jacob, come,
let us walk in the light of the Lord!" Amen.

Grow Strong in the Faith

Address at Blessed Sacrament Cathedral—Detroit, September 18.

Praised be Jesus Christ!

Dear Archbishop Szoka,
Dear Cardinal Dearden,
My Brothers and Sisters,

1. I have been looking forward to this happy moment when in this Cathedral, the Mother of Church of the Archdiocese of Detroit, I would have the opportunity to express *my love for all of you in Christ*. It is indeed fitting that we greet one another here in this place of worship, in *this church dedicated to the Most Blessed Sacrament,* since it is the Eucharist above all that expresses and brings about our unity with Christ and with one another (cf. *Lumen Gentium,* 3, 11). As St. Paul writes, "Because the loaf of bread is one, we, many though we are, are one body, for we all partake of the one loaf" (1 Cor 10:17). In accordance with the whole life and tradition of the Church, the Eucharist unites the People of God with their Bishop in the unity of the Church (cf. St. Ignatius of Antioch, *Ad Phil.*).

This is the relationship that we are celebrating today: the deep reality of the Eucharist, the local Church and the Bishop in the oneness of the universal Church.

The Church Is a Communion

2. The Second Vatican Council refers to the Church as a *mystery*—a mystery of communion. This means that the Church is more than just a community or tradition with shared beliefs and practices, more than an organization with moral influence. Using the imagery of Scripture, the Council also speaks of the Church as a sheepfold, a cultivated field, and a building. The Church is Christ's Body, his Bride, and our Mother (cf. *Lumen Gentium,* 6-7).

We believe that our communion with Christ and with one another comes into being through *the outpouring of the Holy Spirit.* We believe too that the Holy Spirit makes it fruitful. The Council says that it is he, the Holy Spirit, who bestows upon the Church both "hierarchic and charismatic gifts" *(Lumen Gentium,* 4), and by special graces makes all the faithful "fit and ready to undertake various tasks and offices for the renewal and building up of the Church" *(ibid.,* 12). Established by Christ as *an instrument of Redemption,* the People of God are "a communion of life, love and truth" and "a most sure seed of unity, hope and salvation for the whole human race." In this way believers become the light of the world and the salt of the earth (cf. Mt 5:13-14; *Lumen Gentium,* 9).

Dear brothers and sisters: what great opportunities *your city and its suburbs and rural areas* give to the mission that is yours by Baptism: to build up the Body of Christ in unity by means of the gifts you have received (cf. Eph 4). Yours is a mission that unfolds amid the *social, cultural, political and economic forces* that shape the life of the great metropolis of Detroit—forces that also raise questions of fundamental importance for the future of humanity. By *personal conversion and holiness,* and by your daily witness to the Gospel in keeping with your state in life, each of you builds up the Body of Christ, and thus contributes to the further *humanization of the family of mankind,* without losing sight of *that Kingdom to come* which is not of this world and for which we yearn. As the Council also tells us, the Holy Spirit "constantly renews the Church and leads her to perfect union with her Spouse. For the Spirit and the bride both say to Jesus, the Lord: "Come!" (cf. Rev 22:17; *Lumen Gentium,* 4)

"I Come...to Strengthen You"

3. This year is the *fiftieth anniversary* of the designation of this building as your Cathedral. It has witnessed the great events and—more frequently—the great liturgical celebrations that mark your ecclesial life, as well as the daily worship of a parish community. I am very glad that it is so full this evening, *full of God's glory, full of God's praise.*

Within the context of the communion that we share, I come to you as *the Successor of St. Peter,* and therefore, as the Council reaffirms, as the Vicar of Christ and pastor of the whole Church, as shepherd of all Christ's flock. This is because in St. Peter the Lord set up *a lasting and visible source and foundation* of our unity in faith and in communion (cf. *Lumen Gentium*, 18, 22). Yet one has only to read about St. Peter in the Gospels to know that this ministry of his is *a great gift of God's grace* and not the result of any human merit. It is precisely at a moment that reveals St. Peter's human weakness, that is, the moment when Jesus foretells that Peter will deny him three times, that Jesus also adds: "I have prayed for you that your faith may never fail. You in turn must strengthen your brothers" (Lk 22:31-34). And so, dear brothers and sisters, relying on the help of God, I come here today *with the desire to strengthen you,* as together we continue our pilgrimage of faith to our heavenly home.

The Communion of Saints to which we belong embraces all those who have gone before us in faith on this pilgrimage. In particular, *Mary the Virgin Mother of God* is constantly with us on our journey. I commend all of you—the clergy, religious and laity of Detroit—to her, the spiritual Mother of humanity and the advocate of grace (cf. *Redemptoris Mater,* 35, 47). May she be for all of you "a sign of sure hope and solace" and "a model of faith, charity and perfect union with Christ" *(Lumen Gentium,* 63, 69).

To him, Jesus Christ, with the Father and the Holy Spirit, be glory for ever. Amen.

Bear Witness to Christ

Address to Polish Americans at Hamtramck, September 19.

"You are to be my witnesses...to the ends of the earth."
(Acts 1:8)

Dear Polish Brothers and Sisters of America,

1. In the course of my lengthy pilgrimage to the Church in the United States, God has led me to Detroit, the largest community of people of Polish origin after Chicago.

Right from the beginning I wish to tell you two things: first, as St. Paul would say, I have longed to come to you. I have greatly desired to be with you in this important moment, to give prominence to the solicitude of the Church, and my own personal apostolic solicitude for you, and to manifest publicly the natural bonds, the bonds of blood, origin, faith, culture and, to a certain extent also, of language and of love for our common mother, the homeland: your homeland or that of your parents or forebears.

And I wish also to extend our meeting today, which is necessarily limited by time and place, to all the United States, and in a certain sense to all of America. I see it as a meeting with the entire American Polonia, with every American man and woman whose origin is drawn from the old country on the Vistula, with every Pole whose destiny it is to live in this land.

I wish then to meet both those whose roots have been deeply set here for generations and those who, while their hearts are still filled with the scenery of the land of their birth, are seeking a new beginning, certainly not without difficulty. In saying this, I am well aware that I find myself before the largest part of the Polish emigration in the world, which constitutes a large part of the Church in the United States. Even today there are more than eight hundred Polish parishes.

"You are to be my witnesses...to the ends of the earth."

How can we not thank God then for this meeting and for our prayer together? How can we not thank those who have made it possible and those who have prepared this encounter? The American authorities and those of the American Polonia, the Bishops, priests, sisters, lay people, the various organizations.

Together with the host of this encounter, Archbishop Edmund Szoka, I wish to greet most cordially and to welcome all of you who are gathered here and all the guests who honor us with their presence. I cordially greet all those who are spiritually united with us.

I extend a word of cordial greetings to all our brothers and sisters from other Slavic nations, and in particular from the kindred Ukrainian community, who are present here in large number.

In Ukrainian:

I cordially greet the entire Ukrainian community of Detroit. You are close to my heart. As you solemnly celebrate the Millennium of Christianity in the Rus of Kiev and in the Ukraine, from the depths of my Slavic heart I bless all the sons and daughters of St. Vladimir and St. Olga, as well as all the faithful of the Church in the Ukraine and in the diaspora.

Polish-American Achievements

2. Meanwhile today, we wish to be closely united with the sons and daughters of Poland who live on this continent, with all who share or should share in the historical heritage of the same homeland and the same Church. In this way we find ourselves together before the homeland and the whole nation, before its history, its heritage, before its "yesterday" and its "today." And at the same time we find ourselves before all the heritage of Polonia in this vast and rich country which has received and continues to receive so many people from all continents, nations, races and languages; the country that became the homeland for your forebears is also yours.

If we recall the past, if we look attentively at our "today," we do so above all with thought and concern for the future. For, as it has been said: "the nation which lets itself be cut off from its tradition descends to the level of a tribe" (A. Słominski).

We recall briefly the first Poles who, according to the chronicles, came to North America in 1608, and settled in Jamestown, Virginia. And then those who in the second half of the eighteenth century gave the beginning to Polonia in Michigan.

The greatest wave of emigration took place, as is known, at the end of the last century and at the beginning of the present century. It was an economic emigration. There were enterprising, hard-working people, worthy people who in the homeland were unable to find food. They left a Poland which had been torn apart by partitions, and, as the latest arrivals, they were viewed in different ways. Most often they were uneducated. They brought with them no material riches, but they possessed two great values: an innate love of the faith and of the Polish spirit. Besides, many of them had left with the thought of returning after a time. They did not think that their descendants would put down stable roots in a new country and would collaborate fruitfully in its construction at the end of the second and beginning of the third millennium after Christ.

Their tears, suffering, difficulties, humiliations, wanderings and nostalgia are known and described. Yet it was they who built all that is until now, and will remain in the future, the glory and the patrimony of Polonia in North America.

First of all they created a whole network of parishes with monumental churches, schools, hospitals, houses of assistance, organizational structures, the press, publications. We recall here Fr. Leopold Moczygemba and his nearly hundred parishioners who, on Christmas Eve 1854, founded the first Polish parish and gave rise to the village of Panna Maria (the Virgin Mary) in Texas. And also those who in 1872 founded the first Polish parish in Detroit, dedicated to St. Albertus. With great emotion I journey spiritually as a pilgrim to these two places.

Moreover, these immigrants have produced a great number of priestly and religious vocations, and thousands of vocations of women religious, both to Polish Congregations and to others. There arose also the various new Polish Congregations of women. All this served to make the contribution of the immigrants to the development of religious life and to ecclesiastical structures a great and irreplaceable treasure for the Church in America.

The same spirit was deepened and developed by the different Catholic organizations—both by the older ones which have been more than one hundred years in existence, as well as by those which were established more recently. It is not possible to mention all of them here. However, I came to know of them in the course of earlier visits to the United States as Archbishop of Cracow and through their letters to me in Rome on different occasions.

This faithful dedication to the Church is closely tied to a love for Poland and everything associated with it. One has only to think of the volunteers for General Haller's army during the First World War; the financial support for independence activities before the year 1918, and in particular for the support of the Polish Committee in Paris; the enormous gifts and loans to Poland after it regained its independence and began to rise from destruction and ruin. Nor may we forget that this same generation of immigrants, by hard work and sacrifice, also secured a better life for their children and grandchildren.

Another page in the history of Polonia was written by Sts. Cyril and Methodius Seminary, established in Detroit and later transferred to Orchard Lake, which not long ago celebrated its centenary. This seminary grew out of a true love of the Church and out of an attachment to the Polish spirit. Using the language of the Second Vatican Council, we may say that it sought to read "the signs of the times" and to meet the needs of Polish immigration. It developed into a complete scientific and educational complex, from which more than three thousand priests for the service of Polish immigrants and approximately fifteen thousand immigrant leaders have come forth. It disseminates Polish culture and the Liturgy in the Polish language, and contributes to the preservation of awareness concerning the Polish origins of so many Americans. To the representatives of Orchard Lake who are here today I express gratitude for all that has been accomplished in the past; my hope is for a constant fidelity and a new responsiveness to the needs of today's Church and of Polonia as it exists in the world today.

Later history witnessed new events, new trials, and a new wave of emigrants.

As a result of the Second World War and its aftermath, many more Poles came to the United States. These emigrants were different than the first group in that they came with a higher level of culture, and with a different national and political consciousness that retained a strong solidarity with the homeland and the nation. A word of acknowledgment is due to the *Polish American Congress* for its many activities on behalf of the nation, and also to the *Catholic League* which provided great material aid to the Church in Poland after the war, and continues to provide that aid today. For this I wish to express the heartfelt gratitude of the Church in Poland as well as my own personal gratitude.

The most recent great undertaking of Polonia throughout the world, but especially of Polonia in the United States and of some American friends, is the *Foundation in the Vatican* and the Pilgrim House, the Center for Polish Christian Culture and the Documentation Center in Rome which that Foundation operates.

I know that efforts continue; for example, the establishment of Associations of Friends of the Foundation to ensure the continued activity and development of these Institutions. God will surely reward them.

And so, having touched only briefly on past history, we arrive at the present, and the tasks the present creates for Polonia and the Church.

The last wave of emigration, like those that preceded it, also becomes a "sign of the times" for today and a challenge. It calls us to reflection and action. Each emigration has brought with it a new richness as well as new problems. There have been and there continue to be cases of harmful divisions, even splits, which have impeded Polonia in the United States from playing the full role of which it is capable in both the religious and spiritual spheres and the social and political spheres.

The Polish Catholic Tradition

3. Thus there remains, always alive and very real, a process of integration that is twofold. It is integration in the sense of a growth in awareness and maturity in Polonia itself, and integration within the country which is now your home.

Dear brothers and sisters: the more you are aware of your identity, your spirituality, your history, and the Christian culture out of which your ancestors and parents grew, and you yourselves have grown, the more you will be able to serve your country, the more capable will you be of contributing to the common good of the United States.

Precisely out of concern for the common good, this country—in the face of a diversity of peoples, races and cultures unknown elsewhere—has sought integration in various ways. Theories include "nativism," the "melting pot" and others that proved incapable of giving results. Today there is talk of the ethnic principle, of "roots," since from these roots the full personality of the individual, the community and the nation arises.

The Church wishes to be at the service of such personal and social integration. I have spoken of this on numerous occasions and many documents of the Church address this issue. It is necessary to study them and put them into practice.

Today I wish to repeat once again the words of the poet: "There are so many strengths in the nation," and I wish to pray with him: "Make us feel the strength" (S. Wyspianski, "Liberation").

Our strength comes from faith, from God himself, and from our millenary heritage in which there resounds, in such a vibrant way, the Paschal Mystery of Christ: his Passion and Resurrection. This richness has been manifested and continues to be manifested in the love of ideals, of truth, of freedom—"ours and yours," in the love of peace, and in respect for the dignity of individuals and of nations.

In our own day there have been moments when these values have shone before the whole world with special brightness. Who among us, and not only us, can forget first the beatification and then the canonization of that son of

Polish soil and spiritual son of St. Francis, the humble priest St. Maximilian Mary Kolbe, who, in the midst of atrocities and the inhumanity of the concentration camp, exhibited once again before all of contemporary humanity that love unto the end!

These values, this richness, this inheritance were also manifested in a fuller way and acquired a new light during my three pilgrimages to the homeland. I dwell only on the saints and the blessed because they express most fully that which is partially in each of us individually and in all of us together. At the same time they are the most perfect models on our pilgrimage toward our final destiny in Christ.

There is Blessed Brother Albert Chmielowski, a patriot and artist, who wished to be all kindness in the face of Polish poverty and toward the needy; Blessed Raphael Kalinowski; Blessed Ursula Ledochowska; Blessed Caroline Kozka, a simple country girl who gave her life in defense of her dignity; finally, the last in order of time, Blessed Michael Koza, Bishop and martyr of Dachau.

But this inheritance, as a testimony of the Polish soul, has also been manifested in recent years in another form, when the millennial Christian Nation reclaimed its own dignity and legitimate rights.

Among other things, I spoke of this on the Polish seacoast, and much of what I said refers to the whole world, including the United States. There, on the Baltic, "the word 'solidarity' was spoken...in a new way that at the same time confirms its eternal content.... In the name of man's future and the future of humanity, it was necessary to say that word, 'solidarity.' Today it rolls like a wide wave over the face of the world, which realizes that we cannot live according to the principle of 'all against all,' but only according to another principle, 'all with all,' 'all for all.' Solidarity must take precedence over conflict. Only then can humanity survive, can each nation survive and develop within the great human family.... Solidarity means a way of existing, for example, of a nation, in its human variety, in unity, with respect for differences, for all the diversity that exists among people, and so, unity in variety, in plurality. All this is contained in the concept 'solidarity'" (Address in Gdynia, June 11, 1987).

4. With justifiable pride and gratitude we may turn to the great authors of our culture: to writers, poets, artists, politicians, to religious and spiritual guides, to all those who also in this land have pointed out new ways to the human spirit.

Tadeusz Kosciuszko, Kazimierz Pułaski, Włodzimierz Krzyżanowski, Ignacy Paderewski, Helena Modrzejewska, Artur Rubinstein, and the already mentioned Fr. Leopold Moczygemba, Fr. Jozef Dabrowski, founder of the Polish Seminary, Fr. Theodore Gieryk and Jan Barzynski, Fr. Witold Buhaczewski and so many others, without forgetting the authors and leaders alive today.

Polish—American Families

But along with them we remember too the unknown multitudes of mothers and fathers of families who, guided by their force of temperament and sense of faith, living an authentic Christian life and in fidelity to God and their human ideals, were able to mold those lofty ideas into the values that model and determine everyday living. In their daily lives they themselves lived those values, forged down through the centuries, and they succeeded in transmitting them in their families to each new generation. How many priests are there today who bear witness that they owe their priestly vocation in the first place to their saintly mothers.

Perhaps the most threatened institution in today's world is precisely the family. For that reason, the Church "wishes to offer guidance and support to those Christians and others who are trying to keep sacred and to foster the natural dignity of the married state and its superlative value" (*Gaudium et Spes*, 47).

The fundamental task of the family is to serve life, "transmitting by procreation the divine image from person to person" (*Familiaris Consortio*, 28).

Faithfulness to the family extends also to education. The Second Vatican Council teaches that "since parents have conferred life on their children, they have a most solemn obligation to educate their offspring. Hence, parents must be acknowledged as the first and foremost educators of their children" *(Gravissimum Educationis,* 3).

The family is the domestic Church. "You are to be my witness...."

Spiritual Guides of American Polonia

5. I now wish to address you, "servants of Christ and administrators of the mysteries of God" (1 Cor 4:1); you the priests, the pastors of Polonia. I have spoken at length about the priesthood during this present visit to the United States. In the context of the present meeting I wish to thank you for all the good that the American Polonia has received and continues to receive from your ministry. Remember that the Polish emigration is important for Poland, just as Poland is important for the emigration. From your awareness of and relationship to our common Christian heritage will depend, in great part, the bonds between your faithful and the Nation of which they are sons and daughters: bonds of faith, culture and language. Respect for and preservation of this heritage should constitute one of the fundamental principles of your pastoral care. How consoling it is that young people throughout the world are experiencing a growing interest in their past. Young people discover themselves as they search for the foundations of their own identity, its sources and roots, the first strata from which it proceeds.

I know that our young people living here are very much a part of this process, and that more and more they are willing to learn the history, the language and all the richness of the homeland from which their forebears came. They gladly say: "I am proud to be American." But they are no less proud of their origins, especially when they know more about them, because then they feel no complex. Help them in this learning and liberation. Then too, meet the spiritual needs of the most recent emigration. Do not lose heart. Do not be enclosed in the golden tower of prejudice, routine, pastoral minimalism and ease.

Do not diminish, do not reduce, do not close whatever serves the true well-being of the faithful, strengthens their spiritual relationship with the Savior and leads to genuine growth of the spirit.

Witnesses to Christ

6. Dear brothers and sisters: "You are to be my witnesses...to the ends of the earth." This announcement and call was addressed by Christ to the Apostles shortly before his Ascension. Before that, he said to them: "You will receive power when the Holy Spirit comes down on you" (Acts 1:8). That is, you are to be my witnesses when you receive the power of the Holy Spirit. We are witnesses of Christ in the power of the Holy Spirit.

The Holy Spirit is the beginning, the source, the foundation of Christian life in the new era of the history of salvation, in the time of the Church, in the time of mission, in the time of witness. May his power fill your hearts and minds and wills, to enable you to bear witness to Christ with your own witness and that of your forefathers, with the witness of the millenary Christian heritage of that Land that has the right and wishes to call you her sons and daughters.

This heritage is marked in a special way by the presence of the Blessed Virgin, the Mother of God, Mary blessed by God. She who "defends bright Czestochowa, and shines in the morning Gate!" Our Poet cried out to her: "Carry there my soul full of nostalgia!" Your hearts do not feel nostalgia, because you are already sons and daughters of this Land and citizens of this Country. Still, may Mary carry your souls toward everything that is good, beautiful, great; toward those values that make life worth living. This we ask of her, especially today. This we ask of her in the Marian Year.

Now I wish to bless all of you present, your families and dear ones, the children and young people, the sick, the old, those who are alone. I bless the priests, the deacons, the religious families of men and women, the seminarians, the parishes, the places of work and recreation. I bless the whole of Polonia in North America.

The Ministry of the Word, the Altar and Charity

Address to 2,900 permanent deacons and their wives from throughout the U.S.—Ford Auditorium, Detroit, September 19.

Dear Brothers in the service of our Lord,
Dear Wives and Collaborators of these men ordained to the Permanent Diaconate,

1. I greet you in the love of our Lord Jesus Christ, in whom, as St. Paul tells us, God has chosen us, redeemed us and adopted us as his children (cf. Eph 1:3ff.). Together with St. Paul, and together with you today, *I praise our heavenly Father* for these wonderful gifts of grace.

It is a special joy for me to meet with you because you represent *a great and visible sign of the working of the Holy Spirit* in the wake of the Second Vatican Council, which provided for the restoration of the permanent diaconate in the Church. The wisdom of that provision is evident in your presence in such numbers today and in the fruitfulness of your ministries. With the whole Church, *I give thanks to God for the call you have received and for your generous response.* For the majority of you who are married, this response has been made possible by the love and support and collaboration of your wives. It is a great encouragement to know that in the United States over the past two decades almost eight thousand permanent deacons have been ordained for the service of the Gospel.

It is above all *the call to service* that I wish to celebrate with you today. In speaking of deacons, the *Vatican Council* said that "strengthened by sacramental grace, in communion with the Bishop and his presbyterate, they serve the People of God in the service of the liturgy, the word, and charity" *(Lumen Gentium,* 29). Reflecting further on this description, my predecessor *Paul VI* was in agreement with the Council that "the permanent diaconate should be restored ...as a driving force for the Church's service *(diaconia)* toward the local Christian communities, and as a sign or sacrament of the Lord Christ himself, who 'came not to be served but to serve'" *(Ad Pascendum,* August 15, 1972, Introduction). These words recall *the ancient tradition of the Church* as ex-

282

pressed by the early Fathers such as Ignatius of Antioch, who says that deacons are "ministers of the mysteries of Jesus Christ...ministers of the Church of God" *(Ad Trallianos,* II, 3). You, dear brothers, belong to the life of the Church that goes back to saintly deacons, like Lawrence, and before him to Stephen and his companions, whom the Acts of the Apostles considers "deeply spiritual and prudent" (Acts 6:3).

This is at the very heart of the diaconate to which you have been called: *to be a servant of the mysteries of Christ and, at one and the same time, to be a servant of your brothers and sisters.* That these two dimensions are inseparably joined together in one reality shows the important nature of the ministry which is yours by ordination.

Diaconia

2. How are we to understand the mysteries of Christ of which you are ministers? A profound description is given to us by St. Paul in the reading we heard a few moments ago. *The central mystery* is this: God the Father's plan of glory to bring *all things in the heavens and on earth into one under the headship of Christ,* his beloved Son. It is for this that all the baptized are predestined, chosen, redeemed and sealed with the Holy Spirit. This plan of God is at the center of our lives and the life of the world.

At the same time, if service to this redemptive plan is the mission of all the baptized, what is the specific dimension of your service as deacons? The Second Vatican Council explains that *a sacramental grace conferred through the imposition of hands* enables you to carry out your service of the word, the altar and charity with a special effectiveness (cf. *Ad Gentes,* 16). *The service of the deacon is the Church's service sacramentalized.* Yours is not just one ministry among others, but it is truly meant to be, as Paul VI described it, a "driving force" for the Church's *diaconia.* By your ordination you are configured to Christ in his servant role. You are also meant to be *living signs of the servanthood of his Church.*

Threefold Ministry

3. If we keep in mind the deep spiritual nature of this *diaconia*, then we can better appreciate *the interrelation of the three areas of ministry* traditionally associated with the diaconate, that is, the ministry of the word, the ministry of the altar, and the ministry of charity. Depending on the circumstances, one or another of these may receive particular emphasis in an individual deacon's work, but these three ministries are *inseparably joined together as one in the service of God's redemptive plan.* This is so because the word of God inevitably leads us to the Eucharistic worship of God at the altar; in turn, this worship leads us to a new way of living which expresses itself in acts of charity.

This charity is both *love of God and love of neighbor.* As the First Letter of John teaches us, "One who has no love for the brother he has seen cannot love the God he has not seen...whoever loves God must also love his brother" (1 Jn 4:20-21). By the same token, acts of charity which are not rooted in the word of God and in worship cannot bear lasting fruit. *"Apart from me,"* Jesus says, *"you can do nothing"* (Jn 15:5). The ministry of charity is confirmed on every page of the Gospel; it demands *a constant and radical conversion of heart.* We have a forceful example of this in the Gospel of Matthew proclaimed earlier. We are told: "offer no resistance to injury." We are commanded: "love your enemies and pray for your persecutors." All of this is an essential part of the ministry of charity.

The Service of Charity

4. Certainly *today's world* is not lacking in opportunities for such a ministry, whether in the form of the simplest acts of charity or the most heroic witness to the radical demands of the Gospel. All around us many of our brothers and sisters live in either *spiritual or material poverty* or both. So many of the world's people are *oppressed by injustice* and the denial of their fundamental human rights. Still others are troubled or suffer from a *loss of faith* in God, or are tempted to give up hope.

In the midst of the human condition it is a great source of satisfaction to learn that so many permanent deacons in the United States are involved in *direct service to the needy:* to the ill, the abused and battered, the young and old, the dying and bereaved, the deaf, blind and disabled, those who have known suffering in their marriages, the homeless, victims of substance abuse, prisoners, refugees, street people, the rural poor, the victims of racial and ethnic discrimination, and many others. As Christ tells us, "as often as you did it for one of my least brothers, you did it for me" (Mt 25:40).

At the same time, the Second Vatican Council reminds us that the ministry of charity at the service of God's redemptive plan also obliges us to be *a positive influence for change* in the world in which we live, that is, to be a leaven— to be the soul of human society—so that society may be renewed by Christ and transformed into the family of God (cf. *Gaudium et Spes,* 40ff.). The *"temporal order"* includes marriage and the family, the world of culture, economic and social life, the trades and professions, political institutions, the solidarity of peoples, and issues of justice and peace (cf. *Apostolicam Actuositatem* 7; *Gaudium et Spes,* 46ff.). The task is seldom an easy one. The truth about ourselves and the world, revealed in the Gospel, is not always what the world wants to hear. *Gospel truth often contradicts commonly accepted thinking,* as we see so clearly today with regard to evils such as racism, contraception, abortion, and euthanasia—to name just a few.

The Unique Role of the Permanent Deacon

5. Taking an active part in society belongs to the baptismal mission of every Christian in accordance with his or her state in life, but the permanent deacon has *a special witness to give.* The sacramental grace of his ordination is meant to strengthen him and to make his efforts fruitful, even as his *secular occupation* gives him entry into the temporal sphere in a way that is normally not appropriate for other members of the clergy. At the same time, the fact that he is an ordained minister of the Church brings a special dimension to his efforts in the eyes of those with whom he lives and works.

Equally important is the contribution that a married deacon makes to *the transformation of family life*. He and his wife, having entered into a communion of life, are called to help and serve each other (cf. *Gaudium et Spes*, 48). So intimate is their partnership and unity in the sacrament of marriage, that the Church fittingly requires the wife's consent before her husband can be ordained a permanent deacon (Can. 1031, §2). As the current guidelines for the permanent diaconate in the United States point out, the *nurturing and deepening of mutual, sacrificial love between husband and wife* constitute perhaps the most significant involvement of a deacon's wife in her husband's public ministry in the Church *(Guidelines,* NCCB, p. 110). Today especially, this is no small service.

In particular, the deacon and his wife must be a living example of *fidelity and indissolubility in Christian marriage* before a world which is in dire need of such signs. By facing *in a spirit of faith* the challenges of married life and the demands of daily living, they strengthen the family life not only of the Church community but of the whole of society. They also show how the obligations of family, work and ministry can be harmonized in the *service of the Church's mission*. Deacons and their wives and children can be a great encouragement to all others who are working to promote family life.

Mention must also be made of another kind of family, namely the *parish,* which is the usual setting in which the vast majority of deacons fulfill the mandate of their ordination "to help the Bishop and his presbyterate." The parish provides *an ecclesial context* for your ministry and serves as a reminder that your labors are not carried out in isolation, but in communion with the Bishop, his priests and all those who in varying degrees share in the public ministry of the Church. Permanent deacons have an obligation to respect the office of the priest and to cooperate conscientiously and generously with him and with the parish staff. The deacon also has a right to be accepted and fully recognized by them and by all for what he is: an ordained minister of the word, the altar and charity.

Continue to Grow

6. Given the dignity and importance of the permanent diaconate, what is expected of you? As Christians we must not be ashamed to speak of *the qualities of a servant* to which all believers must aspire, and especially deacons, whose ordination rite describes them as "servants of all." A deacon must be known for *fidelity, integrity and obedience,* and so it is that fidelity to Christ, moral integrity and obedience to the Bishop must mark your lives, as the ordination rite makes clear (cf. also *Ad Pascendum,* Introduction). In that rite *the Church* also *expresses her hopes and expectations* for you when she prays:

"Lord, may they excel in every virtue: in love…concern…unassuming authority…self-discipline and in holiness of life. May their conduct exemplify your commandments and lead your people to imitate their purity of life. May they remain strong and steadfast in Christ, giving to the world the witness of a pure conscience. May they…imitate your Son, who came, not to be served but to serve."

Dear brothers, this prayer commits you to *lifelong spiritual formation* so that you may grow and persevere in rendering a service that is truly edifying to the People of God. You who are wives of permanent deacons, being close collaborators in their ministry, are likewise challenged with them *to grow in the knowledge and love of Jesus Christ.* And this of course means growth in prayer—personal prayer, family prayer, liturgical prayer.

Since deacons are ministers of the word, the Second Vatican Council invites you to *constant reading and diligent study of the Sacred Scriptures,* lest—if you are a preacher—you become an empty one for failing to hear the word in your own heart (cf. *Dei Verbum,* 25). In your lives as deacons you are called to *hear* and *guard* and *do* the word of God, in order to be able to proclaim it worthily. To preach to God's people is an honor that entails a serious preparation and a real commitment to holiness of life.

As ministers of the altar you must be *steeped in the spirit of the liturgy,* and be convinced above all that it is "the summit toward which the activity of the Church is directed and at the same time the source from which all her power flows" (cf. *Sacrosanctum Concilium,* 10). You are called to discharge your office with the dignity and reverence befitting the liturgy, which the Council powerfully describes as being "above all the worship of the divine majesty" *(ibid.,* 33). I join you in thanking *all those who devote themselves to your training,* both before and after your ordination, through programs of spiritual, theological, and liturgical formation.

Servants and Friends

7. "Sing a new song unto the Lord! Let your song be sung from mountains high!" *Sing to him as servants,* but *also* sing *as friends* of Christ, who has made known to you all that he has heard from the Father. It was not you who chose him, but he who *chose you, to go forth and bear fruit*—fruit that will last. This you do by loving one another (cf. Jn 15:15ff.). By the standards of this world, servanthood is despised, but in the wisdom and providence of God it is *the mystery through which Christ redeems the world. And you are ministers of that mystery,* heralds of that Gospel. You can be sure that one day you will hear the Lord saying to each of you: "Well done, good and faithful servant, enter into the joy of your Lord" (cf. Mt 25:21).

Dear brothers and sisters, as one who strives to be "the servant of the servants of God," I cannot take leave of you until, together, we turn to Mary, as she continues to proclaim: "I am the servant of the Lord" (Lk 1:38). And in *the example of her servanthood* we see the perfect model of our own call to the discipleship of our Lord Jesus Christ and to the service of his Church.

Global Solidarity

Address on Social Justice Issues—Hart Plaza, Detroit, September 19.

Dear Friends,

1. I am happy that, almost at the end of my second pastoral visit to the United States, I am able to address such a large number of people in this well-known industrial city of Detroit. I greet all of you most cordially: Christian leaders and leaders of other religions; civic leaders from the federal, state and municipal governments; people of various races and ethnic backgrounds, fellow Catholics; Christian and non-Christian brothers and sisters; men and women of good will!

I feel that I must *thank the Lord our God* for this wonderful occasion. Detroit is a place where work, hard daily work—that privilege, duty and vocation of the human person (cf. *Laborem Exercens*, 9)—is a truly distinctive characteristic of urban life. This is indeed *a city of workers*, and very many of you here—men and women, younger people and older people, immigrants and native-born Americans—earn your living and that of your families in and around Detroit through the work of your hands, your mind, indeed your whole person. And many of you suffer from the problems that not infrequently characterize the work situation in an industrial urban setting.

This is why I would like to make reference to a subject which, as you are well aware, is close to my heart. This subject is *social progress and human development* in relation to the requirements of justice and to the building of a lasting peace, both in the United States and throughout the world.

Of course, dear friends, dear people of Detroit and this whole area, it is *you* I have primarily in mind in dealing with such a subject—you who have been created in the image and likeness of God, you who have been redeemed by the blood of the Savior, you who are children of God and brothers and sisters of Christ, you who for all of these reasons possess an incomparable dignity. But in looking at you, assembled here in Hart Plaza, *I see beyond you all the people of this country and the peoples of the whole world*. I see all the men and women who, like you, are confronted anew every day with the

289

obligation and the challenge to provide for their livelihood and for the livelihood of their family through their own work. Work means any activity, whether manual or intellectual, whatever its nature or whatever its circumstances, by which a human being earns his or her daily bread and contributes to science and progress, civilization and culture (cf. *Laborem Exercens*, 1). Human work is such a fundamental dimension of human existence, that one cannot speak about it without touching upon all its aspects.

The Church's Social Teaching

2. *Social progress and human development are the concern of all.* They are of particular concern to *the Church.* From the very beginning of her existence in time, the Church has endeavored to fathom the total richness of the message which Jesus Christ proclaimed both by his words and his actions. Sent by the Father to assume our humanity and bring salvation to all, the Lord Jesus provided us with the key to understanding our humanity. He taught us about our origin and destiny, which are in God. He taught us the transcendent value of all human life and the supreme dignity of the human person, created in the image and likeness of God (cf. Gen 1:27). He taught us that human life is fulfilled in knowing and loving God, and in loving our neighbor according to the measure of God's love for us. He invited us to follow him, to become his disciples. He summoned us to be converted in our hearts by entering into the mystery of his Passion, Death and Resurrection. He revealed that we are God's partners in bringing creation to fulfillment. And he now fashions us into a chosen people, a communion of faith with a commitment to his Kingdom.

In fidelity to Christ, the Church has endeavored *to bring his message to bear on all aspects of life,* throughout the changing circumstances in the course of the centuries, bringing out from the heritage of the Gospel "both the new and the old" (Mt 13:52). New challenges affecting the life of every person individually and of society as a whole have presented themselves at every turn on the path of humanity through history. In trying to meet those challenges, the

People of God have always turned to the message of Jesus, in order to discover the principles and the values that would ensure solutions in consonance with the dignity and destiny of the human person. Throughout her history, the Church has listened to the words of Scripture and has sought to put them into practice in the midst of different political, economic and social circumstances. This has been a truly common effort. Individual Christians have struggled to be faithful to the Gospel inspiration in their daily lives; centers of learning have contributed their specialized studies; groups and associations have addressed issues of particular concern; communities have developed practical initiatives; individual Bishops and Episcopal Conferences have provided guidance; and the Magisterium of the Church has made pronouncements and issued documents. In a continuous interaction the Church has thus developed a tradition of thought and practical guidelines that are called *the social teaching of the Church*. This social teaching has recently been expressed in documents of the Second Vatican Council and in writings of the Popes, who have systematically addressed the rapid changes in contemporary society.

Also today, the various categories of the People of God—according to their respective calling—continue to address the social problems in their various historical and cultural settings.

The Challenge of Domestic Poverty

3. Today, dear friends, on this last day of my second extended visit to the United States of America, I would urge you to continue *your personal involvement in that never-ending quest for justice and peace*. Under the guidance and inspiration of the Church's Magisterium—which is that of the Pope and of the Bishops in union with him—each one of you is called to make a contribution. Each one of you must be instrumental in promoting a social order that respects the dignity of the human person and serves the common good. Each one of you has an irreplaceable contribution to make to secure a social order of justice in peace. In your country today, participation at different levels of economic, social and political life

has greatly intensified the awareness of the unique dignity of every human person and at the same time reinforced your sense of responsibility to yourselves and to others. As Christians you find in your faith *a deep motivation for* your *social responsibility and involvement.* Do not let this hour pass without renewing your commitment to action for social justice and peace. Turn to the Gospel of Jesus Christ to strengthen your resolve to become instruments for the common good! Learn from the Gospel that you have been entrusted with the justice and peace of God! We are not merely the builders of justice according to the standards of this world, but we are the bearers of the life of God, who is himself justice and peace! Let your endeavors to achieve justice and peace in all the spheres of your lives be a manifestation of God's love!

In a setting similar to this one some eight years ago in New York's Yankee Stadium, I proclaimed *the Gospel challenge contained in the parable of the rich man and Lazarus.* You are all familiar with this marvelous lesson in social responsibility which Jesus left us. Knowing your faith and your openness to challenge, I now ask you today: What have you done with that parable? How many times in the past eight years have you turned to that parable to find inspiration for your Christian lives? Or have you put it aside thinking that it was no longer relevant to you or to the situations in your country?

4. In any modern society, no matter how advanced, there will always be situations, some old and some new, that summon your Christian sense of justice to action. Our Lord has said: "The poor you will always have with you" (Mt 26:11). *You must therefore discover the poor in your midst.* There is poverty among you when the old and the weak are neglected and their standard of living constantly declines. There is poverty when illness takes away the wage earner from a family. There is material need and suffering in those areas or groups where unemployment risks are becoming endemic. There is poverty in the future of those that cannot enjoy the benefits of basic education.

Some modern technological developments contain the potential for new hardships and injustice and must therefore be part of our concern. The introduction of robotics, the rapid development of communications, the necessary adaptation of industrial plants, the need to introduce new skills in management—these are but some of the factors that, if not analyzed carefully or tested as to their social cost, may produce undue hardship for many, either temporarily or more permanently.

These are just a few *areas where our social responsibility is challenged.* Others include the situation of marriage and family life and the factors that threaten their underlying values; the respect for the sacredness of unborn human life; the situation of newly arrived immigrants; open or disguised expressions of discrimination based on "race, origin, color, culture, sex or religion" *(Octogesima Adveniens,* 16). To the degree that its social conscience is sensitive, every community will discover where instances of injustice or threats to peace still exist or are potentially present.

But the very attempt to look at some of the challenges in the domestic scene brings us to another important consideration regarding progress and human development. I am referring to *the international dimension.*

International Solidarity

5. Without implying in any way that domestic or national problems do not exist any more—and they most certainly do—it becomes ever more evident that such local or national problems, and their solutions, are fundamentally linked with realities that transcend the boundaries of countries. Not only do decisions taken by one nation affect other regions of the world, but the solution to many domestic problems can no longer be found except on an international, and even, a worldwide level. All major problems that concern the life of the human person in society have become world problems. Any decision that is envisaged in the political, economic or social sphere must be considered within the context of its worldwide repercussions. What now most deeply affects any debate on social progress and human development is the *fact of worldwide interdependence.*

Already twenty years ago, in 1967, Pope Paul VI wrote, at the very beginning of his Encyclical Letter "On the Development of Peoples" *(Populorum Progressio):* "Today the principal fact that we must all recognize is that the social question has become worldwide" (n. 3). In following years, *this affirmation of Paul VI was further vindicated by a succession of events.* There was the emergence on the political scene of peoples who, after centuries of colonial domination and dependence, demanded ever more forcefully their rightful place among the nations and in international decision-making. A worldwide economic crisis brought home the fact that there exists an increasingly interdependent economy. The continuing existence of millions of people who suffer hunger or malnutrition and the growing realization that the natural resources are limited make clear that humanity forms a single whole. Pollution of air and water threatens more and more the delicate balance of the biosphere on which present and future generations depend, and makes us realize that we all share a common ecological environment. Instant communication has linked finance and trade in worldwide dependence.

The poorer nations of the world are inclined to view this interdependence as a continuing pattern of economic domination by the more developed countries, while the latter sometimes view interdependence as the opening up of new opportunities for commerce and export. Interdependence clearly demands that relations between nations be seen in this new context and that *the social question needs an appropriate ethic.* Nobody can say anymore: "Let others be concerned with the rest of the world!" The world is each one of us!

6. When I addressed the participants of the Sixty-eighth Session of the International Labor Organization, on June 15, 1982, I was able to state: "There is a common good which can no longer be confined to a more or less satisfactory compromise between sectional demands or between purely economic requirements. New ethical choices are necessary; *a new world conscience must be created;* each of us without denying his origin and the roots of his family, his people and his nation, or the obligations arising therefrom, must regard himself as a member of this great family, the world community.... This means that the worldwide common good requires *a new solidarity without frontiers"* (n. 10).

The Church's social teaching sees this new solidarity as a consequence of our faith. It is the attitude, in the international reality, of those who heed the Lord's commandment: "Love one another as I have loved you" (Jn 15:12). It is the consequence of our faith in the mystery of Creation: that God has created every human person in his own image and likeness. Every human being is endowed with the same fundamental and inalienable dignity. Every individual is called to acknowledge this fundamental equality within the unity of the human family. Everyone is invited to respect the common destiny of everyone else in God. Everyone is asked to accept that the goods of the earth are given by God to all for the benefit of all.

For the disciple of Christ, *solidarity is a moral duty stemming from the spiritual union of all human beings,* who share a common origin, a common dignity, and a common destiny. In creating us to live in society, in a close network of relations with each other, and in calling us through redemption to share the life of the Savior not merely as individuals but as members of a pilgrim people, *God himself has created our basic interdependence and called us to solidarity with all.* This teaching is formulated in an incomparably effective manner in *the parable of the Good Samaritan,* who took care of the man who was left half dead along the road from Jerusalem to Jericho. We all travel that road and are tempted to pass by on the other side. Referring to the Samaritan, who was moved by compassion, Jesus told his listeners: "Go, and do the same." Today, Jesus repeats to all of us when we travel the road of our common humanity: "Go, and do the same" (cf. Lk 10:37).

The United Nations

7. In speaking to you about social progress and human development, I feel impelled to stress the international dimension because of the objective need to promote *a new worldwide solidarity.*

There is also another reason why I am especially mindful today of the larger international scene. You know well that the Bishop of Rome and the Holy See follow closely *interna-*

tional activities, and therefore have a *special interest in the work of the United Nations Organization* in New York. I would have liked very much to visit once again its headquarters, as I did in 1979, and as Pope Paul VI did in 1965. I regret that I am not able to accept at this time the kind invitation which the Secretary General of the United Nations has extended to me for a new visit. The interest of the Catholic Church in this international organization is linked to the importance of the issues that it treats and to the reasons for which it was founded. To work for *the establishment and maintenance of a just and lasting peace is a goal that deserves support and collaboration.* This is in fact why the United Nations Organization was created in the first place, in that bright daylight which followed the long drawn-out night of the Second World War. I pray that despite its inevitable shortcomings it will be able *to fulfill ever more effectively its unique role of service to the world,* a service that the world truly needs.

The United Nations deals with *disarmament and arms control*—the control of nuclear weapons in the first place, but also biological, chemical and conventional weapons. Its patient, painstaking, and sometimes even frustrating dedication to this cause of paramount importance for the world and all its people is recognized and appreciated as being an incentive and support for the bilateral negotiations by the superpowers for arms reduction. Here it is indeed a question that must be addressed with an unfailing commitment, extreme lucidity and a clear sense of the value of human life and the integrity of creation.

The United Nations is also concerned with many of the *other conditions for true peace.* It is fitting here to reflect on some of them in relation to the international dimension of the social question.

In the first place, I would like to single out the concern for *human rights.* You remember, I am sure, that the United Nations adopted, more than forty years ago, the Universal Declaration of Human Rights. The basic inspiration of this important document was the recognition that the way toward a peaceful and just world must necessarily pass through the respect for each human being, through the definition and recognition of the basic human rights, and through the respect for the inalienable rights of individuals and of the communities of peoples. The adoption of the Universal Declaration was followed over the years by many Declarations and Conventions on extremely important aspects of human rights, in favor of women, of children, of handicapped persons, of equality between races, and especially the two international covenants on economic, social and cultural rights and on civil and political rights, together with an optional protocol. In 1981, the General Assembly also adopted a solemn Declaration against every form of religious intolerance. The United Nations must also be given proper credit for having set up the Commission for Human Rights as a monitoring organ to follow carefully the positive and negative developments in this important field. The *commitment* of the United Nations *to human rights* goes hand in hand with its commitment *to peace*. Experience has taught that disrespect or lack of respect for human rights, oppression of the weak, discrimination because of sex, color, origin, race or religion create conflict and jeopardize peace. Here again, what concerns human beings in any one place affects all human beings everywhere.

Through the different specialized institutions and programs, the United Nations develops its *commitment to a more just and equitable international society*. This work and commitment include the struggle against diseases and illiteracy; action undertaken for the advancement of women; protecting the rights of children and the handicapped; the development of international law; the peaceful use of atomic energy; the protection and preservation of famous monuments which belong to the cultural patrimony of humanity; the defense of the environment; the struggle against hunger, malnutrition and underdevelopment; and the defense of the homeless.

Respect for Other Nations

8. The existence and activities of the United Nations Organization, its achievements and also its failures, underline in a dramatic way *the need for reinforcing international authority* at the service of the global common good. It is

already a sign of great progress that the importance of global social issues and the need for effectively promoting peace are becoming more universally recognized. It is also *a sign of hope* that an international organization, formed by the great majority of states, tries, within the limited means at its disposal, and notwithstanding internal and external difficulties, to increase the awareness of worldwide problems and their appropriate solutions.

It is also a marvelous challenge for all the peoples and nations of the world—now that every day we become more aware of our interdependence—to be called upon by the urgent demands of a new solidarity that knows no frontiers. Now that we move toward the threshold of the third millennium of Christianity, we are given the unique chance, for the first time in human history, *to make a decisive contribution to the building up of a true world community.* The awareness that we are linked in common destiny is becoming stronger; the efforts to reach that goal are being multiplied by men and women of goodwill in a diversity of activities—political as well as economic, cultural as well as social. People in all walks of life and nations and governments alike are being challenged in the name of our common humanity, in the name of the rights of every human being and in the name of the rights of every nation.

In order to succeed and give the correct answer to the many demands that the *de facto* interdependence of all nations makes upon the sense of solidarity of all, we must create a just balance between the constraints put by interdependence upon the nations and the call for effective solidarity addressed to all the nations. In the life of every nation, social progress and human development are ensured by the respect given to the rights of the human person. The human person's very existence in dignity and his or her rightful participation in the life of the community are safeguarded by the deep respect that every person entertains for the dignity and the rights of every fellow human being. In the same way, respect for the rights of peoples and nations must safeguard the existence in liberty of every nation and thus make possible its rightful and effective participation in all aspects of international life. Without this, it would be impossible to speak about solidarity. In order to be capable of global solidarity, *nations must* first of all *respect the human rights of their citizens* and in turn be recognized by their people as the expression of their sovereignty; secondly *nations must respect the full rights of their fellow nations* and know that also their rights as a nation will not be disavowed.

America's Responsibility

9. Dear friends, America is a very powerful country. The amount and quality of your achievements are staggering. By virtue of your unique position, as citizens of this nation, *you are placed before a choice and you must choose.* You may choose to close in on yourselves, to enjoy the fruits of your own form of progress and to try to forget about the rest of the world. Or, as you become more and more aware of your gifts and your capacity to serve, you may choose to live up to the responsibilities that your own history and accomplishments place on your shoulders. By choosing this latter course, you acknowledge *interdependence,* and opt for *solidarity.* This, dear friends, is truly *a human vocation, a Christian vocation,* and for you as Americans it is *a worthy national vocation.*

10. In drawing attention to the need for an ever greater social consciousness in our day, I also wish to draw attention to *the need for prayer.* Prayer is the deepest inspiration and dynamism of all social consciousness. In speaking to the Bishops of America in 1983, I stated: "It is indeed in prayer that a social consciousness is nurtured and at the same time evaluated. It is in prayer that the Bishop, together with his people, ponders *the need and exigencies of Christian service....* Through prayer the Church realizes the full import of Christ's words: 'This is how all will know you for my disciples: your love for one another' (Jn 13:35). It is in prayer that the Church understands the many implications of the fact that justice and mercy are among 'the weightier matters of the law' (Mt 23:23). Through prayer, the struggle for justice finds its proper motivation and encouragement, and discovers and maintains truly effective means" (*Ad Limina Address,* December 3, 1983).

Finally to you, the Catholic people of Detroit and all this area, I repeat the words with which Paul VI concluded his message to the Call to Action Conference that was held eleven years ago in this very City of Detroit: "In the tradition of the Church, any call to action is first of all a call to prayer. And so you are summoned to prayer, and above all to a greater sharing in Christ's Eucharistic Sacrifice.... It is in the Eucharist that you find the true Christian spirit that will enable you to go out and act in Christ's name." And for all of you dear friends, people of every religion, race and ethnic group, I ask God's help so that you may be *ever more aware of global interdependence* and *ever more sensitive to human solidarity.*

Workers in the Vineyard

Homily at the Detroit Eucharist—the Pontiac Silverdome, September 19.

"Conduct yourselves in a way worthy of the gospel of Christ." (Phil 1:27)

Dear Brothers and Sisters in Christ,

1. The Apostle Paul addresses this appeal to the Christians of Philippi. And today *the Church's liturgy repeats this appeal* to all who believe in Christ. As my visit to your country comes to an end, it is my special joy this evening to reflect on those words with you, the people of the Church in Detroit, as well as visitors from elsewhere in Michigan, from nearby Canada and from other areas.

From the humble beginnings of the foundation of Detroit in the year 1701, *the proclamation of God's word* in this region has continued unbroken, despite hardships and setbacks, and has reached a level of maturity and a fruitfulness unimagined by the early missionaries. Many years separate us from the first celebration of the Eucharist by the priests who accompanied Cadillac, the founder of Detroit, and yet we know that our communion this evening in the Body and Blood of Christ also links us with them and with *all who have gone before us in faith.*

With you, I give thanks to God for the courage, dedication and perseverance of the many clergy, religious and laity who worked so hard during all these years, first to share their faith with the Native Americans of this area, and then *to preserve and spread the faith* among those of almost every race and nation who settled here. I also give thanks with you for the intrepid Catholic faith of so many of your parents and grandparents who came to Michigan in order to find liberty and in order to build a better life for themselves and especially for you, their children and grandchildren. Whatever may be the path by which you have received the gift of your Catholic faith, it is due in some measure to those who have gone before you here. *Their voices are joined to that of St. Paul* when he says to us: "Conduct yourselves in a way worthy of the gospel of Christ."

An Image of God's Kingdom

2. We read this exhortation this evening in the light of the Gospel *parable of the workers* sent by the owner of an estate into his vineyard, after he has agreed with them on the daily wage. Our Lord often taught through parables like this one. By using images from daily life, he led his hearers to insights about the Kingdom or Reign of God. Using parables, he was able to raise their minds and hearts *from what is seen to what is unseen*. When we remember that the things of this world already bear *the imprint of God's Kingdom*, it is not surprising that the imagery of the parables is so well suited to the Gospel message.

On the one hand, the vineyard of which Jesus speaks is an earthly reality, as is the work to be done in it. On the other hand, *the vineyard is an image of the Kingdom of God.* This Kingdom is described in the Gospels as the "vineyard of the Lord."

3. Let us reflect for a moment on the first of these realities—*the earthly vineyard*—as a workplace, as the place where you and I must *earn our daily bread*. As I said in the Encyclical *Laborem Exercens:* "Man must work, both because the Creator has commanded it and because of his own humanity, which requires work in order to be maintained and developed. Man must work out of regard for others, especially his own family, but also for the society he belongs to, the country of which he is a child, and the whole human family of which he is a member, since he is the heir to the work of generations and at the same time a sharer in building the future of those who will come after him in the succession of history" (*Laborem Exercens,* 16).

Accordingly, *the Church considers it her task to focus attention on the dignity and rights of workers,* to condemn violations of that dignity and those rights, and to provide guidance for authentic human progress (cf. *Laborem Exercens,* 1). The Church's goal is to uplift ever more the family of mankind in the light of Christ's word and by its power.

Central to the Church's teaching is the conviction that *people are more important than things;* that work is "for man" and not man "for work"; that the person is both the subject and purpose of all work and cannot be reduced to a mere instrument of production; that *the person is to be valued for what he or she is* rather than for what he or she owns (cf. *Laborem Exercens*, 6, 12; *Gaudium et Spes*, 35). This last truth in particular reminds us that the only gift we can offer God that is truly worthy of him is the gift of ourselves, as we discover in the message of today's Gospel parable.

4. That message, as I mentioned, has to do with *a spiritual reality,* the Kingdom of God, toward which Jesus seeks to raise the minds and hearts of his listeners. He begins today's parable with the words: "The reign of God is like the case of the owner of an estate who went out at dawn to hire workmen for his vineyard" (Mt 20:1). That our Lord is speaking about *more than just human work and wages* should be clear from the owner's actions and the ensuing conflict between him and some of the workers. It is not that the owner refuses to honor the agreement about wages. The dispute arises because he gives the same pay to everybody, whether the person worked all day or only part of the day. Each receives the sum which had been agreed upon. Thus the owner of the estate shows *generosity to the latecomers,* to the indignation of those who had worked all day. To them this generosity seems to be an injustice. And what response does the owner give? "I am free," he says, "to do as I please with my money, am I not? Or are you envious because I am generous?" (Mt 20:15)

In this parable we find one of those seeming contradictions, those *paradoxes,* that appear in the Gospel. It arises from the fact that the parable is describing *two different standards.* One is the standard by which justice is measured by things. The other standard belongs to the Kingdom of God, in which the way of measuring is not the just distribution of things but *the giving of a gift,* and, ultimately, the greatest gift of all—*the gift of self.*

The Gift of God Himself

5. The owner of the estate pays the workers according to the value of their work, that is, the sum of one denarius. But in the Kingdom of God the pay or wages is *God himself.* This is what Jesus is trying to teach. When it comes to salvation

in the Kingdom of God, it is not a question of just wages but of *the undeserved generosity of God,* who gives himself as the supreme gift to each and every person who shares in divine life through Sanctifying Grace.

Such a recompense or reward *cannot be measured in material terms.* When a person gives the gift of self, even in human relations, the gift cannot be measured in quantity. The gift is one and undivided because the giver is one and undivided.

How can we receive such a gift? We look to St. Paul for an answer. His words in the Letter to the Philippians are fascinating: "I firmly trust and anticipate that I shall never be put to shame for my hopes.... Christ will be exalted through me, whether I live or die. For, to me, 'life' means Christ; hence dying is so much gain" (Phil 1:20-21).

With these words of St. Paul we find ourselves at the very heart of that standard of measurement which belongs to the Kingdom of heaven. When we receive a gift, *we must respond with a gift.* We can only respond to the gift of God in Jesus Christ—his Cross and Resurrection—in the way that Paul responded—with *the gift of ourselves.* All that Paul is, is contained in this gift of self: both his life and his death. The gift of a person's life cannot be valued merely in terms of the number of hours spent in an earthly vineyard.

St. Paul, and everyone like him, realizes that one can *never match or equal the value of God's gift of himself to us.* The only measure that applies is the measure of love. And love's measure, as St. Bernard says, is *to love without measure (De Diligendo Deo,* I, 1). This makes it possible for the last to be first, and the first last (cf. Mt 20:16).

The Woman of "Great Love"

6. There is another episode in the Gospel of Luke, when Jesus says to one of the pharisees who is scandalized at *the behavior of a woman known to be a sinner:* "Her many sins are forgiven—because of her great love" (Lk 7:47). We do well to reflect upon the love in the heart of this woman, who washed the Lord's feet with her tears and wiped them with her hair. We can imagine the bitter sorrow that led her to

such an extravagant gesture. Yet *by giving herself humbly to God*, she discovered the far greater and undeserved gift of which we have spoken, namely, *God's gift of himself to her.* Through this exchange of gifts, the woman found herself once again, only now she was healed and restored. "Your sins are forgiven," Jesus says to her, "...go in peace" (v. 48).

For us too, sinners that we are, it is all too easy to squander our love, to use it in the wrong way. And like the pharisee, we do not easily understand *the power of love to transform*. Only in the Life, Death and Resurrection of Christ do we come to see that love is the measure of all things in the Kingdom of God, because "God is love" (1 Jn 4:8). We can fully experience love in this life *only through faith and repentance.*

We Are in the World to Bring It to Christ

7. "Conduct yourselves in a way worthy of the gospel of Christ." As Christians we *live and work in this world,* which is symbolized by the vineyard, but at the same time we are *called to work in the vineyard of the Lord.* We live this visible earthly life and at the same time the life of the Kingdom of God, which is the ultimate destiny and vocation of every person. How then are we to conduct ourselves worthily *in regard to these two realities?*

In the *Credo of the People of God* proclaimed by my predecessor Paul VI, we find an answer to that question—an answer that reflects *the faith of the Church* in the light of the Second Vatican Council, particularly the *Pastoral Constitution on the Church in the Modern World:*

> We confess that the Kingdom of God...is not of this world...and that its growth cannot be confused with the progress of civilization, science or technology. The true growth of the Kingdom of God consists in an ever deeper knowledge of the unfathomable riches of Christ; in an ever stronger hope in eternal blessings, in an ever more fervent response to the love of God.... But this same love also leads the Church to show constant concern for the true temporal welfare of people.... Although the Church does not cease to remind her children that

here they have no lasting city, she also urges them to contribute—according to their vocation and means—to the welfare of this their earthly home...and to devote themselves to helping the poorest and neediest of their brothers and sisters. This intense solicitude of the Church...for the needs of people, their joys and hopes, their griefs and labors, is nothing other than her great desire to be present with them in order to illuminate them with the light of Christ and gather them into one in him who alone is their Savior *(Credo of the People of God,* June 30, 1968).

Dear brothers and sisters, these words tell us what is meant by *conduct worthy of the Gospel of Christ*—that Gospel which we have heard and believed, and are called to live every day. And today *in this Eucharistic Sacrifice we offer our work, our activities, our whole lives to the Father* through his Son, Jesus Christ. We call upon God to accept the gift of ourselves.

> 8. "The Lord is just in all his ways
>   and holy in all his works.
>   The Lord is near to all who call upon him,
>   to all who call upon him in truth" (Ps 144[145]:17-18).

In the first reading, the prophet Isaiah speaks in the name of the Lord, who in the Gospel parable is symbolized by the owner of the vineyard. The Lord says: "My thoughts are not your thoughts, nor are your ways my ways.... As high as the heavens are above the earth, so high are my ways above your ways and my thoughts above your thoughts" (Is 55:8-9).

And so, my brothers and sisters, "Conduct yourselves in a way worthy of the gospel of Christ," that is to say, *measure the things of this world by the standard of the Kingdom of God.*

Not the other way around!
Not the other way around!
"Seek the Lord while he may be found,
call to him while he is near" (Is 55:6).
He is near! The Lord is near!
The Kingdom of God is within us. Amen.

The Human Person—
God's Greatest Blessing

Farewell to the people of America—Detroit Metropolitan Airport, September 19.

Mr. Vice President,
Dear Friends, dear People of America,

1. Once again God has given me the joy of making a pastoral visit to your country—the United States of America. I am filled with *gratitude to him and to you.* I thank the Vice-President for his presence here today, and I thank all of you from my heart for the kindness and warm hospitality that I have received everywhere.

Expressions of Gratitude

I cannot leave without expressing my thanks *to all those who worked so hard* to make this visit possible. In particular I thank my brother Bishops and all their collaborators, who for many months have planned and organized all the details of the last ten days. My gratitude goes to all those who provided *security* and ensured such excellent *public order.* I thank all those who have worked to make this visit above all a time of *fruitful evangelization* and *prayerful celebration of our unity in faith and love.*

I am also grateful to the people of *other Churches and creeds* and to *all Americans* of good will who have accompanied me, in person or through the media, as I traveled from city to city. A particular word of thanks goes to *the men and women of the media* for their constant and diligent assistance in bringing my message to the people, and in helping me to reach millions of those with whom otherwise I would have had no contact. Most importantly, I am grateful to *all those who supported me by their prayers,* especially the elderly and the sick, who are so dear to the heart of Jesus Christ.

As I leave, I express my gratitude to God also for what he is accomplishing in your midst. With the words of St. Paul, I too can say with confident assurance "that *he who has begun the good work in you will carry it through to comple-*

tion, right up to the day of Christ Jesus" (Phil 1:6-7). And so I am confident too that America will be ever more conscious of her responsibility for justice and peace in the world. As a nation that has received so much, she is called to continued generosity and service toward others.

America's Greatest Beauty

2. As I go, I take with me vivid memories of a dynamic nation, a warm and welcoming people, a Church abundantly blessed with a rich blend of cultural traditions. I depart with admiration for the ecumenical spirit that breathes strongly throughout this land, for the genuine enthusiasm of your young people, and for the hopeful aspirations of your most recent immigrants. I take with me an unforgettable memory of *a country that God has richly blessed from the beginning until now.*

America the beautiful! So you sing in one of your national songs. Yes, America, you are beautiful indeed, and blessed in so many ways:

—In your majestic mountains and fertile plains;

—In the goodness and sacrifice hidden in your teeming cities and expanding suburbs;

—In your genius for invention and for splendid progress;

—In the power that you use for service and in the wealth that you share with others;

—In what you give to your own, and in what you do for others beyond your borders;

—In how you serve, and in how you keep alive the flame of hope in many hearts;

—In your quest for excellence and in your desire to right all wrongs.

Yes, America, all this belongs to you. But *your greatest beauty and your richest blessing is found in the human person:* in each man, woman and child, in every immigrant, in every native-born son and daughter.

The Ultimate Test of America's Greatness

3. For this reason, America, your deepest identity and truest character as a nation are revealed in the position you take toward the human person. *The ultimate test of your greatness is the way you treat every human being, but especially the weakest and most defenseless ones.*

The best traditions of your land presume respect for those who cannot defend themselves. If you want equal justice for all, and true freedom and lasting peace, then, America, defend life! All the great causes that are yours today will have meaning only *to the extent that you guarantee the right to life and protect the human person.*

— Feeding the poor and welcoming refugees;
— Reinforcing the social fabric of this nation;
— Promoting the true advancement of women;
— Securing the rights of minorities;
— Pursuing disarmament, while guaranteeing legitimate defense:

all this will succeed only if respect for life and its protection by the law is granted to every human being *from conception until natural death.*

Every human person—no matter how vulnerable or helpless, no matter how young or how old, no matter how healthy, handicapped or sick, no matter how useful or productive for society—is a being of inestimable worth created in the image and likeness of God. This is the dignity of America, the reason she exists, the condition for her survival—yes, the ultimate test of her greatness: to respect every human person, especially the weakest and most defenseless ones, those as yet unborn.

With these sentiments of love and hope for America, I now say goodbye in words that I spoke once before: "Today, therefore, my final prayer is this: that God will bless America, so that she may increasingly become—and truly be, and long remain—'One Nation, *under God,* indivisible. With liberty and justice for all'" (October 7, 1979).

May God bless you all.

God bless America!

APPENDIX

Diálogo con Cristo

"Quitáos las sandalias de vuestros pies, que *el lugar que pisáis es sagrado.*" (Ex. 3:5)

1. Estas palabras de Dios marcaron, para Moisés, el comienzo de una nueva manera de vivir. La tierra que pisaba era santa, ya que estaba ante *la imponente presencia del Todopoderoso.* Y en esa tierra santa, oyó una voz que le llamaba a servir al Pueblo de Dios en una misión especial. Desde entonces, la vida de Moisés cambió radicalmente. A partir de ese momento puso su vida a disposición del Dios de Abraham, de Isaac y de Jacob. Ya su vida no le pertenecía. Sería el cabecilla del Pueblo Escogido al conducirlo de Egipto en busca de libertad, hacia la Tierra Prometida. Al encontrarse con Dios, en el suelo sagrado, quien le hablaba y daba órdenes de servicio, Moisés llegó a entenderse a si mismo y se entregó más profundamente a Dios y a su pueblo. *La misión de Moisés comenzó bajo la señal de la santidad de Dios.*

Queridos hermanos y hermanas en el Señor: es para mí motivo de profunda alegría estar con vosotros hoy, en esta histórica *Catedral de San Fernando,* el santuario más antiguo de los Estados Unidos. Es con inmensa gratitud a Dios que me encuentro con vosotros que os estáis preparando para servirle al Señor como sacerdotes y religiosos, vosotros que de una manera particular y notable han escuchado, como Moisés, la voz de Dios llamándoos a la *"tierra santa" de una vocación especial dentro de la Iglesia.* Vosotros habéis permanecido ante la imponente presencia del Señor y habéis escuchado como os llamaba, a cada uno por su nombre. Y escuchándole su voz habéis comenzado jubilosos vuestra formación para el sacerdocio o para una vida religiosa, con discernimiento piadoso.

Toda la Vida Diálogo de Amor

2. Una vocación en la Iglesia, desde el punto de vista humano, *comienza con un descubrimiento,* al encontrarse una perla valiosísima. Descubrís a Jesús: su persona, su mensaje, su llamada. En el Evangelio que oímos hoy, meditamos en la

llamada que Jesús le hizo a sus primeros discípulos. Lo primero que Andrés hizo después de hablar con Jesús, fue buscar a su hermano Simón y decirle: *"Hemos encontrado al Mesías!"* Luego Felipe, de manera parecida, buscó a Natanael y le dijo: *"Hemos encontrado al que Moisés, en la Ley, mencionaba—los profetas también—Jesús,* al hijo de José, de Nazaret" (cf. Jn 1:35-51).

Después del descubrimiento inicial, comienza un diálogo en oraciones, un diálogo entre Jesús y el llamado, *un diálogo que va más allá de las palabras* y que se expresa en el amor.

Las *preguntas* son importantes componentes de este diálogo. Por ejemplo, en el relato de la llamada de los apóstoles, en el Evangelio, se nos cuenta que "cuando Jesús se volvió y notó que le seguían, les preguntó: *"¿Qué buscáis?"* Ellos le dijeron, "'Rabbi' (que quiere decir maestro), '¿dónde te alojas?' *'Venid y ved'* les contestó" (Jn 1:38-39).

Lo que comienza como un descubrimiento de Jesús se convierte en un mayor entendimiento y compromiso a través de *un piadoso proceso de preguntas y de discernimiento.* En este proceso se purifican nuestros motivos. Enfrentamos preguntas puntudas como son "¿qué buscas?" E incluso nos preguntamos acerca de Jesús, como lo hizo Natanael: *"¿Cómo es que me conoces?"* (Jn 1:48) Solo después de haberlo pensado, dentro del silencio y candor de nuestros corazones, es que comenzamos a convencernos de la verdadera llamada del Señor.

Sin embargo, aún entonces, el proceso de discernimiento no se ha concluído. Jesús nos dice, como se lo dijo a Natanael: *"Verás cosas más grandes que esas"* (Jn 1:50). A lo largo de nuestras vidas, después de habernos consagrado y permanentemente comprometido y después de comenzar a prestar un servicio activo al Señor, necesitamos aún más el diálogo en la oración para que profundice de contínuo nuestra sabiduría y el amor de nuestro Señor Jesucristo.

Queridos estudiantes para el sacerdocio y candidatos para la vida religiosa: Vosotros os encontráis haciendo *una enorme fila, con otras personas que se han entregado totalmente* por causa del Reino de Dios, que han participado del Sacrificio del Señor y entrado en su victoria Pascual. Durante generaciones, sacerdotes y religiosos generosos, que han servido a la Iglesia, en el estado de Texas, han llegado como emigrantes, o en calidad de misioneros, de otras tierras. Deseo dar las gracias a Dios por la contribución de éstos a la Iglesia aquí. A la vez alabo al Señor por vosotros todos y por el creciente número de vocaciones nativas, fervientemente rogándoles que sigan en aumento.

Como todos los que os han presidido, tendréis pruebas. Vuestra fidelidad se asegurará solamente cuando invoquéis la fortaleza de Jesús, solo cuando dependáis de su gracia. Pero si Cristo es el centro de nuestras vidas, por quien vivís y morís, entonces vuestro servicio generoso por vuestros hermanos y hermanas no conocerán los límites. Amaréis a quienes es difícil amar, y *enriqueceréis el mundo con el Evangelio* de Jesucristo.

La Vocación Sacerdotal

3. Quisiera hablarle ahora *a los seminaristas*. Queridos hermanos en Cristo: en calidad de hombres en preparación para la ordenación sacerdotal, que sóis, os es importante *entender con claridad la vocación* para la cual os sentís llamados con el fin de que la fidelidad a ella durante toda la vida sea una promesa madura y fielmente guardada. Vuestras vidas en el sacerdocio os unirá a la Eucaristía más estrechamente. Seréis ministros de los misterios de Dios; estaréis dispuestos a predicar y a enseñar en nombre de la Iglesia.

La Eucaristía es la razón principal de la ordenación sacerdotal. Como lo dije en mi carta del Jueves Santo, de 1.980: "Por medio de nuestra ordenación, estamos los sacerdotes unidos de manera particular y excepcional a la Eucaristía. De cierto modo somos *fruto* y existimos *para* la Eucaristía" (no. 2). Ningún otro trabajo que hagamos como sacerdotes tiene tanta importancia. La celebración de la Eucaristía es la forma en que servimos mejor a nuestros hermanos y hermanas en el mundo, porque es la fuente y centro del dinamismo en sus vidas cristianas.

Qué tan crucial es, entonces, tanto para nuestra felicidad como para llevar un ministerio productivo, el que *cultivemos un profundo amor por la Eucaristía.* Durante vuestros días de seminaristas, el estudio a fondo de la teología y de la naturaleza del misterio de la Eucaristía y un conocimiento preciso de las normas litúrgicas, os prepararán bien para sobrellevar plenamente, una consciente y activa participación de la comunidad en la liturgia. El futuro sacerdote está llamado a profesar, de acuerdo con el Concilio Vaticano II, que "los sacramentos, al igual que cualquier otro ministerio de la Iglesia y cualquier otro trabajo de apostolado, están estrechamente ligados a la Sagrada Eucaristía y se dirigen a la misma. La Sagrada Eucaristía contiene la mayor salud espiritual de la Iglesia, es decir, Cristo mismo" (*Presbyterorum Ordinis*, 5).

La tarea de predicar el evangelio es de suprema importancia en el sacerdocio. Como dice San Pablo "la fe viene a través de la predicación y lo que se oye es la palabra de Cristo" (Rom 10:17), la formación del seminarista debe estar dirigida a una profunda comprensión de la palabra de Dios, tal como la vive y la proclama la Iglesia. Recuerdo siempre las palabras del profeta Jeremías: "cuando oí tus palabras, las devoré; ellas se convirtieron en el gozo y la felicidad de mi corazón porque llevaba tu nombre, oh Señor" (Jer 15:16).

En orden a obtener fruto de vuestra predicación en las vidas de aquellos a quien servís, debéis nutrir en vuestra mente y en vuestro corazón una adhesión interna y real al magisterio de la Iglesia. Por ello, tal como el Concilio os recordaba, "la tarea de los sacerdotes no es enseñar su propia sabiduría, sino la palabra de Dios y compulsar urgentemente a todas las gentes hacia la conversión y la santidad" (*Presbyterorum Ordinis*, 4).

El sacerdote necesita saber las condiciones reales de la vida de quienes ellos sirven y debe vivir entre ellos como un verdadero hermano en Cristo. El no puede separarse jamás de la comunidad. Sin embargo, hay un sentido en el cual, como el apóstol Pablo—en las palabras de la Escritura— "debe separarse para proclamar la palabra de Dios" (Rom 1:1). En su identidad sacerdotal recibe el encargo de un servicio especial—un servicio único—al Cuerpo de Cristo. Por esta razón, el Concilio Vaticano II lo expresa de la siguiente manera: por su vocación y ordenación, los sacerdotes del nuevo testamento son separados en un cierto sentido del medio del pueblo de Dios. Sin embargo, ello no quiere decir que deban separarse de este pueblo y de los hombres, sino que deben dedicarse totalmente al trabajo al cual el Señor los ha elegido. Ellos no pueden ser ministros de Cristo a menos de ser testigos y dispensadores de la vida venidera (*Ibid.*, 3).

Cada uno de vosotros está llamado a abrazar, libremente, la vida de celibato en nombre de Cristo y de su Reino, en orden a llegar a ser un "hombre para los demás." Si el celibato se modela sobre el generoso amor divino y humano de Jesús, hacia su Padre y hacia todos los hombres, mujeres y niños, entonces vuestro celibato significará un realce de vuestra vida, una mayor proximidad al pueblo de Dios, un anhelo a darnos sin reserva. Abrazando el celibato en el contexto del sacerdocio, os estáis comprometiendo vosotros mismos a un amor más profundo y universal. Por encima de todo, el celibato significa el don de vosotros mismos a Dios. Será la respuesta en Cristo y en la Iglesia a los dones de la creación y la redención. Será vuestra participación, en la muerte y resurrección de Jesús, al más profundo nivel de libertad humana y generosidad. Humanamente hablando este sacrificio es difícil debido a nuestra debilidad humana; sin oración es imposible. Requiere disciplina y esfuerzo así como perseverancia en el amor por vuestra parte. Pero en vuestro don de celibato a Cristo y a su Iglesia, el mundo será capaz de ver el significado de la gracia del Señor y el poder de su misterio pascual. Esta victoria debe estar siempre visible en vuestro gozo.

El Concilio señala la diferencia esencial entre el sacerdocio de los ordenados y el de todos los bautizados y prescribe una formación sacerdotal en los seminarios, la cual es diferente a las otras formas de formación (cf. *Lumen Gentium*, 10; *Optatam Totius*, 4). En el centro de esta diferencia esencial está la verdad que Jesús confió a los doce para proclamar el Evangelio con autoridad, celebrar la Eucaristía, perdonar los pecados y atender el cuidado pastoral de la comunidad. Esta autoridad, conferida para un propósito específico y a través de la ordenación, es participada por todos los sucesores de los apóstoles y sus colaboradores en la ordenación sacerdotal. Es conferido como un ministerio particular de servicio a ser llevado a cabo, en imitación del Hijo del Hombre que vino a servir. El ministerio del sacerdote ordenado es esencial a la vida y desarrollo de la Iglesia; es un servicio esencial para el resto de la Iglesia. Es evidente que todos aquellos que se están preparando para este ministerio específico, *tendrán especiales necesidades y exigencias* que difieren de aquellas del resto de la comunidad.

Todos los miembros de la Iglesia están compulsados a participar en su misión por razón del bautismo y la confirmación. Los sacerdotes deben asistir y estimular a los otros en el servicio al Evangelio, siendo ellos mismos fieles en su ministerio sacerdotal en la Iglesia. "Por consiguiente, ya sea en la oración y la adoración, predicando la palabra, celebrando el servicio eucarístico y la administración de los otros sacramentos, o ya sea realizando cualquiera de los otros trabajos de su ministerio para las gentes, los sacerdotes contribuyen a la extensión de la gloria de Dios, tanto como al desarrollo de la vida divina en su pueblo" (*Presbyterorum Ordinis,* 2).

La Vocación Religiosa

4. Y ahora me dirijo a vosotros, mis hermanos y hermanas que se están preparando para la vida religiosa: El vuestro es un gran y específico don del amor de Dios. A cada uno de vosotros, al igual que a los primeros discípulos, Jesús ha dicho: "Ven y sígueme" (Jn 1:39). No existe fuerza o coacción por parte de Cristo, sino una invitación extendida simple y personalmente a venir y permanecer en su casa, a estar en su presencia, y con El, alabar a su Padre, en unidad del Espíritu Santo.

Una vocación religiosa es un don, libremente otorgado y libremente recibido. Es una profunda expresión del amor de Dios por vosotros y por vuestra parte requiere un cambio, un total amor por Cristo. De esta manera, la vida entera de un religioso se dirige a estrechar los lazos de amor que inicialmente se forjaron en el sacramento del bautismo. Estáis llamados a esta consagración religiosa a través de la profesión de los consejos evangélicos de castidad, pobreza, y obediencia (cf. Can. 573 secciones 1-2).

Durante vuestros años de preparación, la Iglesia está ansiosa en que recibáis una formación que os prepare para vivir vuestra consagración religiosa con fidelidad y gozo, una formación que sea a la vez profundamente humana y cristiana, una formación que os ayudará a aceptar aún más generosamente las exigencias radicales del Evangelio y a convertiros en un testimonio público de las mismas. Vuestra vida significará una confiada y convincente afirmación de que Jesús es "el camino, la verdad y la vida" (Jn 14:6).

Pero debéis desarrollar primero y ante todo, el hábito de la disciplina y de la oración, que para vosotros son más fundamentales que cualquier servicio que realicéis. A este respecto, el Concilio Vaticano II dijo que los religiosos deberían "buscar, ante todo, a Dios en todas las cosas" y "combinar la contemplación con el amor apostólico" (*Perfectae Caritatis*, 5). Esta no es una tarea fácil, porque la oración tiene muchas dimensiones y formas. Es personal y comunitaria, litúrgica y privada. Profundiza nuestra unión con Dios y alimenta nuestro amor apostólico. Se necesita un clima de silencio, al igual que un estilo de vida personal que sea simple y dispuesto al sacrificio.

La vida litúrgica de la comunidad influye notoriamente en la oración de todos sus miembros. La Eucaristía será siempre la fuente y la culminación de vuestras vidas en Cristo. Es el sacramento por el cual la alabanza de vuestra entera existencia es presentada a Dios en unión con Cristo (cf. Can. 607:51).

La Eucaristía es el punto en el cual la ofrenda de vuestra castidad, pobreza y obediencia se hacen una con el sacrificio de Cristo.

En vuestra consagración religiosa, el sacramento de la Penitencia es un constante recordatorio de la llamada de Jesús a la conversión y a la renovación de la vida. Precisamente porque estáis llamados por vuestra profesión religiosa a ser testigos de la santidad de Dios, debéis ayudar al Pueblo de Dios a nunca perder el sentido del pecado. Para ser auténtico al seguir a Cristo en la perfección de la caridad, debéis ser los primeros en reconocer el pecado en vuestro corazón, en arrepentiros y en glorificar la gracia y la misericordia de Dios. La conversión es un proceso de toda la vida que requiere de un amor arrepentido. El sacramento de la

Penitencia es el sacramento en el cual nuestra debilidad se encuentra con la santidad de Dios en la misericordia de Cristo.

De mil maneras la Iglesia os llamará al servicio de su misión por el Reino de Dios. Ella necesita vuestros talentos, vuestra disponibilidad de ir y venir de acuerdo a las necesidades del momento, las cuales son a menudo las necesidades de los pobres. Ella necesita vuestra colaboración en la causa de la fe y la justicia. Ella necesita vuestro trabajo y todo lo que podáis hacer por el Evangelio.

Pero, sobre todo, la Iglesia necesita lo que sóis; ella os necesita, a vosotros hombres y mujeres consagrados a Dios, viviendo en unión con Cristo y con su Iglesia, buscando la perfección del amor. ¿Por qué? Por la santidad de Dios! Queridos hermanos y hermanas, lo que hacéis es importante, pero lo que sóis lo es mucho más. Es más importante para el mundo, para la Iglesia y para Cristo.

En María, la madre de Cristo y de la Iglesia, comprenderéis la identidad de vuestras propias vidas. Ella mostró durante toda su vida el sentido de los consejos evangélicos a los cuales vuestra consagración religiosa está dirigida. Las palabras al ángel: "Yo soy la esclava del Señor. Hágase en mí según tu palabra" (Lucas 1:38), demuestra la obediente y total sumisión que requiere nuestra consagración a Dios expresada en nuestros votos.

La Missión del Laico

5. Por supuesto, *el llamado a la santidad,* es un llamado UNIVERSAL. Todos los miembros de la Iglesia, sin excepción, están llamados por Dios a crecer en santidad personal y a compartir la misión de la Iglesia. Una conciencia más clara de esta verdad ha sido uno de los frutos del Concilio Vaticano II. Y ha ayudado a fomentar un conocimiento mayor *del papel del láico* en la construcción del Reino, así como también una colaboración más cercana de los láicos con el clero y los religiosos. Como personas que se preparan para el sacerdocio y la vida religiosa, será vuestro privilegio ayudar a explorar aún en formas más efectivas de colaboración en el futuro. Pero incluso más importante es que esta-

réis en posición de animar a los láicos a cumplir *esta misión que es exclusivamente suya* en esas situaciones y lugares, en los cuales la Iglesia puede ser la sal de la tierra, sólo a través de ellos.

El Concilio habló claramente sobre su misión especial. Entre otras cosas, dijo: "el laicado, por su vocación , busca el Reino de Dios, emprendiendo tareas temporales y ordenándolas de acuerdo al plan de Dios. Viven en el mundo, es decir, en cada una de las profesiones y ocupaciones seculares. Viven en las circunstancias ordinarias de la familia y de la vida social, de las cuales depende su propia vida" *(Lumen Gentium, 31).*

Gratitud y Súplica

6. En ésta ocasión no puedo dejar de expresar mi gratitud especial y aliento a aquellos de vosotros que son responsables por la formación de candidatos al sacerdocio y a la vida religiosa. Estad seguros que todos vuestros esfuerzos, trabajos y sacrificios son profundamente apreciados por la Iglesia y por mi personalmente. Vuestra labor es vital para el futuro de la Iglesia y vuestra contribución a la vida del Pueblo de Dios será duradera. Ciertamente es crucial que vosotros mismos viváis intensamente la doctrina, la experiencia pastoral y la Santidad de Vida. De gran importancia es vuestra actitud hacia la fe y particularmente vuestro ejemplo personal de amor filial por la Iglesia, así como vuestra leal adherencia al auténtico magisterio ordinario (ver *Lumen Gentium,* 25). San Pablo nos dice: "Cristo amó a la Iglesia. Se entregó por ella para santificarla (Eph 5:25-26). Rezo para que vuestras propias vidas estén siempre animadas por este tipo de amor sacrificado.

Deseo añadir una palabra de profunda apreciación a todos aquellos padres que mantienen y animan a sus hijos a seguir a Criso. El apoyo, entendimiento y amor de la oración que les daís es de inmenso valor.

7. En este momento deseo rogar a la Iglesia en los Estados Unidos por vocaciones para el sacerdocio y la vida religiosa. El deber de fomentar esas vocaciones descansa en la totalidad de la Comunidad Cristiana, y ciertamente la

familia por tradición ha hecho la contribución más grande. Debemos siempre recordar también el impacto que ejercen los fervientes sacerdotes y religiosas sobre las vocaciones, a través de su ejemplo de servicio, por el testimonio de su caridad, su bondad y su alegría. Por encima de todo la clave para las vocaciones es la oración perseverante como Jesús ordenó: "La mies es mucha pero pocos los sembradores. Pidan al Maestro sembrador que envíe más obreros a su mies (Mt 9:37-38).

Queridos hermanos y hermanas: Deben llegar a conocer al Señor Jesús. *Habéis oído su voz descubierto su amor y respondido a su llamado.* Que el Señor Jesús, quién comenzó ésta buena obra en vosotros la complete para gloria de su Padre y por el poder de su Epíritu. Recordad siempre "el lugar en donde estáis es tierra Sagrada" (Ex 3:5).

Y que la bendita Virgen María os ayude con sus oraciones y con el ejemplo de su amor.

A la Gente de Nuevo México

*Mensaje emitido por radio durante el vuelo de San Antonio a Phoenix—
14 de Septiembre*

Querido pueblo de Nuevo México:

1. Aunque no ha sido posible incluír a *Nuevo México* en esta visita pastoral a los Estados Unidos, me alegro de tener esta ocasión para extender a todos mis más cordiales deseos. Quiero incluír en este saludo a todos los pueblos de todas las culturas y tradiciones religiosas, particularmente a los americanos nativos. Las antiguas viviendas indias todavía hoy hablan elocuentemente de la riqueza de vuestra herencia. Que siempre conservéis y saquéis fuerzas de vuestras tradiciones recibidas del pasado.

Ofrezco saludos especiales a mis hermanos y hermanas en la *fe católica* que viven en Nuevo México. Los comienzos en la fe se remontan al tiempo de los primeros misioneros que vinieron de México. El impacto del Evangelio en vuestra historia y en vuestra cultura se refleja claramente en el nombre de vuestras ciudades,como Las Cruces, Santa Rosa y Socorro. Incluso vuestras montañas luminosas se refieren a Cristo y a los Santos, con nombres como Sangre de Cristo, San Andreas y San Mateo. Parece muy lógico que la capital de vuestro Estado y la sede de la Arquidiócesis tenga el nombre de *Santa Fe*. Verdaderamente la fe católica influenció mucho en la historia y la cultura de Nuevo México.

2. Mis sentimientos hacia ustedes se encierran en las palabras de San Pablo: "*Damos siempre gracias a Dios por todos vosotros recordándoos en nuestras oraciones,* acordándonos sin cesar ante nuestro Dios y Padre de *ejercicio de vuestra fe, del esfuerzo de vuestra caridad y de la constancia de vuestra esperanza en nuestro Señor Jesucristo*" (1 Tes 1:2-3).

Nuestra *identidad* como cristianos tiene sus raíces en el *don de la fe*. Hemos llegado a conocer y creer en el Señor. Estamos convencidos que El es "el camino, la verdad y la vida" (Jn 14:6). Y mientras valoramos este don de la fe, sabemos que tenemos que guardarlo y desarrollarlo, fortalecerlo y compartirlo. Debemos ejercitar nuestra fe en el amor, poniéndolo en práctica en todos los aspectos de nuestra vida diaria.

Este precioso don perfila toda nuestra visión de futuro. Cuanto mayor sea nuestro amor a Cristo, mayor será nuestra confianza en el cuidado providencial de Dios sobre nosotros y todos nuestros seres queridos y para el futuro del mundo. Como dice la carta a los Hebreos: *"La fe es una firme confianza en aquello en lo que esperamos, y una convicción en las cosas que no vemos"* (Hb 12:1-2).

Entonces queridos hermanos y hermanas en el Señor: "Hagamos a un lado cualquier lastre del pecado que pueda atraparnos y perseveremos con constancia en la carrera que nos espera. *Mantengamos nuestros ojos fijos en el Señor, el autor y consumador de la fe"* (Hb 12:1-2).

Que el Señor os fortalezca a cada uno de vosotros en la fe y os llene de amor y alegría. Dios bendiga a Nuevo México!

To the People of New Mexico

Message broadcast during flight from San Antonio to Phoenix, September 14.

Dear People of New Mexico,

1. Although it has not been possible to include *New Mexico* in this pastoral visit to the United States, I am happy to have this occasion to extend to all of you my cordial good wishes. I wish to include in this greeting all the people of every cultural and religious tradition, particularly the *Native Americans*. The ancient Indian dwellings which still remain today speak eloquently of the richness of your unique heritage. May you always preserve and draw strength from the worthy traditions which have been handed down to you from the past.

I offer a special greeting to my brothers and sisters of *the Catholic faith* who live in New Mexico. The first beginnings of the faith in this area go back to the time of the first Spanish missionaries who came from Mexico. The impact of the Gospel on your history and culture is clearly reflected in the names of your cities, such as Las Cruces, Santa Rosa and Socorro. Even your colorful mountains refer to Christ and the Saints, with names such as Sangre de Cristo, San Andreas and San Mateo. It seems very fitting, then, that the capital of your state and your Archdiocesan See should bear the name of *Santa Fe,* the holy faith. For indeed the Catholic faith has greatly influenced the history and culture of New Mexico.

2. My sentiments in your regard are captured by the words of St. Paul who said: *"We keep thanking God for all of you and we remember you in our prayers,* for we constantly are mindful before our God and Father of the way you are *proving your faith,* and *laboring in love,* and *showing constancy of hope in our Lord Jesus Christ"* (1 Thes 1:2-3).

Our *identity* as Christians is rooted in *the gift of faith.* We have come to know and to believe in Christ. We are convinced that he is "the way, and the truth, and the life" (Jn 14:6). And while we treasure this gift of faith, we know too that it must be guarded and developed, strengthened and shared. We must exercise our faith in love, putting it into practice in every aspect of our daily lives.

This precious gift shapes our whole vision of the future. For the deeper our love for Christ, the more confidently we trust in God's providential care for ourselves and those who are dear to us, and for the future of the world. As the Letter to the Hebrews says: *"Faith is confident assurance* concerning what we hope for, and conviction about things we do not see" (Heb 11:1).

And so, dear brothers and sisters in the Lord: "Let us lay aside every encumbrance of sin which clings to us and persevere in running the race which lies ahead. *Let us keep our eyes fixed on Jesus, who inspires and perfects our faith"* (Heb 12:1-2).

May the Lord strengthen each of you in faith, and fill you with love and joy. God bless New Mexico!

INDEX

Daughters of St. Paul

ALASKA
750 West 5th Ave., Anchorage, AK 99501 **907-272-8183.**
CALIFORNIA
3335 Motor Ave., W. Los Angeles, CA 90034 **213-202-8144.**
1570 Fifth Ave. (at Cedar Street), San Diego, CA 92101 **619-232-1442.**
46 Geary Street, San Francisco, CA 94108 **415-781-5180.**
CONNECTICUT
Bridgeport: Please check your phone book for current listing.
FLORIDA
2700 Biscayne Blvd., Miami, FL 33137 **305-573-1618.**
HAWAII
1143 Bishop Street, Honolulu, HI 96813 **808-521-2731.**
ILLINOIS
172 North Michigan Ave., Chicago, IL 60601 **312-346-4228; 312-346-3240.**
LOUISIANA
423 Main Street, Baton Rouge, LA 70802 **504-343-4057; 504-336-1504.**
4403 Veterans Blvd., Metairie, LA 70006 **504-887-7631; 504-887-0113.**
MASSACHUSETTS
50 St. Paul's Ave., Jamaica Plain, Boston, MA 02130 **617-522-8911.**
Rte. 1, 450 Providence Hwy., Dedham, MA 02026 **617-326-5385.**
MISSOURI
1001 Pine Street (at North 10th), St. Louis, MO 63101 **314-621-0346.**
NEW JERSEY
Hudson Mall, Route 440 and Communipaw Ave.,
  Jersey City, NJ 07304 **201-433-7740.**
NEW YORK
625 East 187th Street, Bronx, NY 10458 **212-584-0440.**
59 East 43rd Street, New York, NY 10017 **212-986-7580.**
78 Fort Place, Staten Island, NY 10301 **718-447-5071; 718-447-5086.**
OHIO
616 Walnut Street, Cincinnati, OH 45202 **513-421-5733.**
2105 Ontario Street (at Prospect Ave.), Cleveland, OH 44115
  216-621-9427.
PENNSYLVANIA
1719 Chestnut Street, Philadelphia, PA 19103 **215-568-2638;
  215-864-0991.**
SOUTH CAROLINA
243 King Street, Charleston, SC 29401 **803-577-0175.**
TEXAS
114 Main Plaza, San Antonio, TX 78205 **512-224-8101.**
VIRGINIA
1025 King Street, Alexandria, VA 22314 **703-549-3806.**
WASHINGTON
2301 Second Ave. (at Bell), Seattle, WA 98121 **206-441-4100.**
CANADA
3022 Dufferin Street, Toronto 395, Ontario, Canada.